W9-COF-923

Sacred Rights

Sacred Rights

*The Case for Contraception and Abortion
in World Religions*

EDITED BY DANIEL C. MAGUIRE

UNIVERSITY PRESS

2003

OXFORD
UNIVERSITY PRESS

Oxford   New York
Auckland   Bangkok   Buenos Aires   Cape Town   Chennai
Dar es Salaam   Delhi   Hong Kong   Istanbul   Karachi   Kolkata
Kuala Lumpur   Madrid   Melbourne   Mexico City   Mumbai   Nairobi
São Paulo   Shanghai   Taipei   Tokyo   Toronto

Copyright © 2003 by Oxford University Press, Inc.

Published by Oxford University Press, Inc.
198 Madison Avenue, New York, New York 10016

www.oup.com

Oxford is a registered trademark of Oxford University Press

All rights reserved. No part of this publication may be reproduced,
stored in a retrieval system, or transmitted, in any form or by any means,
electronic, mechanical, photocopying, recording, or otherwise,
without the prior permission of Oxford University Press.

Library of Congress Cataloging-in-Publication Data
Sacred rights: the case for contraception and abortion in
world religions / edited by Daniel C. Maguire.
p. cm.
Includes bibliographical references and index.
ISBN 0-19-516000-2—ISBN 0-19-516001-0 (pbk.)
1. Birth control—Religious aspects.   2. Contraception—Religious
aspects.   3. Abortion—Religious aspects.   I. Maguire, Daniel C.
HQ766.2.S23 2003
291.5′66—dc21
2002008363

9 8 7 6 5 4 3 2 1

Printed in the United States of America
on acid-free paper

Contents

Contributors

Rev. Gloria H. Albrecht
Chair, Religious Studies Department
University of Detroit Mercy
P.O. Box 19900
Detroit, MI 48219-0900

Dr. Jose Barzelatto
Center for Health and Social Policy
5800 Nicholson Lane #1201
Rockville, MD 20862-2964
josebarzel@aol.com

Marcy C. Churchill
Women's Studies
Campus Box 246
University of Colorado at Boulder
Boulder, CO 80309-0246
churchil@stripe.colorado.edu

Christine Gudorf
Florida International University
Department of Religious Studies
University Park
Miami, FL 33199
gudorf@fiu.edu

Ping-chen Hsiung
Institute of Modern History
Academia Sinica
128 Yen-Chiu-Yuan Road, Section 2
Nankang, Taipei, Taiwan
Republic of China
mhpch@ccvax.sinica.edu.tw

Sandhya Jain
300-SFS, DDA Flats
Gulmohar Enclave
New Delhi 110 049 India
jsandhya@satyam.net.in

Anrudh Jain
Senior Director of Policy
  and Regional Programs
The Population Council
One Dag Hammarskjold Plaza
New York, NY 10017
ajain@popcouncil.org

Daniel C. Maguire
Religious Consultation on Population,
  Reproductive Health, and Ethics
2717 East Hampshire Street
Milwaukee, WI 53211
consultation@igc.org

Geling Shang
Philosophy Department
Grand Valley State University
1 Campus Drive
Allendale, MI 49401
shangg@gvsu.edu

Arvind Sharma
McGill University
Wm. and Henry Birks Bldg., Room 103
3520 University Street
Montreal, Quebec
Canada H3A 2A7
cxlj@musica.mcgill,ca

Sa'diyya Shaikh
Religious Studies Department
University of Cape Town
Private Bag, Rondebosch, 7700
South Africa
sshaikh@nimbus.ocis.temple.edu

Funmi Togonu-Bickersteth
Department of Psychology
Obafemi Awolowo University
Ile Ife, Nigeria
togonub@infoweb.abs.net

Parichart Suwanbubbha
Department of Humanities
Faculty of Social Sciences
Mahidol University, Salaya
Nakornpathom, 73170 Thailand
shpsw@mahidol.ac.th

Laurie Zoloth
Program in Jewish Studies
College of Humanities
San Francisco State University
1600 Holloway Ave.
San Francisco, CA 94321
lzoloth@sfsu.edu

Sacred Rights

Introduction

DANIEL C. MAGUIRE

This book is written in the conviction that religion is *a* if not *the* shaper of culture. Religion is a response to the sacred. However we define that sacred—theistically or nontheistically—we can't avoid the word or the experience. Life is not just good. In some of its manifestations it is sacred—our code word for the peaking of preciousness. There is no one who finds nothing sacred, and there is nothing that adds power to human motivation like the tincture of the sacred. As John Henry Newman once observed, people will die for a dogma who will not stir for a conclusion. So if we would mobilize cures for the ills of earth, religion will be a player, for good or for ill. Mysteries like birth and death stimulate the emotion of the religio-sacred, making religion an inevitable presence—again, for good or for ill—in the ethics and policies of family planning.

It is notoriously difficult to say with certainty how much religion has to do with fertility decisions since education, affluence, the status of women, and so many other factors are involved in fertility motivation. Also positions held by religious leaders are not necessarily shared by the body of the faithful. The Catholic hierarchy stands virtually alone among religions in its opposition to contraception (although there are defections even there: see chapter 3), and yet France was the first country to experience a fertility transition and Italy (which hosts the Vatican) and Spain have two of the three lowest fertility rates in the world. Only Hong Kong is lower.[1] However, realistic fertility analysis must deal with the widespread belief in theistic religions—particularly in areas of low literacy—that we must accept the number of children that God sends. My mother, born in nineteenth-century Ireland, assured us that "God will never send a mouth without sending the food to feed it." Even the still-fresh memory of the potato famine did not expunge that mythology.

What is *not* notoriously difficult to say is that religions seriously affect national and international policy on contraception and abortion. The Vatican from its unduly privileged perch in the United Nations along with the "Catholic" nations, newly allied with conservative Muslim nations, blocked reference to contraception and family planning at the United Nations conference in Rio de Janeiro in 1992. This alliance also disrupted proceedings at the 1994 UN conference in Cairo and impeded any reasonable discussion of abortion. As the then Prime Minister Brundtland of Norway said of the Rio conference: "States that do not have any population problem—in one particular case, even no births at all [the Vatican]—are doing their best, their utmost, to prevent the world from making sensible decisions regarding family planning."[2]

This volume developed under the auspices of the Religious Consultation on Population, Reproductive Health, and Ethics with support from the David and Lucile Packard Foundation and the Ford Foundation. This international group of distinguished authors came together twice over a period of a year for intense four-day conferences to conceptualize and plan this book. The project dispels the illusion that the world's religions are uniformly conservative and unhelpful on issues of family planning. The anomalous and influential presence of the Vatican in the United Nations and its alliance with conservative Muslim states on family planning issues give only one narrow view from the field of religious ethics. We seek to counter that undue and deceptive monism because the classical wisdom traditions that we call the world's religions have considerably greater depth and breadth, and this volume seeks to give that voice. On the subjects of contraception and abortion, there are "pro-choice" as well as "no-choice" positions solidly grounded in these religions.

This moves the debate away from the sterile either/or, "pro-choice"/"pro-life" stalemate. Our scholars show that almost all religions admit of both the no-choice and the pro-choice options. The religions of the world are not so much seamless garments as patchwork quilts. They are rich, though flawed, classics, and on many specific moral issues such as abortion and contraception they support a valid moral pluralism. Even in a religion such as Roman Catholicism, the no-choice position on abortion is indeed one plausible reading of that tradition. It is not, however, the only plausible and orthodox reading. A more moderate pro-choice position is also solidly grounded there.

Obviously this flexibility has important implications for law because nations that claim religious freedom should not privilege one religiously grounded position on abortion over another. This is comparable to the ethics of war. Persons who on religious grounds believe all war is wrong are permitted conscientious objection. Those who understand their religion to permit war may serve in the military. Persons who on religious grounds consider all abortion evil should not be forced to have one or to participate in one if they are in the medical profession. Those who find solid moral and religious grounds for abortion for serious reasons should not have their civil and religious freedom curtailed.

Religion Normatively Defined

Our use of the term "religion" differs from the usage in the social sciences. There the term is used descriptively and includes all the phenomena that call themselves religion, however innocent or guilty, destructive, magical, or superstitious they may be. We work out of a normative definition of religion. We study religion as a positive, life-enhancing response to the sacred. Each of these religions, though burdened with negative debris from their journeys through time, is a classic in the art of cherishing. The study of religion is a mining effort that seeks to bring to light the renewable moral energies lost in the mess we can make of all good things. Good religious studies do not fudge the downside—the sexism, the patriarchy, the superstition, and the authoritarianism abundantly found in religions. Amid the corruption we are ferreting out the good. And on issues of family planning, the good is there.

The religions we study are all philosophies of life. As Morton Smith says, in the ancient world there was "no general term for *religion*." Thus, for example, "Judaism to the ancient world was a philosophy."[3] It presented itself as a source of wisdom. Look at Judaism's self-portrait in Deuteronomy: "You will display your wisdom and understanding to other peoples. When they hear about these statutes, they will say, 'what a wise and understanding people this great nation is!' " (Deut. 4:6). So, too, were the other religions' quests for enlightenment and betterment. They contain ore from which rich theories of justice and human rights can be extracted. Often these treasures have not been applied helpfully and healthily to issues like sexuality, sexism, family planning, or ecological care, but that is precisely our mission in these pages. We are studying the human right and obligation to bring moral planning to our biological power to reproduce. We support what should be the obvious right to contraception, but we do not shy away in this book from the moral right to an abortion. The authors here would agree with the position stated by Asoka Bandarage: "Abortion should not be used as a contraceptive method, but safe and legal abortions should be available to women who choose to have them. Abortion is, almost always, a painful decision for women. Instead of punishing women for that difficult moral and emotional decision, society should develop compassion and support systems for women in making their own choices."[4] And we find the reasons for that position in the major and indigenous religions of the world. We believe that women should make the decision for abortion themselves and that it is a misuse of governmental power to take this sacred right from them.

To criminalize a right that is grounded in the world's major religions is criminal itself. It is also a form of religious persecution. Criminalization is also lethal in its effects. It is estimated that 200,000 women die every year from illegal, unsafe abortions, and the number could be higher because many nations do not report maternal mortality statistics to the World Health Organization.[5]

Justice-Based Family Planning

We humans have noticed that, all of a sudden, there are more of us. We could hardly miss this rapidly swelling bulge. It took ten thousand generations to produce the first two and a half billion people and only one generation to double it. One might rush to the conclusion that such a quantum leap on a finite planet has to be the biggest problem ever to face our species. Population growth, however, is part of a family of problems and cannot be taken by itself as the biggest problem in our world. Let us dare to look at some of the related problems before looking at the real problems relating to overpopulation.

The maldistribution of wealth, privilege, and resources is, in fact, a neglected and unpopular problem. Eighty-two percent of the world's income goes to the top 20 percent of humanity, leaving 18 percent for the remaining 80 percent. More than a billion people have an income of about one dollar per day. Racism and ethnic hatreds split nations and control the allocation of resources in genocidal ways. And there are other problems that are more ruinous than population growth: sexism is viciously woven into the texture of our economics, politics, and religions with lethal effect. It effectively sinks women into poverty and illiteracy. Militarism that sucks up money like a giant vacuum is a disabling problem for the world economy. More money goes annually into international military spending than the bottom half of the human race has to live on. Not surprisingly, if you spend for war you go to war. There were 149 wars between 1945 and 1992. We impoverish ourselves and our spirits by spending too much on kill-power and not enough on health, education, and the arts. The nation-state that we have been trying to civilize with law and constitutions for the past several centuries is being eclipsed by corporations whose dominant passions are not justice, peace, and environmental health, but profit and growth. Of the top 100 economies in the world today, 50 are corporations, not nations. No one can say that too many people are the cause of all this craziness and earth-wrecking mayhem or that overpopulation is the root of all evil. It's not that simple.

In fact, according to most experts, population growth is a passing problem and will level off in the next 50 years. Some 30 industrialized nations are already at or below replacement levels of fertility, and even some poor states in India like Kerala and Goa have stabilized their populations. As Dr. Nafis Sadik, former head of the United Nations Fund for Population Activities, says, more women today have the means to manage their fertility than the total number of women of reproductive age in 1950. As a result, she says, "fertility is half what it was in 1960."[6]

So do we conclude that population is a non-issue? Not at all. In fact, population pressures affect many of the problems just listed, in direct and indirect ways. It is not the only cause of any of those problems, but it is a factor not to be denied. Lester R. Brown of the Worldwatch Institute says that the projected growth in population can exacerbate "nearly all the other environmental and social problems." He notes that the population increase will occur mostly "where countries are already overpopulated, according to many ecological measures."[7] Right now, we are faced with what is called "population momentum," the amount of growth that will occur if our fertile youth only reproduce themselves. They may do more than that. We have on earth at this time the largest class of fertile persons in the history of the world, as many fertile people as there were people on this planet in 1960. Half of the world's residents are under 25; there are one billion adolescents. Their unpredictable reproductive behavior is one factor in the varying predictions of whether the planet in the middle of this century will peak at nine, ten, or eleven billion people.

Dismissing population problems by happy-talking the fact that world population will level off sometime around the middle of this century is small comfort for poor nations like Ethiopia, Pakistan, and Nigeria, whose numbers will probably triple in the next 50 years with economic and political effects that can hardly be imagined. Half the children in Ethiopia today are undernourished, and if Pakistan triples its numbers as expected, that would leave about a tennis court of Pakistani grain land per person. Ninety percent of the coming population increase will be in the already straining poorest nations of the world. It is only the hard of heart and the weak of mind who could dismiss overpopulation as one of the serious problems for humans and for the rest of nature.

The Infinity Illusion

What the planet needs is a declaration of finitude. Orgies are not conducive to reflection, and the elite part of the human family has been on an orgy orbit for the past two centuries. The finite treasures of the planet are being spent with ominous abandon. Agriculture is a water glutton. It takes up to 70 tons of water to make a ton of beef and 3,000 tons to make a ton of grain. Orgy talk boasts that we are turning petroleum into food. The reference is to the petroleum-based fertilizers that supplement the marvels of manure and the complex machinery that supplants the horse-drawn plow. But a now foresee-able tomorrow will bring the end of oil and even now overwatered fields grow white with salinization, the fatal residue of evaporated water. Revealingly, budgets for alternative energies like solar and wind are paltry, and politicians, even if they see the problem, are not about to offend the revelers whose votes they feed on.

When the facts come home to roost, moderation in all things will be an ideal imposed by necessity and family planning will be seen for what it is: a permanent necessity for successful living on this limited planet. Family planning will be needed until we stabilize world population, and then forever after. Family planning is quite simply essential to a reasonable and just world. Why, then, is the term so mired in controversy?

Toward a New Definition of Family Planning

Words, like people, have relatives. When you marry one, you may get all those relatives in the bargain—both the good and the bad.

The term "family planning" has a clan of relatives, and not a peaceable clan at that. To some people, family planning is the cornerstone of feminism, lifting women from their patriarchally defined role as domestic managers and brood mares, defined by their reproductivity in ways that men are not. For others it is a euphemism for abortion, which they see as always an immoral choice. Family planning must entail contraception and that, too, is objection-able to some. Others see it as part of a "Malthusian" elitism that would see all the problems of the world as caused by what one writer a century ago called "the untrammeled copulation of the poor." But there are others who see family planning as the sensible wedding of two good ideas, *family*, and that alternative to chaos that we call *planning*. That is the way it is seen in this book.

The human animal is, by definition, the planning animal. So why is family planning so hotly controversial? It's because of those relatives. Family planning relates to sensitive issues such as sexuality, the begetting of children, gender roles, sharing, social and distributive justice, the proper role of government, and the overall health of this fragile earth. That is a heavy bunch of relatives. What that means is that it draws us into those heated areas of human discourse that we call ethics and religion. All those issues just mentioned are ethical issues and issues in which the religions of the world are deeply and influentially involved. All moral and religious values generate a certain amount of heat, and these issues generate a lot.

Family Planning and the Common Good

A few years ago I was speaking to a group of executives from the Ford Foundation near Athens, Greece. During my presentation I mentioned "the common good." As I left for a short break, the group asked that when I returned I address "the common good" and tell them precisely what it is. For my break I took a walk down a dirt path toward the lovely Aegean Sea. Ahead of me was what looked from a little distance to be a black ribbon stretched across the path. As I got closer I saw that it was not a ribbon, but two columns of ants moving back and forth in single file. Those in one row were all carrying something; the others were going back for a new load. A real estate change was in process. Every ant was committed to the project. There were no special interest groups. There were no shirkers or apostates from the effort. All these insect/citizens were bonded to the common good of that community.

What a pointed illustration nature had given me to take back to the Ford officers. The needs of the common good are inscribed on the genes of the ants. It is both our glory and our tragedy that our human genes have no such inscription. We, like the ants, have need of common-good considerations since the common good is the matrix of minimal livability within which individual good can be pursued.[8] With our species, this need for which our genes do not adequately provide is met by ethics and by that powerful cultural motivator and value-bearer that we call religion. Religion is a response to the value of human life and always plunges into moral questions about what befits or does not befit that life. Ethics and religion therefore are concentric circles.

Ethics, quite simply, is the systematic effort to study what is good for people and for this generous host of an earth. At times it almost seems as though our genes are perversely disposed to egoistic good in opposition to the common good. Ethics and religion would appear then to be no match for the efficacy of genetic inscription. The good news is that our motivation is not simply genetic and history shows that we can rise above selfishness, individually and collectively. In Christian terms, there is in the human story evidence of "grace" as well as "original sin." Even the gloomy Augustine conceded that we have within us the seeds of virtue. But human power is a challenge. We are the most powerful actors in the history of the planet, and because our common good includes the good of the whole of nature, our moral flaws show our readiness to wreck the planet that is our home. The current state of that home suggests what a dangerous mix humanity is.

Here we are, a species with prodigious talents but with a feeble ecological and social conscience. Add to that our pathological resistance to planning where we need it most and you can understand why some biological historians suggest that the two greatest disasters to befall planet earth are these: first, the blasting of this gentle planet by asteroids sixty-five million years ago, which seems to have ended, among other things, the life of the dinosaurs; and second, the arrival of the human race. We are assaulting all the basics of life: topsoil, water, air, and the cross-fertilizing, sustaining web of diverse life forms. In our hands, that web is being torn to shreds. Every hour of every day several species of life become extinct due to human rapacity. We are deaf to the grim reminder that death is the end of life but that extinction is the end of birth. Dying canaries warned miners of danger. The disappearing species are our canaries. And it is not just other species that we are killing. We have turned upon our own kind, using not just war, but hunger and the maldistribution of resources as our weapons of choice. War is actually an inefficient and picayune killer, no competitor at all for hunger. Some 40 million people die every year from hunger and poverty-related causes—the equivalent of 300 jumbo jet crashes daily—with half of the passengers being children.[9] What war ever did anything like that?

So in a word, family planning means contraception with access to safe abortion as an option when necessary. But it also includes, in Protestant theologian James Martin-Schramm's words, a redistribution "of land and income, improvement in access to education and employment, the elimination of discrimination based on race or sex, and substantial improvement in access to affordable housing, food, and health care."[10] Family planning wholistically understood involves a lot more than condoms: it is an issue of social and distributive justice. If this is not recognized, it will not achieve its goals.

So What of the Numbers?

There are those who think that the only or at least the main problem is too many people, especially too many poor people. Would that it were that simple!

Numbers, of course, can be a problem. Too many people in too little space with not enough to meet their needs is a problem. That is not a new or brilliant insight. Thirty-five hundred years ago, a Babylonian tablet gave a history of humankind. The story it told was already an old tale when it got carved on stone. It said that the gods made humans to do scut work that was unworthy of the divinities but that huge problems developed when the humans over-reproduced. So the gods sent plagues to diminish the population and made it a religious obligation for the remaining humans to limit their fertility. Joel Cohen says that this "is perhaps the earliest extant account of human over-population and the earliest interpretation of catastrophes as a response to over-population."[11] Over two thousand years ago, Aristotle sensibly insisted that the number of people should not exceed the resources needed to provide them with moderate prosperity.[12] Thomas Aquinas, the Catholic saint, agreed with Aristotle that the number of children generated should not exceed the provisions of the community, and he even went so far as to say that this should be insured by law as needed. If more than a certain number of citizens were generated, said Thomas, the result would be poverty, which would breed thievery, sedition, and chaos.[13] (Thomas sidestepped the question of how this would be legally enforced.)

All this was centuries before Thomas Malthus in the eighteenth century famously and pessimistically proposed that human population is caught in a vicious cycle of population exceeding food supply, leading to famine and disease, which would bring population back to a manageable level. Then the process would begin again. Malthus underestimated the capacity of the planet to produce food; he was uninformed of the complex dynamics of fertility increase and decline, and he also failed to see overconsumption by the rich, not the numbers of the poor, as a more crucial problem. There is enough, as Gandhi said, for our need, but not for our greed. The 2.9 million people in Chicago consume more than the more than 100 million people in Bangladesh. If, with an eye on consumption, you compare Germany with a poor African country, Germany consumes like the equivalent of one billion people.[14] Seventy-five percent of the world's pollution is caused by the "well salaried and well calo-ried." Malthus also did not see how the need for children could be changed by technology and by the move to cities. (You don't need as many children in the city as you did on the farm. As recently as 1800, only 2.5 percent of humans lived in cities. By the 1980s that figure had risen to more than 50 percent.[15]

Still, numbers do count. Too many people on a finite planet can be a problem, especially too many greedy, economically comfortable people, but also too many poor people. Too many rich people are high-speed wreckers. Too many poor people makes for slow earth wrecking, but both are wreckers.

Many of us living in Western countries look down our streets and do not see too many people. We don't see that human population right now is a triangle, with the fertile young at the bottom, and the infertile older folks at the narrow top. Until this changes into a rectangle, the population surge will continue. We do know, of course, that even big affluent cities are jammed, but even folks who live there can take a ride and find open spaces and solitude. Those of us who are comfortably ensconced in the garden spots of the world can easily miss the fact that too many people on the earth—even the ones we don't see—makes problems for everyone else on earth. We are more connected than we know. The interdependence that Buddhism taught as theory is now, more and more, an empirically verifiable fact.

Most of the population increase going on now is in the poorest nations. Ninety percent of the increase in the next 50 years will be in the poorest parts of the world where people are already starving. There are almost 900 million hungry and malnourished people in the world—and some put the figure higher. That is nearly as many people as lived in the world when Malthus wrote his famous essay. That causes problems that don't stay overseas. "Too many" *over there* leads to big problems *here.* As populations rise in the poorest countries, wages go down and industries move from the affluent countries to take advantage of the cheap labor. Desperate poor people can destroy an environment. More farmland is needed; forests are destroyed. How does that affect us? In many ways. As forests are destroyed, microbes need new hosts and move to humans. Microbes and viruses that used to find a life for themselves in the forests have accepted deforesting humans as their new hosts. It's not the tigers coming out of the forest that we now fear. It's the microbes. And those microbes travel. As Nobel Laureate Joshua Lederberg says: "The bacteria and viruses know nothing of national sovereignties. . . . The microbe that felled one child in a distant continent yesterday can reach yours today and seed a global pandemic tomorrow."[16] Poverty is as global as the economy. The poison spreads. The poisons of poverty are blowing in the wind and falling in the rain and coming home to us in the strawberries and the beef. As historian Paul Kennedy says, for the first time in history the poor can now hurt the rich.[17] The words of the ancient Jeremiah take on a fresh contemporaneity. He warned that it is hard to escape the effects of moral malignancy: "Do you think that you can be exempt? No, you cannot be exempt" (Jer. 25:29).

Desperate poor people also migrate. The wealthy nations are worrying about the poor people sneaking in or being smuggled across their borders in a desperate search for work. Shortsighted people just want to build walls or tighten immigration laws. That is like trying to stop the flow of water by jamming the faucet, rather than turning off the spigot. The spigot is *desperate need at home.* Ask the Roman Empire. If you have it and they do not, they will come, and walls or dangerous seas will not stop them. The only cure is helping them find what they need at home—the jobs, the health care, the education for their children, human rights—all the things we all want and need. And we all would rather find them at home.[18]

Overpopulation and poverty conspire with the overconsumption of the comfortable to kill our life support systems. We have lost a fifth of tropical rainforests since 1950. These natural treasures provide oxygen, absorb excess carbon, and supply medicine, not to mention their intrinsic value apart from us. (Seventy-five percent of our pharmaceuticals come from plants.) We all get hurt when the planetary womb in which we live gets hurt. Professor David Orr records some of the results: male sperm counts worldwide have fallen by 50 percent since 1938. Human breast milk often contains more toxins than are permissible in milk sold by dairies . . . signaling that some toxins have to be permitted in the dairies. At death some human bodies contain enough toxins and heavy metals to be classified as hazardous waste.[19] Newborns arrive wounded in their immune systems by the toxins that invaded the womb. One report from India is that "over 80 percent of all hospital patients are the victims of environmental pollution."[20] Human consuming is stressing the oceanic fisheries to their limits, and water tables are falling as there are more of us to share this limited resource. This leads us to a dire conclusion: if present trends continue, we will not.

Population growth is one of the significant co-conspirators in this wasting of the environment. And the environment is where we all live. We and the rest of nature form one fragile and precious community, perhaps the only one like it in all the folds of the universe. The world's religions, with all their variety, seem united in challenging our two indigenous moral failings: *the selfishness that smothers our compassion and our lack of gratitude.* The importance of the world religions lies in their targeting what may be the heart of our "original sin," these fatal flaws that could be our undoing. The diminished influence of those religions is central to the modern crisis.

Why Do People Make Too Many Babies?

Beware of simple answers to that question! Simple answers make for simple solutions. Among the simplest—and wrongest—is to say that all we need is more condoms. That ignores the reasons why people—even those with access to contraception—go on making babies anyway. Family planning that is reduced to mere condom distribution is a form of self-deception. It ignores the reasons, good and bad, why people feel they need more children. Let's look at just some of these reasons, good and bad.

My father was one of 13 children born at the end of the nineteenth century. Only he and four of his siblings grew into adulthood. When I asked him what happened to the others, he would reply: "One wee girl died of the fever, another wee boy died of the cramps, etc." Nutrition was poor and medicine almost absent. That is the state of a lot of the world today. You need to make many babies because most will die. In Sudan many feel they need to have 12 or more children to see 3 or 4 survive. That, after all, is family planning of a very desperate sort. The last thing those people feel they need is condoms! What they need is social and economic justice, and family planning that does not know that is morally bankrupt and myopic.

For many people in areas with no old-age social security, children are the answer. In 1984 the World Bank reported that 80 to 90 percent of the people they surveyed in Indonesia, South Korea, Thailand, and Turkey expected to rely on their children for support in their old age.[21] Poverty is a major stimulant of fertility. "The poverty of the poor is their ruin," says the Book of Proverbs (10:15). Studies show that for young women in desperate circumstances, the only love relationship they can count on is the mother-child relationship.[22] As political economist Asoka Bandarage says: "Fertility declines require alleviation of poverty and improvements in the living conditions of the poor, especially women."[23] As a German Episcopal Conference put it: "The maxim of development policy cannot be to reduce poverty by means of reducing population growth but must be to reduce the population growth by eradicating mass poverty."[24]

Religions and the Problem of Undemanded Need

Religions contribute to the desire for large families. Small wonder. They were spawned in a world where the problem was depopulation. The Emperor Augustus penalized bachelors and rewarded families for their fertility.[25] Widowers and divorcees (of both sexes) were expected to remarry within one month! Only those over 50 were allowed to remain unmarried. Remember that Augustus presided over a Roman society with an average life expectancy of less than 25 years. It was a society where, as historian Peter Brown says, "death fell savagely on the young."[26] Only four out of every hundred men—and fewer women— lived beyond their fiftieth birthday. As a species, we formed our fertility habits in worlds that were, in Saint John Chrysostom's words, "grazed thin by death."[27] Such instincts are deep-rooted. If, as Teilhard de Chardin sagely says, nothing is intelligible outside its history, this reproductive thrust, especially in stressful conditions, is the defining story of our breed. These religions, as we shall see, also contain the cure for this problem, but we concede that for most of history their concern was for more, not fewer, children.

It is true that there is "unmet need" for contraceptives, where women want them but have no access. "Half of all pregnancies may be unwanted," according to Nafis Sadik, former head of the United Nations Fund for Population Activities.[28] And there is a glaringly unmet need for research on male contraceptives. But there is also what I would call *undemanded need* where people would benefit from fertility limitation but through cultural and religious prejudice don't feel free to seek it. It is that religious prejudice that this book addresses, and, through a kind of homeopathic medicine, finds the cure for religious ignorance in the very religions themselves.

Early marriage is another cause of excessive fertility, as is illiteracy, especially of women. In India overall, the literacy rate for women is 39 percent and the fertility rate is more than three children per woman. However, in the remarkable state of Kerala in India, the literacy rate for women is 86.3 percent and the fertility rate is 1.8. Small wonder that the United Nations Population and Development Conference in Cairo in 1994 saw that the economic and educational empowerment of women is the key to fertility limitation.

So, in a word, family planning means more than providing contraception with safe abortion as a backup option when necessary. Families do not exist in a void. They live in a cultural, religious, economic, and political matrix that helps shape their goals and limits or enhances their possibilities. Recognizing that is the beginning of justice-based family planning wisdom.

How Many Is Too Many?

Professor Joel E. Cohen in his monumental book *How Many People Can the Earth Support?* concluded that this is a questionable question.[29] It is a question that imports an army of other questions. But it is a question that started teasing the human mind in the seventeenth century, when the first estimates were made of the population that the earth's "land if fully peopled would sustain." The estimate back then that the earth could support at most 13 billion is not far off from contemporary estimates. Most estimates today range from four to sixteen billion. If we were content to live at the level of Auschwitz or the Artic Innuit or the Kalahari bushmen, you would get certain numbers. If you face the reality that most people have rising not lowering expectations, you get other numbers. Some estimate that only 3 billion people can eat a diet like that enjoyed in the United States, Western Europe, or Japan. One particularly pessimistic study done at Cornell University estimated that the earth can support only a population of 1 to 2 billion people at a level of consumption roughly equivalent to the current per capita standard for Europe.[30]

Most nations live beyond their means. Take the Netherlands, for example. It is estimated that the Dutch require the equivalent of 14 times as much productive land as is contained within their own borders. To consume the way they consume takes the equivalent of 14 Hollands.[31] Where does it get the other 13 Hollands? It imports from the rest of the world. In one of the gargantuan lies of modern parlance, we refer to the gluttonous nations of the world as "developed" and the poor nations as "developing," implying that they can consume like we do and someday will. But if we can return to reality, where is Zimbabwe going to find 13 Zimbabwes if it tries to match us in overconsumption?

Professor Cohen reaches this sensible conclusion: "The Earth has reached, or will reach within half a century, the maximum number the Earth can support in modes of life that we and our children and their children will choose to want."[32] Family planning is necessary now lest population momentum carry us into chaos, and it will be necessary when population stabilizes to keep families and overall population at sustainable levels. As Harold Dorn says with elemental logic: "No species has ever been able to multiply without limit. There are two biological checks upon a rapid increase in numbers—a high mortality and a low fertility. Unlike other biological organisms [humans] can choose which of these checks shall be applied, but one of them must be."[33]

Operis Personae

Reproductive ethics is complex and multifaceted, and undertaking the task of exploration is a group of scholars rich in variety and talent. From Taiwan's Academia Sinica comes Ping-chen Hsiung, a professor of Chinese cultural history, with special interests in sexuality and reproductive patterns. Parichart

Suwanbubbha comes from Mahidol University in Bangkok, Thailand to represent some of the teachings of Buddhism. Sa'diyya Shaikh from South Africa is a major young reforming theologian in Islam. Sandhya Jain lives in New Delhi and studies Hinduism, Jainism, and Indian culture. Laurie Zoloth heads the Program in Jewish Studies at San Francisco State University. Christine Gudorf is a prominent Catholic theologian teaching at Florida International University. Mary Churchill of the University of Colorado comes out of the American Cherokee tradition and works on the various native American religions. Geling Shang, a native of China, is an expert on Taoism and Confucianism. Arvind Sharma, an expert on Hinduism, but also on the comparative study of world religions, completed our group of world religionists, and he has written a concluding overview of our project.

Jacob Olupona, a native of Nigeria and an expert on native African religions, was a consultant in this project. Other consultants were Riffat Hassan, a native of Pakistan and an expert on Islam. Also, we were aided by Beverley Harrison, recently retired from Union Theological Seminary in New York, who wrote the first book by a Protestant on the moral right to choose an abortion. At our first meeting we were assisted by Dr. Oyin Sodipe from the Department of Primary Health Care in Abeokuta, Nigeria.

To keep the religious scholars informed on the multiple aspects of demography, science, and policy relating to our topic, we were joined by Dr. Anrudh Jain, the senior director of policy at the Population Council. Funmi Togonu-Bickersteth came to us from Obafemi Awolowo University in Ile Ife, Nigeria, where she is a professor of social psychology. Dr. Jose Barzelatto, an endocrinologist natively of Chile, has been an international leader in population and fertility issues for years. Dr. Barzelatto was assisted by Elizabeth Dawson of the Center for Health and Social Policy in San Francisco.

Where Science and Religion Meet

It is a typically modern illusion to think that we have entered a postreligious age where the superstitions of "religion" have been replaced by the demonstrable verities of science. Scientists know better. In January 1990, 34 major scientists issued "An Open Letter to the Religious Community."[34] In this manifesto, the scientists insisted that the complex problems of our planet have a religious as well as a scientific dimension and they begged the religions of the world to rise to the occasion. The solution will not be merely technical or narrowly "rational," What is needed, they said, is "a vision of the sacred." They almost echoed the words of Jewish theologian Abraham Heschel that we will not perish from a lack of technology but from a lack of reverence and appreciation. In October 1993, representatives of 58 scientific academies signed a report called "Population Summit of the World's Scientific Academies."[35] The report was not a one-rubric "Malthusian" approach to the world crisis. It cited the maldistribution of wealth, the ethnic, class, and gender biases that, along with overpopulation in many areas, are threatening the state of the earth. And they recognized the need for a sophisticated understanding of the role of religion relating to all of these problems, including population.

This volume is an urgent and earnest response to such enlightened concerns.

NOTES

1. Joel E. Cohen, *How Many People Can the Earth Support?* (New York: W. W. Norton, 1995), pp. 288–91.

2. See *Harvard Magazine*, July–August 1992, p. 48.

3. Morton Smith, "Palestinian Judaism in the First Century," in Moshe David, ed., *Israel: Its Role in Civilization* (New York: Harper and Brothers, 1956), pp. 67–81.

4. Asoka Bandarage, *Women, Population, and Global Crisis* (New Jersey: ZED Books, 1997), p. 336.

5. See Jodi L. Jacobson, "The Global Politics of Abortion," *World Watch Paper*, no. 97, July 1990, p. 38.

6. Nafis Sadik, "Reproductive Health and Gender Equality in the Twenty-First Century: A New Reality," a paper in the International Lecture Series on Population Issues of the John D. and Catherine T. MacArthur Foundation, July 2000, p. 5.

7. See Joel E. Cohen, *How Many People Can the Earth Support?* pp. 288–91, and Lester R. Brown, "Challenges of the New Century," in *State of the World: 2000* (New York: W. W. Norton, 2000), p. 5. Brown also cites the need for the economic and educational empowerment of women and increased contributions to reproductive and general health as basic. He is not presenting a "lower the numbers and all is well" simplism.

8. I developed the meaning of the common good in *A New American Justice* (San Francisco: Harper and Row, 1980, chap. 5, "What's So Good About the Common Good?" See also Daniel C. Maguire and A. Nicholas Fargnoli, *On Moral Grounds: The Art/Science of Ethics* (New York: Crossroads Publishing Co., 1991, pp. 27–32, 68–69. Briefly, the common good is both a descriptive and normative category. It *describes* the fact that the conditions for surviving and some thriving are to some degree present but it *prescribes* our common obligation to meet the indispensable needs that make our communal existence possible. Humanity's absolutely indispensable needs, I submit, are respect and hope. The opposite of respect is insult, and insult is the root of all rebellion. The opposite of hope is paralysis. The common good is a context in which minimal amounts of respect and hope are available to all. Social justice is simply our ongoing obligation to contribute—with taxes, obedience to just laws, civic participa-

tion, breakup of monopolies, voting, affirmative action, etc.—to creating a context where no one will lack the essentials of life.

9. See Clive Ponting, *A Green History of the World: The Environment and the Collapse of Great Civilizations* (New York: Penguin Books, 1991), p. 254.

10. James B. Martin-Schramm, "Population Growth and Justice," in Azizah al-Hibri, Daniel Maguire, and James B. Martin-Schramm, eds., *Religious and Ethical Perspectives on Population Issues* (Milwaukee, Wisc.: The Religious Consultation on Population, Reproductive Health, and Ethics, 1993), p. 17.

11. Cohen, *How Many People Can the Earth Support?* p. 6. Jack Miles, in *God: A Biography* (New York: Alfred A. Knopf, 1995), pp. 47–48, notes that the Genesis story at the time of the flood "suggests that the unchecked multiplication of humans also played a part." God is presented as in "an ongoing struggle" with humankind over the control of human fertility.

12. *The Basic Works of Aristotle*, ed. Richard McKeon (New York: Random House, 1941), *Politics*, bk. 2, chap. 6.

13. Thomas Aquinas, *Omnia Opera, Tomus XLVIII, Sententia Libri Politicorum* (Rome: Ad Sanctae Sabinae, 1971), A 140–41.

14. *How Many People Can the Earth Sustain? Ethical Reflections on the Growth of the World Population*, a study by the EKD Advisory Commission for Development Affairs, Evangelical Church in Germany, Herrenhauser Strasse 12, 30419 Hannover, Germany.

15. See Ponting, *A Green History of the World*, p. 295.

16. Joshua Lederberg, "Medical Science, Infectious Disease, and the Unity of Humankind," *Journal of the American Medical Association* 260 no. 5, 1988, pp. 684–85.

17. Paul Kennedy, *Preparing for the Twenty-First Century* (New York: Vintage Books, 1994), p. 96.

18. Harvard political scientist George Borjas points out that it is not those well-off folks fretting about immigration who are most hurt by it: "Current immigration redistributes wealth from unskilled workers whose wages are lowered by immigrants, to skilled workers and owners of companies that buy immigrants' services." "The New Economics of Immigration," *Atlantic Monthly*, Nov. 1996, p. 72.

19. See David W. Orr, *Ecological Literacy: Education and the Transition to a Postmodern World* (Albany: SUNY Press, 1992), pp. 3–5, and *Earth in Mind: On Education, Environment, and the Human Prospect* (Washington, D.C: Island Press, 1994), pp. 1–3.

20. Quoted in Kennedy, *Preparing for the Twenty-First Century*, p. 191. Kennedy is quoting H. Govind, "Recent Developments in Environmental Protection in India: Pollution Control," *Ambio* 18, no. 8 (1989), p. 429. Kennedy notes that this use of the term "environmental pollution" is broad and looks to more than respiratory effects.

21. World Bank, *World Development Report, 1984* (New York: Oxford University Press, 1984), p. 52.

22. See Bandarage, *Women, Population, and Global Crisis*, p. 164.

23. Ibid., p. 174.

24. Quoted in *How Many People Can the Earth Sustain? Ethical Reflections*, p. 13.

25. See Peter Brown, *The Body and Society: Men, Women, and Sexual Renunciation in Early Christianity* (New York: Columbia University Press, 1988), p. 6.

26. Ibid.

27. John Chrysostom, *De Virginitate*, 14, 1.

28. Sadik, "Reproductive Health and Gender Equality in the twenty-first Century," p. 8.

29. Cohen, *How Many People Can the Earth Support?* pp. 356–70.

30. David Pimentel, Rebecca Harman, Matthew Pacenza, Jason Pecarsky, and Marcia Pimentel, "Natural Resources and an Optimal Human Population," *Population and Environment* 15, no. 3 (1994).

31. See David C. Korten, *When Corporations Rule the World* (West Hartford, Conn.: Kumarian Press, 1995), p. 33.

32. Cohen, *How Many People Can the Earth Support?*, p. 367.

33. Harold F. Dorn, "World Population Growth: An International Dilemma," *Science* (26 January 1962), reprinted in George W. Cox, ed., *Readings in Conservation Ecology* (New York: Appleton-Century-Crofts, 1969), p. 275.

34. This letter is available from the National Religious Partnership for the Environment, 1047 Amsterdam Ave., New York, N.Y. 10025.

35. *Population Summit of the World's Scientific Academies*, Washington, D.C.: National Academy of Sciences. Reprinted in *Population and Development Review* 20, no. 1, pp. 233–38.

I

"Each One an Entire World"

A Jewish Perspective on Family Planning

LAURIE ZOLOTH

Three million and three hundred thousand Jews lived in Poland before the war, three million died. Two million eight hundred and fifty thousand Jews lived in Russia. More than a million died. The synagogues stand empty now, our brothers and sisters were murdered everywhere in the days of destruction.

Let us say Kaddish not only for the dead, but also for the living who have forgotten the dead. And let the prayer be more than a prayer, more than lament; let it be outcry, protest and defiance. And above all let it be an act of remembrance.

—Elie Wiesel (1999)

Shoah

Every spring, just after the celebration of Passover, Jews commemorate Yom HaShaoh (the Day of Remembrance of the Holocaust). It is a new holiday, made distinctive by new ritual: in the United States, the community gathers in the evening, and for the next 24 hours, reads lists of names of the dead. It continues overnight, by the light of memorial candles, at dawn, and into the evening darkness of the next day, in synagogues and on college campuses: the names, the ages of each one, one by one, specific: the listing of the children is particularly poignant. The tradition is to stand and listen, and take a turn in speaking a name, knowing that even in

24 hours, even reading every hour, even with one's entire community, one cannot hope to list them all.

Why begin a discussion on a Jewish perspective on reproductive health, ethics, and family planning policy with this story? In a world clearly facing significant, vexing issues with justice, with environmental challenges, with a steady increase in human population and consumption, and significant shifts in worldwide fertility, why not begin the discussion of Jewish ethical and re- ligious perspectives on family planning with a far more general description of Jewish perspectives on reproduction, contraception, abortion, families, and health?

Tradition, Location, Polity, and Text

This chapter will argue that to fully understand, describe, and reflect on Jew- ish perspectives on reproductive health and ethics one must have a clear un- derstanding of both history and text. A Jewish contribution to the debate on family planning is based on both what is written and what is performed. Normative Jewish practice is one that is based on a textualized reasoning: an analysis of the problems of a tangible sensory and social world. Hence, both the concerns of historical context and the rigor of traditional canonical texts create social policy. When new historical situations arise, and the daily en- actment of community and faithfulness shifts against political, scientific, or physical contingencies, a process of heightened discourse reshapes the new enactments. In critical ways, the questions of the environment, of population are in constant flux. For Jews, the cultural and economic realities of modern- ity affect religious practice, social justice, and ethical norms. Family life, families, childrearing, and sexuality are part of the practice of religion. In re- flecting on Jewish ethics, one considers the whole of human activity and the whole of the community as well: women as well as men are moral agents, and the lifeworld of the family, of women and of children, is a central con- cern of religion. This discourse is primarily contained in the extensive liter- ature of debate and exegesis of the rabbinic literature, which is primarily al- though not exclusively collected in a set of volumes called the Talmud. It is a record of an oral discourse, in which contention and casuistic narrative ethics both determine and discuss the Hebrew scriptures and struggle to ap- ply them to daily life. In an elaborate, linguistically complex oral debate, later codified in the written Talmud, the teachers of the period described 613 com- manded acts named as "the mitzvot" (200 B.C.E. to 500 C.E.). Both the study of this linguistic world and the ongoing efforts to shape and be shaped by the practice of the commandments defined the moral universe of observant Jews in the centuries since this time.

Jewish law develops in the 1,500 years since the redaction of the Talmud by an ongoing series of "responsa" to questions about the legal code discussed in the Talmud. Difficult cases of social crisis of all types are brought before decisors and scholars who ruled on the facts of the cases, on the methodological principles of logical discourse, and on certain key principles of relationships in the familial, ritual, civic, and commercial spheres. Each commentator is engaged in discourse with those who came previously, yet is confronted by changes in context: political and cultural shifts as well as scientific understandings that could not have been available to previous generations. This process of query and response continues into the present. Nowhere is this more publicly evident than in the rapidly changing field of reproductive health.

Statement of the Problem

This chapter will argue that we face a time of intense historical challenge in halachic Jewish thought and in the Jewish polity. It is a time of serious environmental threat to a shared global environment, which necessitates a call for reclaiming central rabbinic texts by creative rereading. Here, I will make the claim for a particular one: placing the parent-child relationship, in particular the nursing relationship (and all that this meant thematically), at the center of the texts about birth control allows Judaism to contribute creatively and substantially to the critical issues of population, family policies, and imperiled world resources.

My thesis is this: First, there is nothing new about survival as an issue for the Jewish community. The question of survival is at the heart of the covenant with the God of Israel. Second, women's position as prime moral agents in the covenant is central to the textual account of Jewish survival in which child-rearing is at the core of the spiritual activity of much of Jewish ritual life. Third, how the "faithful remnant of the People Israel," always understood liturgically as small in number but as universally critical in the larger human fate, is preserved is a deep concern for Jewish thought. The tension between the promise of fecundity and maintenance of covenant in the biblical account, and the realities of the fragility of Jewish existence in exile is at the core of a theological and social struggle. Finally, the Jewish tradition itself is suggestive of a principle for Jewish views on the ethical problem of population and family planning. Such a view forms the duty toward a specific future in the presence of a specific other. Each child calls on each parent to enact a duty toward her, of providing a world of abundance and generosity and attention. In fact, much of Jewish law is a discourse on how to provide and maintain such a world for a Jewish child faced with injustice, exile, and danger—hence, by extension, a world of justice for each human child.

The collection of essays in this book is devoted to seeking traditional reflections on the call for family planning, abortion, and birth control. It is a task undertaken out of a sense, emerging from a long history of concern about "overpopulation" of the globe, that we live in a world that is unable to sustain human society, a world burdened by scarcity of water, food, clean air, and arable land. This analysis understands that population growth alone is not the only issue, and that careful innovations in how we use the earth we live on will need to be made by all. In fact, even if world population stabilizes at present levels, the question of how to share the already crowded and degraded world environment persists.

How are Jews, such an infinitesimal part of the world population, part of this problem? First, in many of the venues in which Jews find themselves, the burdened cities of the Diaspora, and the small, densely populated, and fragile desert environment of Israel, we are already struggling with serious issues of water scarcity, pollution, and air quality.[1] Second, since Jews have strongly made the claim that minorities who have been persecuted ought to be allowed to procreate in larger numbers as a kind of reparative justice, consideration of the case of the Jews after the Shoah warrants special attention. It is important to understand the justice and limits of such a powerful claim. Third, many American Jews, like American Christians, Muslims, Hindus, and Buddhists, live as Americans, consuming resources of the world at rates wildly disproportionate to those in developing countries, and hence we must ask ourselves what the faith commitments we live by say about such consumption. Finally, because Jewish texts are at the heart of an Abrahamic tradition shared by Christians and Muslims, a Jewish perspective on these Jewish texts can make a unique contribution in and of itself, offering new considerations on families and women that lie at the heart of the debate. The reproductive health of families is key to the discourse of ecology and population—and it is religion that exercises one powerful influence over the meaning and intention of the well-lived life of families and of a just response to the use of the earth.

Notes on the History of Populations—The Demographic Shifts and Their Meaning

Let me begin the discussion by reflections on the historical idea of overpopulation itself and on the way that our society speaks of rights-claims that tends to shape our relationship to that idea. Before 1800, the world population grew only slightly, at a steady, but incrementally slow rate. Since the 1800s, the world population has been growing exponentially. This was certainly not framed as a problem by many, since Europeans, including Jewish leaders, understood the world as intended for increase, available for full human use, in fact invoking biblical references to "fill the earth and subdue it" in service of expansion. But the sudden population increase—called the first "demographic shift"—was the result of a change not in fertility patterns but in mortality patterns of early childhood. The early modern period enabled strategies for preventive health, clean water, and pest control that allowed many more children to survive to reproductive ages;[2] increased food production allowed for more robust offspring; and this reduction in mortality altered the basic social reality of families. What followed the population increase, in every society, transculturally and transhistorically, with a few notable exceptions, was called the second "demographic shift." This shift becomes apparent after a transitional period that lasted between 25 and 100 years (25 years in countries in the developing world, 100 years in Europe). Fertility patterns changed in response to the decreased threat to childhood—one did not need to give birth to many children in order to assure the continuity of family or lineage. Parents began to conceive smaller families, in essence counting on each child to reach adulthood safely. This is not only a historical or European phenomenon. This has occurred in nearly every country as modernity, with clear water, vaccinations, and antibiotics arrived, including Latin America, China, and South Asia—countries thought to be unable to control population.[3] Population overall has begun to stabilize in many countries: in Italy and Japan, for example, the negative fertility rate is on a slow decline. While the numbers of persons and our consumption still threaten a fragile environment, the specter of unbridled population increases simply no longer fits the new demographic understandings.

This worldwide phenomenon of a demographic shift is observed across religious and cultural differences. Most diasporic and Israeli Jewish communities[4] follow similar trends, much to the alarm of the leadership, both secular and religious, who tend to see the decline, not as part of a worldwide historical phenomenon but as a special problem for post-Holocaust Jews. Hence, in many Jewish religious communities—especially but not exclusively in Orthodox ones—young parents are urged to have larger families. For many, a classically observant family is typically portrayed as a nineteenth-century one, with many children, as was (as we see, rather briefly) the case at that period in Jewish history. Many commentators attribute this norm to the influence of classical Jewish texts supportive of a generalized pronatalism, and of the eagerness of Jews to return to what is perceived as authentic Jewish normative practices, here again, largely understood as the social praxis of the nineteenth century. However, let me suggest a concurrent factor—one that affects even nontraditional Jewish families. For many Jews, the *perceived* childhood mortality rate has not yet declined. For Jews raised one generation after the Shoah, for Jews who annually (at least) hear the list of the lost and who are enjoined to remember, the specter of death and the fragility of the survival of the community creates an emotive, passionate appeal.

For while there is little in the contemporary ethical literature about an environmental crisis, there is much about the meaning and the danger of the current demographic shift in light of Jewish survival. The 1990 Council of Jewish Federations National Population Study showed that American Jews, once 3.7 percent of the population were now only 2.4 percent and of that, 52 percent were married to non-Jews. In these families, only 25 percent were raising their children as Jews. Religious Jews account for only 1.9 percent of the population.[5] Faced with this decline, Jews are enjoined to "re-create the nation" in the face of extinction. One finds such language in both Orthodox and Conservative rabbinic authorities when they address the issue of birth control and family policy. Consider the following from Elliott Dorff:

> Maimonides says, "whoever adds even one Jewish soul is considered as having created an entire world." This is an especially important teaching in our time, when low reproductive rates among Jews, caused in part by their extended education . . . and the late age at which they marry and attempt to have children, have combined with assimilation and intermarriage to create a major demographic crisis for the Jewish community. Nothing less than the future of the Jewish community and of Judaism depends upon fertile Jews having three or four children per couple.[6]

Dorff continues this theme:

> We as a people are in deep demographic trouble. We lost one-third of our numbers during the Holocaust. . . . The current Jewish reproductive rate among American Jews is between 1.6 and 1.7. That statistic means we are killing ourselves off as a people. . . . This social imperative has made propagation arguably the most important mitzvah of our time. . . . To refuse to try to have them, or to plan to have only one or two is to refuse to accept one of God's great gifts. It is also to renege on the duty we all have to create the next generation.

Dorff is the leading ethicist and theologian of the Conservative Movement, a thoughtful, liberal author of the authoritative text for that movement on matters of sexuality and reproductive health. Dorff urges the community to offer monetary incentives for such large families, with private school tuition reduction. He counters concerns about population and ecology by urging Jews to "support . . . efforts in Africa or other overpopulated countries" to produce fewer children. In fact, the Conservative Rabbinate's official policy statement repeats this theme, consistently articulating a powerful argument heard in the Jewish community: that the miniscule number of Jews worldwide has little impact on the world population in any way, that since Jews number only 0.2 percent of the world's population, this is, in essence, not our problem.

In the Orthodox community, the same clarity about the need to have more Jewish children and the link to the losses of the Shoah pervade the texts: Immanuel Jakobowitz, leading commentator on Jewish medical ethics and former Chief Rabbi of Britain, in remarking on abortion in Israel, noted that "abortion deprived the Jewish state of over a million native-born citizens."

In secular texts, as well, for example, in the social research of Gary Tobin, author of the federation's report, the attitude is the same: falling fertility rates and increasing intermarriage can be graphed to show a point a generation or two in the imagined future in which there are no Jews at all.

However, as we see, the rates of fertility for Jews are not exceptional—they are consistent, and have been consistent, with worldwide trends for populations in modernity, with rare exception. For Jews, then, living in a shared world narrative, not to mention a shared physicality with the nations of the world, is the claim for exception a legitimate claim? How should Jews respond to the challenge of the environmental crisis? Can Jews claim an exemption to the need for environmentally driven population policies after the Shoah? And do Jewish women have a special and distinctive obligation to have many children to assure the survival of the Jewish people?

For it is the broader constraints that face us that must be held in tension with this claim. We live in a world facing global climate changes, critical water shortages, maldistribution of food supplies, significant epidemic diseases potentiated by poverty, and a scarcity of arable land. Far too many children cannot get education in basic reading and writing skills, and far too many women lack access to even the social goods promised within their culture, much less to a wider aspirational goal of universal human rights. For many families, Jews, Muslims, Catholics, Hindus, Protestants, and other faiths, the imperative to have children despite a social inability to care for, feed, or house them adequately is understood as a religious imperative. It is the task of this chapter to see whether Jewish law, or Jewish history, mandates such a course.

Are Jews Exempt from Broader Concerns About the
Effect of Population on the Environment Because
of the History of Persecution?

Let me now turn toward arguments for and against this claim and assess them.

*Warrants for an Affirmative Response: The Context of the
Normative Readings That Have Dominated the Discourse*

One can construct a credible case for an affirmative answer. Clearly, the normative weight of contemporary texts seem to point us in this direction. First,
the murders in the Holocaust reduced the entire Jewish population by a third,
a loss potentiated in every generation at an exponential rate. Next, modernity
and secularity claim many Jews each generation. If a people might be eliminated, the special warrant for continuance and creation of "new Jews" creates
a strong moral appeal.[7] The tradition is strongly pronatalist: many of the essential rituals mandate families in which to enact them, and there are specific
commandments about the necessity for a man to produce heirs. In fact, key
source texts clarify the actions that must be taken to assure the continuance
of lineage. The rules of levirate marriage state that if a man dies without having
had a child, his widow can ask his surviving brother to marry her. This allows
her child to be counted, and to receive the name and property as the child of
the dead—clearly an overriding of even the prohibition of incestual sexuality
taken in a desperate, emergent situation. One could argue that mandating children to "replace" ones lost in the Shoah is an equivalent step, assuring that the
many who have died without children need to have some sacrifice by the living
made on their behalf. And one could argue that in a reparative justice sense, Jews
might be entitled with special rights, parallel to levirate entitlements for special
considerations, granted from the world's global community—as could other minorities persecuted and murdered and endangered, for example, the Roma, Native Americans, Armenians, and others.

*Warrants Against an Affirmative Answer: A Second Look
at the Reading of Tradition*

But one can argue from the opposite position with equal justification, and let
me suggest that it is this alternate, nuanced stance that is far more consistent
with both Jewish source texts and history. The argument for this position pro-

ceeds as follows. Jews faced the issue of near total annihilation at many times in history, in particular after the destruction of the Second Temple, and have not used mere fertility as a device to increase the nation. If one looks carefully, then, at the response after catastrophe, one can develop a richer response to our current situation.

What has been the response of tradition in all of these other historical moments? Rather than calls for the physical "replacement" of the nation, the text called for the development of innovations in ritual and in education to maintain the constancy of Jewish life. Indeed, there are scant textual accounts of women increasing their fertility after other catastrophes, or being urged to do so. Women and men are urged to continue to have families in situations of oppression, to be sure, as noted in the biblical text itself and the attendant midrash that describes the birth of Moses to his enslaved parents even after the edict to kill all sons is delivered.[8] One can search in vain for a textual account of enlarging families in the face of destruction. In fact, in the quintessentially shaping catastrophe of the destruction of the Second Temple, there is no such mandate. Here, where the risk of complete extermination was even more valid than at any other time in Jewish history, the rabbinical authorities did not enact emergency measures to "make up" or attempt to "replace" Jews lost to Roman invasion. Rather, they developed scholarly and communal leadership, and enhanced a system of *yeshivot*, or houses of study. It was here that the world was preserved, via the creative act of polity-creating study, in which the canonical texts were debated, and in which the speech act, the story, and the debates set up the new normative universe. This collective, social, and textual response is key. In urging the renewal of study, the Torah and its teaching are at the center of communal response, rather than the cause and the biological quest of any individual or family. The world is made for the "sake of the Torah" and the word precedes the physicality of creation, an idea intricately discussed in the Talmud.[9] Hence, the primary institutions that needed building were collective and communal in nature: the house of study, the system of charity, and the educational study accessible to all.

In reflection on this phenomenon, Edward Feld comments:

> To the question, "How did Jews respond to other catastrophes?" I
> would answer, "not by having increasingly large numbers of chil-
> dren, but by formulating a new interpretation of themselves in his-
> tory and relation to God. The sixty years between the destruction of
> the Temple and the Bar Kochba revolution were among the most
> hermeneutically and legally creative in Judaism's history. The fabric
> of Jewish life was interwoven with study, creative interpretation, and

legal disquisition. Thus, when the rabbis of the generation of Bar Kochba had to decide which were the most central Jewish institutions to protect, the study and transmission of Torah stood out as the essential instrument of religious preservation."[10]

Such emphasis continued throughout the medieval period. Even at the height of the fertility rate of Jews in Europe, the normal family size was six— only slightly larger than that of other Europeans.[11] Average birth rates range between five and eight for immigrant Jewish communities outside of Europe, but only for a brief time. Jews returned to smaller families, along with other ethnic groups, as the society made the transitions that adjusted to changing infant mortality. But despite pogroms, war, and associated epidemics, the Jewish birth rate follows the general trends of surrounding cultures—first rising in response to improved material conditions, then falling in the face of improved childhood mortality. No textual or historical evidence exists for a special distinction. In fact, population increase is not seen as a factor that makes Judaism relevant or significant—on the contrary, it is the power of the *text* and the transmission of the *text* that asserts continuity—no matter how small the population.

Indeed, it is clear, in general, from the legal (*halachic*) accounts that the concerns of the text are specific and protective: (1) To assure that women are not *required* to have children, since childbirth is seen in the Talmudic period as potentially life-threatening, and life-threatening acts are as a rule never required; (2) To assure that the temptation for men to immerse themselves entirely in a life of study is avoided; so that every man was married and in a family with children, but not to require an unlimited, large family; (3) To allow for the pleasure of nonreproductive sexuality after reproduction of two children—the required number that, like for Adam and Eve,[12] allows for human family to continue; (4) Finally, to allow both women and men to pursue, within limits, options for family planning based on a complex assessment of personal need and social context. The discursive method of Jewish ethical reasoning follows from close analysis of key texts—but it is never a history of unanimity—rather, it is a centuries-long argument with sharply disagreeing authorities making definitive and, in some cases, contradictory statements. In thinking about the resources within the tradition that allow us to understand how Jewish tradition understands ethical questions, such as how to respond to the continuing crisis of the environment, let us turn to the development of the internal argument of selected texts to illustrate both the mutability of the tradition and the argumentative nature of the normative debate. Here, I want to briefly reflect on three classic textual traditions that are used to rule on matters of family planning.[13] Since the historical account clearly suggests that Jews did in fact limit family size in concert with other communal obligations for women, are there sources in the text that speak for this? Can one find textual justification for this side of the argument? Let us turn to the way traditional texts in two areas—birth control and abortion—are used to mobilize normative action.

Birth Control: Is a Woman Commanded
to Propagate the Race?

The drama of the biblical texts is the problem of infertility. The promise that is the basis of the covenant itself is the repeated assurance that the tribe of Abraham will be continued, made numerous, and that the Jewish future and, through it, the human future is safe. The key text on the issue of family planning arises in a Yevamot,[14] one of six tractates or sections of the Mishnah,[15] written in the earliest Talmudic period (200 B.C.E.). In this passage, the rabbis begin by discussing the problem of how to continue the line of a man who has died childless. While his wife can remarry, his line will end, and the concern of the biblical text was to enact a system to avoid this—hence, the idea that his closest biological kinsman will marry his widow, and she will claim the children born as her dead husband's, entitled to his inheritance. The Mishnaic text deepens the question about the nature and meaning of the obligation to have children:

> A man may not desist from [the attempt to] procreate unless he al-
> ready has children. Bet Shammai says, two sons, but Bet Hillel says,
> one son and a daughter, for it says "male and female He created
> them" (Genesis 5:2). If he took a wife and remained with her for ten
> years and she did not give birth, he is not allowed to desist [from
> the attempt to have children]. If he divorced her, she is permitted to
> marry someone else. And the second husband is allowed to remain
> with her for ten years. . . . A man is commanded to procreate but
> not a woman. R. Yohanan b. Baroka [disagrees and] says: About *both*
> of them it says "And God blessed them and said to them be fruitful
> and multiply."

What is occurring here? The biblical text sets the standard for the halachic requirement that a person must have children. There is debate among the sages of the Mishnah about whether a girl child will "count," and this is debated. After these children are born, the text implies, a man's sexual relations with his wife, clearly required in other places, may continue without procreative intent, which implies further that birth control can be used. (In texts of the Mishnah, there is reference to both women and men drinking a "sterilizing potion" to achieve this.) Some commentators add that it means that a man may, after he has had two children, and his wife has died, or he has divorced, marry a woman who cannot have children, or that he may even stay single.[16] The text continues with a concern about infertility. The implication here is that both women and men desire children, and hence, after a childless marriage, they both are permitted to marry someone else. The text ends with an argument about the obligations that women hold toward childbearing, and the argument stands.

The Gemora, the subsequent generational commentary on the Mishnah, continues where we left off. In the Gemora, the rabbis debate whether the command to "replenish and subdue the earth" is addressed to both women and men. Typically, there is a debate, first about gender and nature, with Rabbi Ile'a declaring that it is not "the nature of women to subdue."[17] After more debate, a consensus emerges. Women are not *required* to procreate. Then three critical cases are brought into the debate, stories that will allow for two centuries of discourse. In the first, a woman who is childless comes to ask for a divorce so she can marry and have children in another marriage.[18] There is debate: if a woman is obliged to create, then she must be given a divorce—but is she obligated? Or is it a matter of choice? Another story is told in which a woman comes with a similar plea, her desperation evident in the text "What will become of a woman like myself in old age [without children?] . . . Does not a woman like myself require a staff in her hand and a hoe for digging a grave?" It is a compelling plea: the rabbis decline her request at first, but when they consider her argument, they accept it and they allow her to divorce—a woman may make her own decisions and take on this obligation to bear children. But then a third case is told: If procreation is a woman's choice, may a woman decide to refrain from childbearing, *even if her husband wants more children?* Here, the textual account continues: Judith, the wife of Rabbi Hiyyah, endures an odd and painful twin pregnancy. As soon as she can, she disguises herself and comes to the house of study, where her husband is deciding cases of law. She asks about the halachic texts that define the obligation for procreation as having two children, and queries whether one must continue childbearing once that has been fulfilled: "Is a woman commanded to propagate the race?" "No," he replied. And relying on this decision, she drank a sterilizing potion. When her action became known, he exclaimed, "Would that you bore unto me only one more issue of the womb!"

As Rachel Baile notes: "Though Rabbi Hiyyah reacted with an outcry of grief, he did not challenge the legality of her actions." Here, we see Judith acting in the classic biblical way: like Tamar, who disguises herself to trick her father-in-law Judah into acting in accordance with the law to allow her to have children he would otherwise deny her (a kind of levirate marriage), this rabbinic Judith will also use disguise to force Hiyyah to act according to the law as well, allowing her to choose to have only two children. Thus, the discussion over the authority of women's reproductive choices ends.

The *Bariata* of the Three Women

Such texts clearly give warrant for chosen limits on family size. In other texts, specific conversations about family planning and contraception allow us to see other critical ethical values in the tradition. In these texts one sees a central—I would argue for perhaps *the* central—concern: that every child, once born, needs a protected, nurtured infancy. "The *Bariata* of the Three Women," a *bariata* being a textual argument not written in the Mishnah, but debated in the Gemora as part of the oral tradition of the Mishnah, is a central text, repeated in five different places in the Talmud[19] and once more with a few changes in the later commentary called the *Tosefta*. In it, the rabbis discuss the time when women must or may use a birth control device to prevent pregnancies, times when a pregnancy must be avoided.[20]

> R. Bebai recited before R. Nahman: Three [categories of] women use
> a *mokh* in marital intercourse: a minor, a pregnant woman, and a
> nursing mother. The minor, because she might become pregnant
> and die. A pregnant woman, because she might cause her fetus to
> become a *sandal* [flattened or crushed by a second pregnancy]. A
> nursing woman because she might have to wean her child prema-
> turely and the child would die.

What is occurring in this text? The rabbis set a requirement for birth control using a device called a *mokh*, a soft cotton pad worn internally against the cervix.[21] It may be worn during coitus, or it might be used after as a kind of absorbent—these details are left unanswered. The text is concerned with women for whom pregnancy might carry additional risks, and must be avoided, and in what cases these risks mean that even the male obligation to procreate must be forestalled. The reasons to prevent pregnancy are both to protect the woman and, importantly, to protect her child from danger. In the first, the rabbinic understanding that married minors (girls under the age of 12 years and a day) are at higher risk should they become pregnant is straightforward.[22]

In the second case, the rabbis, who at this point debate whether superfetation (second pregnancy) is biologically possible, are concerned primarily that the fetus might be compromised by intercourse. To avoid this, a complex discourse emerges over the centuries. Some suggest that the *mokh* would prevent the kind of deep penetration that might put pressure on the cervix in the last months of pregnancy; others argue that it is only in the first three months that the problem exists. The intent, however, is to allow the existing pregnancy to continue to term.

The Centrality of the Nursing Mother—Reclaiming a Core Text

This protective spirit animates the final and, for us, the most interesting, category of women who must use birth control to avoid pregnancy—nursing mothers. Nursing is understood to suppress pregnancy. It is further meant as a prolonged period which lasts two to three years. (Weaning ceremonies reenact the biblical narrative in which Sarah weans Isaac at three, and were commemorated in European tradition by deferring the first haircut to age three, a practice observed in many communities today, called "the *upsharin.*") Rabbinic texts refer to two years of nursing.[23] During this entire two-year period, pregnancy was forbidden. In fact, in Talmudic texts, the threat of another pregnancy to the health of the nursing child was considered so important that a divorcee or widow who is nursing, or who is pregnant (and will be nursing soon) cannot marry until her child is two years old. This point is clearly made in several tractates of the Talmud. It is a stronger prohibition than that which applies within marriage, since in the case of a nonrelated child, the rabbis feared that birth control might not be used with diligence. The violation of this law carries severe punishment, according to Feldman: if a couple cannot withhold from unprotected sex, the couple must divorce and cannot remarry before the full 24-month period. It is a law that assures family planning and spacing of at least 33 months between each child. Over the next centuries this law is debated closely: the question arises about the reason for the ruling, and later responsa try to sort it out and understand how to apply it in the societies in which Jews find themselves. What follows from this "*Bariata* of the Three Women" is a long and complex argument. On the one hand stand those who would use the cases in as expansive a way as possible, permitting both a widening circle of cases in which contraception could be used, and the clear use of barrier methods of birth control.

Let us look at two divergent views. In the eleventh century, R. Hai Gaon cites the risk that a pregnancy might impair the nursing mother's milk and explores the argument that one could risk a pregnancy if supplementation of the nursing child's diet with milk was used. He then *rejects* this argument in favor of the *mokh*—it is more assured to avoid pregnancy altogether. It was, he argues, consistent with the biologic plan—birth control was to be understood as a supplement of the natural protection against pregnancy that nursing physiologically provides. The idea of avoiding a second pregnancy until the child was fully weaned was so strongly held by some, including R. Y'hudah Ayyes in early eighteenth-century Italy, that R. Ayyes writes a response allowing an abortion for a nursing mother, to protect her nursing child.[24]

But by the nineteenth century, just as the birth rates are rising in European societies, and, interestingly enough, just as external pressures to reexamine women's positions in society begin to have an impact even on Jewish culture, textual arguments seem to change. Later rabbinic responsa literature, to explain this shift, offers what will become a specific tool of the responsa literature (used selectively), namely, that human biology has changed since the Talmudic era, and hence, earlier ruling and justifications are no longer binding. (Clearly, changing human physiology is easier in this view than declaring canonic texts incorrect.) R. Y. L. Don Yahya is representative of a large literature of later commentators who enter the debate:

> [Though the rabbis of the Talmud] required a *mokh* during the nursing period, I suspect that natures have changed in this matter . . . for in our times we see many women wean [before the 24-month period] and their children live and thrive. Perhaps then the permission of contraception is not applicable today. . . . Nevertheless, in questions of physical health we cannot depend on such reasoning because perhaps the majority of [such infants] live, while a very small number become thereby weak and die young.[25]

This text is intriguing in two ways. First, because it is one of several responsa that seem to allow for radical changes in interpretation based on new understanding of science and biology, and next, since even while acknowledging this, it still offers a protective opinion. Later responsa debate the point: since lactation itself reduces the risk of pregnancy (although not reliably) the *mokh* is only a supplement.

As the argument develops, however, those with a more restrictive view come to the fore, offering new opinions limiting the use of contraception to ever narrowing categories of women, and allowing for changes that limit this further, as in allowing supplemental feeding of infants to supplant the intent of the protection for a nursing mother, and describing the *mokh* as a postcoital "absorbent" only.

No less an authority than R. Solomon Luria (Polish, c. 1573) supports the use of the *mokh*, saying that "Precoital *mokh* is assumed, and it is not improper" during the entire nursing period. But despite this clear support of birth control for women during the nursing period, far stricter views that limited birth control devices to situations of morbid threat to women prevailed. This promoted a decreased interval between pregnancies. Lost was the premise of protection of the nursing infant, and hence lost were the cultural practices that this might have suggested.[26] In part this was because of a lack of knowledge of Luria's opinion, but in part, it was a nineteenth-century faith in medicine and its progress, and a growing social norm of larger families in this era, consonant with social practices of the time. Finally, the entire idea of the careful (and indeed mandated) prohibition on a second pregnancy during the two-year nursing period becomes nearly lost—it is now barely mentioned in contemporary texts.[27] This once-central, nuanced, and protective discussion has nearly been replaced by the calls for rapid fecundity and newly stated obligations.

But the philosophic point that is made by the notion of prohibited conception during nursing and in the other cases as well allows a key insight for our discussion about what can be reclaimed at the core of Jewish texts on reproductive practice. Here we see that what is at stake is the creation of a family, and what matters in the "*Bariata* of the Three Women" is the health of each woman, each pregnancy, and the careful, particular nurturing of each child in turn.

Abortion: A History of Discourse

Abortion is a part of any discussion of religion and family policy for reasons that are large driven by discourses external to Judaism. Texts about abortion as the final extreme of reproductive practices are not a matter of deep contention in Jewish thought, since there is wide agreement on textual warrants for abortion under certain circumstances. Such texts nevertheless serve as a marker of the boundary questions for reproductive health, occasionally seen, as in the case mentioned earlier as extreme examples of particular halachic codes.

Of all of the religious and philosophical issues that mark the contemporary American discourse, and the realpolitik of public policy, there is perhaps none that divides as deeply as the question of the meaning and morality of abortion. How this came to be the case and how the stance on abortion became the definitive linguistics for religion, politics, and ethics in the popular imagination requires an exploration of historical and textual positions of various religious faiths, of the place and meaning of moral status, of the changing abilities of medical technology, and of the evolving understanding of the role of women in society.

The debate about abortion is one that is divisive and painfully difficult to resolve, touching on the deepest moral issues of the meaning of the responsibility of one to another, the problem of who we will include in the community, and the persistent issues of power. For all religious traditions, abortion is a crisis, a failure of the public and the private spheres. What is at stake is the moral justification for the act, and what can be done to limit the deep symbolic disruption of this act within a social community and a personal and family narrative. The medical language itself raises critical issues and limits. However, the essential thinness of the description obscures the critical questions of morality and meaning that surround issues of life and death. For that genre of discourse, human societies have turned to religious considerations, and on the issue of abortion the discourse is intensely shaped by the understanding of the body, the issue of forbidden sexual liaisons, the view of health, the definition of personhood, and the role of women. Religions debate the permissibility of interruption and termination of pregnancy, and the nature of maternal and fetal health itself. For most religious traditions, the medical aspects of the procedure are not central—what is central is the moral meaning of the human fetus, the power of women over reproduction, birth, and lineage, the embodied and terribly fragile nature of human existence, and the paradoxical conundrum that elective abortion presents: that of the regulation of the boundary between death and birth. Similarly, all religious traditions are the carriers of a strong pronatalist position, particularly in contrast to modernity. This pronatalist view creates a lay pastoral norm that in some cases shapes the choice of text used for counseling, but is held in tension with the widespread praxis of abortion even in faith communities where the act is forbidden.

The first, and for some traditions, the final consideration of the question of abortion is the moral status of the embryo from the moment of conception to birth. Moral status is a consideration of the obligations and responsibilities of the human world toward the entity that is in question. If the embryo is considered a fully ensouled human person, of equal moral status as the mother in whose womb the embryo is carried, a carrier of a unique and sacred human life, then to end that life is tantamount to murder and could only be considered in situations in which one would murder a born human child.

For Jewish theologians, the debate is rooted in context and temporality. If the mother's life, or physical or mental health, is at risk (including, for some, the situation in which having a severely disabled child, such as a child with Tay-Sachs, would threaten her mental health) the abortion is not only permitted, it is mandated. Not only does Jewish tradition have a developmental view of the moral status of the embryo and fetus but also the tradition's focus on life and health for the mother is the primary ground for the debate. Moral status of the embryo in Jewish considerations of abortion is based on age and proximity to independent viability.

In that capacity, there are discussions about the nature and character of the contents of the womb at various stages of embryonic and fetal development. There are other considerations, such as quickening (the development of a spinal cord) and the external visual changes in a woman's body that also warrant differing social responses and a different consideration of the pregnancy. The discussion and commentary takes two courses, either that the fetus is a part of the body of a woman *ubar yerickh imo*[28] and hence does not have an equal moral claim; and a later understanding, put forward by Maimonides, that in the case where a pregnancy is endangering the life or health of a woman, the fetus can be considered a *"rodef"* (an aggressor, lit: one who pursues), and killing a *rodef* is a permitted act of self-defense. The decision about the language of the choice is framed by the woman herself (it is she that names the situation as unendurable and thus asserts her moral voice over the voice of the fetus), but the discourse is to be made in conjunction with a spiritual teacher, a rabbi, and a discourse is not wholly private, nor wholly public, opening the possibility that the discourse is primarily based in the context of a supportive and caring community.

Abortion appears as an option for Jewish women from the earliest sources of the Bible and Mishnaic commentary. Clearly seen as an emergency option, it was nevertheless clearly available under several circumstances. Most sources begin with the one biblical text that refers to an interruption in a pregnancy: "And if men strive, and hurt a woman with child, so that her fruit depart and yet no harm follow, he shall be surely punished, according as the woman's husband will lay upon him; and he shall pay as the judges determine. But if any harm follow, you shall give life for life" (Exodus 21:22–23).[29]

What is occurring here? The biblical text assumes that the following conditions obtain: that the event described—an induced abortion—is an accidental occurrence, that it is not in the woman's control, that the being lost is of value since it is perhaps the property of the husband, that the being that is "departed" is not a life in the way that the woman is a human life, that a crime of some sort has been committed, but that it is not a capital crime. Since the penalty for the loss of the fetus is a monetary fine, which is typical of a property dispute, subsequent commentators understood the fetus as distinct from the mother.

Argument One: Moral Status of the Fetus

This argument is developed in Mishnah (Arakin), which argues that abortion is permitted as a health procedure, part of normative reproductive health care when necessary, since a fetus is not an ensouled person. Not only are the first 40 days of conception considered "like water" but also even in the last trimester, the fetus has a lesser moral status. Consider the following text:

> Mishneh: If a woman is about to be executed, one does not wait for her until she gives birth; but if she has already sat on the birthstool [*yashvah al ha-mashber*] one waits for her until she gives birth. . . .

And the Gemora continues, in this particularly gruesome account:

> Gemora: But that is self-evident, for it is her body! It is necessary to teach it, for one might have assumed since Scripture says, "according as the woman's husband shall lay upon him" that it [the woman's child] is the husband's property, of which he should not be deprived. Therefore, we are informed [that it is not so] . . . "But if she had already sat on the birthstool": What is the reason? As soon as it moves [from its place in the womb] it is another body [*gufa aharina*]. Rav Judah said in the name of Samuel: If a woman is about to be executed one strikes her against her womb so that the child may die first, to avoid her being disgraced. That means to say that [otherwise] she dies first? But we have an established principle that child dies first. . . . This applies only to [her natural] death because the child's life is very frail. The drop [of poison] from the angel of death enters and destroys its vital organs but in the case of death by execution she dies first. (Arakhin 7a–b)

What is occurring here? This is the introduction of an argument that the fetus is simply not a *nefesh* and therefore, as a part of a woman's body, until the head is born, that it is not a matter of property, and that the avoidance of disgrace, even for a convicted murderer, is a valid reason for an abortion. What is at stake is the personhood of the woman, not the fetus, and we are given the most extreme account to prove this point. Rashi, commenting on Arakhin and on Sanhedrin 72b, argues that as long as the fetus has not emerged into the light of the world, it is not a *nefesh*. This argument continues in later responsa. In fact, some later commentators extend the liminal moral status even after birth: Because when a child dies within thirty days (being then considered a stillborn and not mourned like a person who had died) it becomes evident only in retrospect that it was a stillborn [*nefel*] and that the period of its life was only a continuation of the vitality of its mother that remained in him" (Ben Zion Uziel, *Mishpetei Uziel*, Hoshen Mishpat 3:46).[30]

An early modern response notes a broad definition of how the law can be interpreted. Jacob Emden, writing in 1770, suggests that we might permit an abortion in the case of a woman who has gotten pregnant out of wedlock, or in an adulterous union she now regrets. He reasons that since such an act used to warrant the death penalty for adultery, and since in our Mishnaic text of Arakhin, we saw that if a woman was convicted of capital crime she could be hung and her fetus killed to prevent her being shamed, then surely Emden can justify ending the pregnancy to avoid shame in this case as well:

> Therefore, it seems to me simple that there is also no prohibition against destroying it. . . . And even with a legitimate fetus, there is reason to be lenient for the sake of a great need as long as it had not yet moved even if it is not a case of threat to the mother's life, but to save her from it because it causes her pain. And the matter needs further deliberation. Nevertheless, it is evident that there is still a prohibition *a priori* on destroying the fetus. . . . [C]learly it is not forbidden when it is done because of a [great] need. . . . Therefore, our ruling is: if there is no reason [that is, in the case of legitimate fruit] it is forbidden to destroy the fetus. But in the case before us of a married woman who went astray, I have pronounced my lenient opinion that it is permitted [to abort], and perhaps it even almost has the reward of a *mitzvah*. (Jacob Emden, *Responsa* She'elat Ya'avetz, no. 43)[31]

Here we see the use of the argument of moral status (not a *nefesh*) and the argument of need both in play. That later argument has its source in earlier interpretations, also drawn from Mishnaic sources.

Argument Two: The Arguments of Self-Defense—the Fetus as *Rodef*

This argument states that the fetus is a danger to the woman and can be aborted because of the more general rule of self-defense: this argument becomes articulated as the argument called the *rodef* (pursuer). We see this in Mishnah 6: "If a woman suffer hard labor in travail, the child must be cut up in her womb and brought out piecemeal, for her life takes precedence over its life; if its greater part has [already] come forth, it must not be touched, for the [claim of one] life can not supersede [that of another] life." Here the text assumes three things: abortion is deliberate, the decision to abort is a conjoint one and somewhat in a woman's hands (she is the sufferer, so it is her suffering that calls the question, and it must have something to do with her stated limits) and that all can agree that a child is in her womb, but not a child who counts as a *nefesh* (fully ensouled human person) until the head is out.

An expanded commentary begins in later periods. A central extension of the *rodef* argument is made by Maimonides (the Rambam) (1135–1200): "This, too, is a mitzvah: not to take pity on the life of a pursuer [*rodef*]. Therefore the Sages have ruled that when a woman has difficulty in giving birth one may cut up the child within her womb, either by drugs or by surgery, because he is like a pursuer seeking to kill her. Once his head has emerged he may not be touched for we do not set aside one life for another; this is the natural course of the world" (Maimonides, *Mishneh Torah*, Hilkhot Rotze'ah U-Shmirat Nefesh 1:9). Rambam assumes three things: that the fetus is in fact a *nefesh*, hence has full moral status, but is a pursuing *nefesh* (*rodef*), and that a life must be at stake to allow the killing of the *rodef*. Maimonides argues that abortion is not permitted if a woman herself merely desires to end the pregnancy—she must *need* to end the pregnancy for his argument to hold. The act is permitted even though Maimonides understands that the person has no right to inflict harm on herself, and that abortion "diminishes the divine image" because a potential life is thwarted. Contemporary authority Hayyim Soloveitchik explains the alternate basis for this argument:

> The reason for the opinion of Maimonides here, namely, that the fetus is like a pursuer pursuing her in order to kill her, is that he believed that a fetus falls into the general law of *pikuah nefesh* [avoiding hazard to life] in the Torah since a fetus, too, is considered a *nefesh* and is not put aside for the life of others. And if we intend to save [her] life through the life of the fetus and he were not a pursuer the law would pertain that you do not save one *nefesh* through [sacrificing] another. . . . And it is only because of the law of saving the one who is pursued that there is the ruling that the fetus's life is put aside to save the mother's life. (*Hiddushei Rabbi Hayyim Soloveitchik* to *Mishneh Torah*, Hilkhot Rotze'ah 1:9)[32]

Ben Zion Uziel, writing in the 1950s, then extends this argument to include permission to end pregnancies that threaten not just life, but health:

You have checked with me about a question brought before you
where a woman who was suffering some ailment in her ear became
pregnant and then became dangerously ill and the doctors told her
that if she does not abort her fetus she should become totally deaf in
both ears. She and her husband fear God and keep His laws and
they ask if they are permitted to follow the doctors' orders and abort
the fetus by means of drugs, in order to save her from total deafness
for the rest of her life. . . . Therefore, it is my humble opinion that
she should be permitted to abort her fetus through highly qualified
doctors who will guarantee ahead of time that her life will be preserved, as much as this is possible. (Ben Zion Uziel, *Mishpetei Uziel*,
Hoshen Mishpat 3:46)

Finally, Rabbi Eliezer Waldenberg, a contemporary of Uziel's, interprets
the text to include protection of not just physical health, but mental health,
allowing abortions in the case of a diagnosis of Tay-Sachs, where the mother
would suffer mental anguish:

One should permit . . . abortion as soon as it becomes evident without doubt from the test that, indeed, such a baby [Tay-Sachs baby]
shall be born, even until the seventh month of her pregnancy. . . . If,
indeed, we may permit an abortion according to the halachah because of "great need" and because of pain and suffering, it seems
that this is the classic case for such permission. And it is irrelevant
in what way the pain and suffering is expressed, whether it is physical or psychological. Indeed, psychological suffering is in many ways
much greater than the suffering of the flesh. (Eliezer Waldenberg,
Responsa Tzitz Eliezer, part 13, no. 102)

Normative Definitional Criteria: Families, Religion, and the Sacredness of Daily Life

While these texts of exception are important to understand in any review of
Jewish tradition and family planning policy, it is my contention that attention
ought also be paid to quotidian concerns that reside at the core of families,
and not, as in the abortion texts, used in the most extreme cases. The proof
text that might be of more use is the classic one in which Jacob returns home
with his wives and all his children and encounters his brother Esau. The rabbis
who understood Esau to stand for Rome, oppression, and dominance by mil-

itaria, note that he travels with his armed men, while Jacob-who-is-named-Israel is marked by the fact that he travels always with children, burdened but blessed, with many details to deal with. Daily family life is the concern of most of the texts one encounters in this arena.

We have seen this to some extent in the discourse surrounding the nursing mother, but there are other texts that we ought to employ in a full account of reproductive health. Thinking about our particular texts that describe strategies for attention to family planning must be done against the larger background of how Jewish tradition has constructed family life and the daily practice of religion in more general ways. Religion for Jews is not a set of external institutional events visited on occasions of crisis or celebration—religion, "leignedness," is a binding to a commanded life, in which every single daily act of practice and attention is a part of the being of the faithful person. It is the totality of life that Jewish belief is after—the inescapable call of the stranger, the constancy of the demand for justice in every interaction, and the mattering of minute details of daily life. The commanded life is a matrix of competing and complementary and contentious strands. There is both a temporal aspect to the matrix, in that interpretations contend over more than two thousand years of discourse, and an analytic aspect, in that any act can be judged in a variety of ways. It can be prohibited, but unpunished; prohibited and punished; permitted but not approved of; permitted and accepted; obligatory, but with many exceptions; or obligatory in all cases.

Much of our understanding about families comes not from these texts that describe odd variations and extreme exceptions, but from the far broader range of normative texts that support a pronatalist family life. How to be a good Jew begins with the assumption that Jews live in families and begin these families early in life. Such families must live in communities with other Jews, and in fact have specific obligations to the wider community, as the community has to each family. In large measure, the community and the family are both oriented toward care of the most vulnerable, with a wide set of obligations to the nurturance, protection, and support of each family. Here, the biblical patriarchs and matriarchs set the template. A good family is intended to be a productive economic unit;[33] a venue for ritual acts; a place of protection for vulnerability, aging, illness, and childbearing; the core educational unit for the young children and for older girls; and a place for sensual pleasure and erotic sexuality, intimate comradeship as well as the reproductive unit of society. Hauptman notes as well that marriage is also the check on two clearly troubling impulses of men—that they might engage in "sexual misadventures" or, even more tempting, that they might fall so deeply in love with the intense encounter with the study of Torah, the passion for faith and the male partnership of study (the *cheverutah*), that they may abandon the task of childrearing entirely. She cites the case of R. Sheshet, who appears at the end of our text on leverite marriage, who became sterile as "a result of going (diligently) to R. Huna's classes." Too much immersion in study and the neglect of family life is widely understood as problematic.[34]

Laws of "Family Purity"

In large part, the sexual and social activity of women and men within families was structured by the practice of the laws of *niddah*. In traditional Jewish households, women and men do not have sexual contact for two weeks of each lunar month, based on the menstrual cycle of the wife: when she is menstruate and for a week after she is no longer menstruate (checked daily by the women and verified by her). After this period, she goes to a ritual bath, called a *mikvah*, in which she first bathes carefully, for cleanliness, is checked by an attendant, and then immerses herself in the waters of the ritual bath, while saying special prayers. Modern scholars argue about the meaning and intent of this practice. For some, it marks the deepest moment of estrangement within the tradition, a ritual to mark the negative, objectified, and degraded way that women are often seen in talmudic literature—degraded and made dangerous by her very blood. For others, the practice is a positive and powerful social construction that allows for women to live within marriage without being always the object of sexualized attention, for a valuing of both sexual and nonsexual companionate relationships in marriage, and an ongoing strategy to enhance sexual anticipation. In this later understanding, the ritual is an enactment of the realization that she has in some way "touched" death—her menses marks the nonpregnancy of that month, a kind of a loss, a theoretical death. For the second half of the month, sexual relations are to be enjoyed fully, and are, in fact, mandated. Infrequent sexual activities are grounds for divorce, on the part of either the man or the woman, and the schedule of the minimal frequency is described in the Gemora.

The Centrality of Children and Childhood Education

Considerable care is to be given to each child. Normative duties are also described: each child is the responsibility of the parents until he or she is no longer a minor. Until that time, even the responsibility of the enactment of the commandments is the task of the parents. And the careful education of each must be attended to as well: each father, or mother if the father is not able, must teach each child Torah and a trade, make sure the child has a marriage partner, and finally, some add, must teach him how to swim! It is a considerable investment of time and social resources: hence the need, as in our texts, to allow each child the best start.

The Rupture of Modernity

Against this ordered world, modernity and the *Haskalah*, or the intellectual shift following the Enlightenment, created a significant threat. Even prior to the Shoah, Jews were leaving the daily rigor of the practice of *mitzvot* for a generalized American-informed liberal Judaism. Reform and Conservative Jews drifted away (in some cases fled) from the practices of family life and the constraints on passions: keeping kosher, keeping the Sabbath, and the practice of *mikvah* with its implications that women and men would lead radically separate lives even within marriage. Jews lived in large part in cultures swept by the same demographic forces as the other populations they lived within, and consumed in large part as others did. Issues of empowerment and education for women affected all sectors of the Jewish community.

But the Shoah accelerated some processes of change and obliterated others: after the great loss of rabbinic leadership, the broad range of divergent scholarship and the broad knowledge of textual sources are far more constrained. For many nonreligious Jews, the rupture of the Shoah creates deep unease about the ideas of faith commandments, or the sacred, much less a powerful and loving God—what remains is an allegiance to Israel and a certainty that the Holocaust must be remembered—and both of these are issues of physical survival, arenas in which Jews can feel constantly at risk. For many secular Jews, Judaism itself is an enactment of attention to these two issues.

For Orthodox and neo-Orthodox, what is at stake is the betrayal of modernity itself. For many, this has meant a reassessment and a reembrace of traditional European practice, a practice in some circles that is nearly completely interpreted by rabbinic authorities since many have no history of familial customs or context. For many, the practice of Judaism is concomitant with an affiliation with the moment in Jewish history just prior to this betrayal: the late 1800s, when European Jewry enjoyed a growing community, and benefited from 400 years of stability and intense and creative interpretive study. This was, not coincidentally, the period of the most rapid demographic growth and the highest fertility as well. Jewish families, like all European families, had on average six children. Affiliation with this moment is clearly understandable.[35] But this period was not typical of other periods of Jewish history: not in biblical text, nor in Talmudic texts, nor in earlier periods in Europe—all, of course, equally valid emulative moments for custom, costume, and halachic standards. Large families were not a demographic option for human populations prior to modernity, were not seen as a strategy for Jewish survival.

In the contemporary period, the post-Shoah Jewish community after the costly and tragic failure of modernity, the deconstruction of the universal narrative has called into prominence a significant turn toward the most conservatizing elements in the tradition. This is utterly understandable, albeit a limiting of the deep and rich possibilities in the tradition. In many circles, faithful Jews perform this faithful continuity by literally wearing the garb of that earlier century in which they flourished. It will come as no surprise that since that period (c. 1877) was one of a heightened fertility rate, and family sizes were large, that aspect of life is rehearsed as well. Some Orthodox communities have birth rates among the highest in the world.[36]

Conclusions

This chapter is a partial effort to critically reflect on the central thematization of Jewish family policies in the contemporary period. And indeed, in the face of arguments for a reparative, post-Shaoh family policy made so strongly by so many diverse elements of the Jewish community, one can defend a strong case for the argument of exceptionalism. But there are both theoretical and practical limits to this argument, and, ultimately, it fails to reflect fully the rich and complex cultural and textual world of Jewish tradition.

First, we cannot bring back the lost world of Eastern European Jewry, calling after them by a genre of faithful, ritualized enactments of an imagined past. To be sure, wearing the clothes of the past, or performing the beloved moment of the past over and over has always been a limited part of rabbinic Judaism. The tradition maintains traces of this everywhere, in the liturgy, in the Passover Seder, in the Yom Kippur liturgical choreography where one reenacts, via prayer, the Temple sacrifice. But all of these acts are self-conscious, transparent, aware of the call and necessity of modernity, the need for continuity and memory, aware of their strangeness and of the need to return to the world of work. Held in tension with such enactments are two moral constraints, the necessity of tradition and the necessity of an ongoing, mutable discourse that simultaneously participates in and seeks to interpret the acts.

Let us be clear: Jews did not survive the terrible, genocidal losses of the past by population increase. In fact, there is nothing in the textual account to suggest this, and the only time that Jews increased fertility was right along with all other Europeans at a time of relative peace.

How did Jews respond to other catastrophes? With education, with the small but tenacious *beit midrash*, the house of study, which was the educational innovation at the time of the worst previous crisis for the Jewish people. The mandate of procreation begins in Genesis, in which the central drama of the first narrative is the struggle to define humanness as distinct from that which is animal. Here, the text is clear: we do not after our creation "swarm" over the earth, and make "each to his kind" in an anonymous way. We are born each into a genealogy and a name list, each particular one created, as Maimonides reminds us, "as if a whole world is created." This is not a call for multiplicity—it is rather a call of respect and attention to each.

If childbearing is world making, then the notion of acting like God begins to shape the gravitas of the enterprise: what would be more important than making an entire world? It is this particularity, and not abundance, that is stressed—it is not enough to be fruitful; one is also entasked, and it is the ability to meet the demands of the task that is critical.

Further, in countless other texts, what is key is not fecundity or numbers of persons, but the enactment of justice—the common good is not created by women's ability to make many children *in and of itself* but in her ability to create a household of justice. In such a household, her hands, beyond obligations to her "own" children, "stretch out to the poor and her palms to the destitute."

What Would a Normative Policy Be?

Given this argument, how can we envision a family planning normative practice that is both respectful of tradition, exquisitely sensitive to history and memory, and protective of women in the way that *halachic* texts remind us is key? Let me suggest a feminist philosophy that is consonant with our tradition, yet aware of our current situation.

First, such a norm, to be authentic, must advocate procreativity. Children and families have and will stand at the center of Jewish practice. This should be taken, I believe, to encompass the entire obligation toward the next generation. We can robustly reclaim the narratives of adoption in service of this goal, and of the primacy of education, as in the texts that stress that having students is also akin to childrearing.

Next, any such practice would be regulated commitments to long-term family relationships—not only between couples who intend to be parents but to the task and duty of being grandparents, uncles, aunts, and kin. It is self-evident within the tradition that children need long-term commitments from parents and from the larger families who nurture, support, and celebrate the continuance of family life. Real reproductive choice means that the Jewish community needs to pay serious attention to how family life is supported and how women, in particular, within families can lead lives enlivened by the delight of the Torah in the ways similar to men—this means strategies for the study of texts that could open the world of the textual tradition of the issues we have briefly explored.

Such a norm would understand the historic place of nonprocreative sexuality, in that any norm that is truthful to the tradition must contain within it a delight in the erotic and sensual aspects of sexuality as well as the procreative ones. This is in large part the point of the textual issues about obligation and its limits. The Jewish tradition contains complex and conflicting views on this—some frankly patriarchal, to be sure, but others that are deeply curious, insightful, and liberatory for both women and men.

Finally, justice constraints need to be a part of our reflection on families. In a clear way, Jewish tradition does not focus on rights but on obligations and duties. Hence, for Jews the question needs to be reframed in this way: what are the obligations about reproduction, family planning, contraception, and abortion? How can we struggle to be faithful Jews and faithful citizens to the world, indeed, live as if chosen, not for our oppression, but for the "light" carried in the Torah, which is to say, the long history of meaning and language that the textual tradition presents us with? Jews in most of the Diaspora and to a far lesser extent in Israel consume like all Americans, using many times more resources, water, land, energy, and food than our counterparts in Africa and Latin America. This alone raises questions of justice (not to mention the self-interest that is a part of ecological concerns). Justice means that within families, resources need to be regulated by needs of childrearing, health, and education. Justice considerations mean that a community's resources also need to be fairly used—we need to ensure that larger families do not overwhelm a community's ability to care for the poor and to respond to calls for justice outside the community as well.

In calling for serious reflection on our aspirations for family planning and reproductive health, we need to call for more study of the complex matrix of competing textual history in this arena. In particular, we need to reenter the metaphor and the practice of the protection of the nursing infant to allow for careful spacing between children, on behalf of both women and of each child.[37] As this chapter demonstrates, the textual resources for compassion are already fully intact within the tradition. Even if women understood and practiced only the restrictions on becoming pregnant while nursing, allowing for a slower pace of childbearing, this would be a tremendous change for many women and would certainly allow for the careful attention to each child.

Finally, we must come to some understanding about the historical question of the legacy of the Shoah, where we began this chapter. Like other groups considered in this volume, Jews press for unique claims for our people, our tribe. At the deepest level these claims are understandable. *A claim of this sort carries, however, serious responsibilities: the obligation for social justice runs as deep as the right to survival.* It must be acknowledged that the tension about Jewish survival is one of the deepest themes of Judaism—Abraham is never completely free of the doubt that his line will continue. Yet volume of children is never the issue. As a proof text I can offer the fact that Abraham has many other children, with other wives, yet it is not they, but only Isaac, one boy, that matters, and this is a theme that is repeated throughout Genesis.[38] Endurance, we are carefully reminded, is the work of the faithful remnant, continuity, to teaching the child the meaning of the covenant. Less than half come out of Egypt with Moses, fewer than 15 percent may have survived the Romans, but what remains is a community with a narrative, a law, and a discourse, and that is what matters when survival is at stake.

Against destruction there is only the commanded life of faith, argue the prophets, but it is elaborated by the rabbis who carefully debate the details of this life, of blood and birth and nursing babies, along with ritual and prayer in the catastrophic social and environmental collapse after the Second Temple. There we see the important suggestion, calling for further study of the question, of the primacy of the nursing mother, and there we see also the certainty of the need for *tikkun olam*, repair of the whole world, not only the Jews in the world, always the imperative of the Torah. Jews in our period struggle with ever deeper issues of scarcity and limits, and Jews now relearn to care for an Israel whose survival is precarious, whose every hill, every wadi, every tree matters deeply, a literal as well as a spiritual Israel whose survival is not ensured by creating more and more Jewish bodies, unless each one carries the knowledge and commitment to the tradition that marks them as Jews. This is why Jewish tradition counts teachers nearly as important as parents.

In rethinking Jewish ethical discourse on reproductive health and family planning, like all ethical discourse, we must reflect on the complexity and the power of the practice we pass on and create in language, responsa, and the struggle with our texts. And it is these texts that demand that the generations continue in a world of justice, as clearly as they insist we support and nurture each child—this is the legacy and a heritage that can participate in the salvation of the world.

NOTES

The author wishes to acknowledge the invaluable research support of Janet Danforth, a graduate research assistant in the spring and summer of 2000 at the University of Virginia, and the support of San Francisco State University.

1. Think, for example, of Los Angeles and New York, the two major venues for American Jewish life.

2. Primarily sewage disposal and pest control.

3. Important exceptions to this include the sudden devastation of the AIDS epidemic in Central and Southern Africa.

4. And secular Israeli communities as well.

5. Gary Tobin et al., "Jewish Population Survey," Council of Jewish Federation Report, 1991.

6. Elliott Dorff, *Matters of Life and Death* (Philadelphia: Jewish Publication Society, 1999), p. 40.

7. At a conference of the Religious Consultation in 1996 one participant, after hearing me make such an appeal, gently asked *why* it mattered if Jews disappeared.

8. See Exodus, Midrash Rabah, and Aviva Zornberg, *Genesis* (New York: Jewish Publication Society, 1989).

9. Midrash Rabbah, Bereshit, III.

10. Edward Feld, *The Spirit of Renewal: Finding Faith After the Holocaust* (Woodstock, Vt.: Jewish Lights Publishing, 1994), pp. 58–59.

11. Roberto Bachi, *Population Trends of World Jewry* (Jerusalem: Institute of Contemporary Jewry, 1976), p. 42.

12. This is based on a notion of replacing oneself. Hence, a boy and a girl are the ideal norm.

13. Many other issues related to this topic could also be addressed, such as the entire literature about infertility and fertility. This will not be explored in this chapter, but is governed by the same general principles I have listed earlier. In essence, however, one would need to ask the same questions here that one asks about population issues: What is the goal of the family? How far is one permitted to go in achieving that goal? Janet Danforth suggested these helpful queries.

14. *Yevamot* means "sisters in law," or levirate wives.

15. The Mishnah is the first level of textual commentary on the text of the Bible and interpretive laws derived therein. The word means "to study." With the Gemora, a later commentary on the Mishnah, it makes up the Talmud, a record of oral debates that spans five centuries, containing narrative, exegesis, and legal opinions on public policy and faith rituals.

16. See Judith Plaskow, *Standing Again at Sinai* (San Francisco. Harper, 1991).

17. And then, about grammar: "subduing" requires two. "Thou" means two—so it must apply to both men and women!

18. Alert readers will recognize this interesting reversal of the usual case.

19. Yeyamot, 12b and 100b, Ketubot 39a, Niddah 45a, Nedarim 35b.

20. There is a long argument about whether the term is "must" use birth control or "may" use birth control, and another about the type, placement, and timing of the devices. The details of this are important, but lie outside the scope of this chapter. It is my intent to note only the intense concern with the problem of the nursing child, and the intent to both protect that child's infancy and allow for sexuality during the space between procreative sex.

21. The actual description is obscure.

22. Even today, the risk of maternal morbidity in women between 12 and 17 is higher.

23. Yevamot 34b; Tosefta Niddah, ch. 2, with emendation of Gaon of Vilna, as cited by David Feldman, *Birth Control and Jewish Law* (New York: New York University Press, 1968).

24. See Feldman. R. Y. L Don Yahya, Responsa Bikkurei Y'Hudah, II, 121. Also see Magen Avaraham, by Abraham Gumbiner in his seventeenth-century commentary on the Shulkan Arukh, Responsum Shem MiShim'on, No. 7, Yad, Eliyahu, P'sakim No. 70, Mosheh Shick in Responsum Maharam Schick, Hoshen Mishpat No. 54. One sees this argument even in the Lubavitcher Rebbe Menahem Shneirson in the late nineteenth century, Rep. Tzemah Tzedek, (Ha-hadshot), Even HaEzer, vol. I, no. 89. All as cited in Feldman, p. 190.

25. Feldman, 190.

26. Far more research is called for to explore what these practices of childrearing and prolonged nursing might have been.

27. Indeed, one can see this with a review of contemporary Orthodox marriage manuals, popular texts, etc.

28. Literally, "part of the thigh of the mother." See Hulin, 58a; Gittin, 23b.

29. "The Greek translation, from which the Christian tradition emerges, is different, and assumes the exact opposite. The word in question is *ason*, which we have rendered as "harm" . . . but the Greek renders the word as "form," yielding something like "if there yet be no form, he shall be fined, but if there be form, shalt thou give life for life. The 'life for life' clause was thus applied to the fetus instead of the mother." This is of critical importance here. See Victor Aptowitzer, as noted in Feldman, p. 257.

30. "But if one should kill it within the thirty days because its life is only a continuation of the mother's vitality, since there is no way of ascertaining whether it indeed was a stillborn or not, that is not a crime for which one is executed, because of the doubt. Nevertheless it is certainly prohibited to kill it, because of that doubt." Ben Zion Uziel, Mishpetei Uziel, Hoshen Mishpat 3:46.

31. You asked if it is prohibited to destroy a fetus in the womb of a mother who is known to have been whoring, whether a single woman or a married woman . . . permitting her [to abort]. [This is] found [in] the responsum in the book *Havat Yair* where the rabbi [Yair Bachrach] was asked about it. . . . And this is his answer. . . .

There is no difference between her being single and available, and the fetus being a *mamzer* [bastard] from a married woman. . . . And I, most junior among my peers, say that in my humble opinion there is a big difference in this matter . . . between a [married woman who committed adultery] and a single woman, or, certainly, a married woman who is pregnant from her husband. . . . Indeed, the one asking the question asked about a married woman who had whored and it is a very good question, and I, according to my views, would lean toward leniency. . . . For, it seems to me that there is room to be lenient since she had committed adultery and "the blood is on her hands." From now on she is doomed to execution according to the law of the Torah. Even though her life is not given into our hands to end, nevertheless she is condemned to death by the judgment of Heaven . . . and if her sentence were in our hands we would have executed her and the fruit of her womb, just as it is in Arakhin where you do not wait for her [to give birth]. And this case is even stronger since there [Arakhin] it is in reference even to a legitimate fetus and here it is a fetus conceived through transgression that is also condemned to death. It is evident that you do not worry about it [the fetus] and it is killed through [the execution of] its mother. (Jacob Emden, Responsa She'elat Yaavets, No. 43)

32. There is a problem in the argument, and alert readers are not the first to note it. What of the fetus who is a *rodef* but whose head is out of the birth canal? See for example this quote:

And the difficulty in the ruling of Maimonides is that he considers the fetus before its head emerges to be a pursuer, and after its head emerges he does not consider him a pursuer for that is "the natural course of the world." And this is peculiar since before the head emerges it is also "the natural course of the world"! Unfortunately, this matter has not been clarified for me and I find no clear way to explain it, and to explain it away with excuses— that has already been done in previous generations. (Yehezkel Landau, Noda bi-Yehudah, 2nd ed., Hoshen Mishpat No. 59)

33. For a longer explanation of this, see my essay on economic ethics "Her Work Sings Her Praise," in Stewart Herman, ed., *Spiritual Goods* (New York: Philosophy Documentation Center, 2001), pp. 220–235.

34. And in fact, M. Sotah 9:15 singles him out as an example of diligence and dedication to the study of Torah—the temptation of the text is clearly seen as a powerful lure. "The Tannaim in the Tosefta remark that one who does not procreate both denies God and commits murder (T 8:7). They turn to Ben Azzai who conceded these points to them, and note that he had no children. He responds, "What can I do, my soul lusts after Torah. Let the world be populated by others." Hauptman, p. 143.

35. It is important to note that dressing in costumes of an earlier period was certainly not a practice of these Jews, who did not imitate the apparel of, for example, Rashi.

36. See Gary Tobin, "Trend in World Jewish Population," unpublished report to Northern California Jewish Community Federation, 1995.

37. And in formulating our questions, we ought to ask for explanations about why the allowance for the creative use of exceptions has waned in recent decades, and why the idea of a changed biology was allowed to change this most basic of child-rearing practices. The heart of the method of Jewish ethics is the idea that all can take hold of the text, study it, and articulate it in practice.

38. Janet Danforth has noted that in fact it is precisely Isaac, weaned at three, that is the template case for weaning at that age. Here, she notes, is an example of a child-focused attention that lends itself to continuity.

2

Contraception and Abortion in Roman Catholicism

CHRISTINE E. GUDORF

This chapter will examine the experience of contraception and abortion within Roman Catholicism rather than focus solely on the teachings of the Church regarding these practices. Critical questions include the extent of knowledge and use of contraception and abortion before the twentieth century, the degree of uniformity between and within theological, episcopal, and papal teaching on contraception and abortion, and the range of pastoral practice regarding contraception and abortion. Data on these questions helps determine the extent to which Catholic teachings on contraception and abortion are reformable in the future.

Fertility Control in Christian History

There is a fair amount of scholarly agreement that knowledge of contraception preceded Christianity in the ancient world, and that it was never eclipsed within Christianity. John Noonan, Rosalind Petchesky, and Linda Gordon, among many others, agree on this point.[1] A variety of methods of contraception, including coitus interruptus, pessaries, potions, and condoms, were known and apparently widely practiced by the Egyptians, Jews, Greeks, and Romans. Abortion, too, appears to have been a universal phenomenon. What Petchesky writes of abortion is similarly true of contraception:

Moreover, since most abortions until the present century either were self-induced or were administered by midwives or through the remedies of local lay healers, herbalists or female kin or neighbors, they have no recorded history; they are not "cases" in a medical sense. Only in France in the late eighteenth and nineteenth centuries and in America and England in the nineteenth century, when a rising male-dominated medical profession exposed the practice of abortion and its lay practitioners to scrutiny and attack, did abortion acquire a history, both demographic and medical. Under surveillance of physicians and populationists, it acquired an incidence (social measurement) and a politic (state regulation). In this regard abortion is similar to mental illness and homosexuality; it is historically constructed and takes on a particularly ideological form through the scrutiny and "recordings" of positivist medicine.[2]

This is an important point. Christianity over the centuries attempted to suppress the ancient world's knowledge and practice regarding limiting family size, first by its original suppression of Near East and European paganism[3] and later in the witchcraft persecutions of the fourteenth to eighteenth centuries.[4] But it never achieved broad success. Abortion is too closely linked to childbirth for knowledge of its techniques to ever be suppressed; too many women had interest in contraception for its suppression to be entirely effective.

At the same time, neither abortion nor contraception was the primary means of limiting fertility in Europe even before the coming of Christianity. Infanticide was the principal method, as it was throughout the world.[5] Infanticide had a number of advantages as a method of limiting fertility: it was more effective than contraception, less dangerous to the mother than abortion, and it allowed for sex selection, which was a prime concern for premodern groups who generally wanted to maximize their males to increase production without either increasing community size beyond available resources or draining family resources to pay daughters' dowries. Late medieval and early modern records suggest that "laying over" and stillbirths were very common public explanations for infanticide, in that the numbers of infants who were "stillborn" or "accidentally" smothered by parents rolling over on them in sleep is surprisingly high; it was so high as to bring legal suspicion on many after infanticide was made illegal under Christianity.[6] Doubtless some of these deaths were what we call today sudden infant death syndrome, and some of the parents prosecuted were undoubtedly innocent; nevertheless, the level of layings over could hardly have been fully accidental. Infanticide was relatively easy as a method; infants were likely to sicken and die if one did not take special efforts to keep them warm and nourished, or failed to care for them when they took ill.[7]

Rome attempted to substitute abandonment for infanticide as the predominant form of fertility control; for Romans abandonment was more civilized and respectable than infanticide. John Boswell's study *The Kindness of Strangers: The Abandonment of Children in Western Europe from Late Antiquity to the Renaissance* explains child abandonment as distinct from, though related to, infanticide and as having two forms.[8] Some infants were abandoned (exposed) in the forests at the mercy of animals and with little hope of human rescue, in which case abandonment seems to have the same intent and consequence as infanticide. Most abandoned infants in the Roman Empire before and after the coming of Christianity were left at crossroads, on the doorsteps of individuals, or in marketplaces, in the hope that the child would be accepted and reared by passersby, which, according to the many family records, literature, folktales, and official documents, frequently happened, though most of those rescued were reared as slaves, not as children of the household. During this period (600–1600) abandonment seems to have outnumbered infanticide by a factor of several hundred to nearly a thousand.[9]

By the Middle Ages oblation offered families with too many children in Christian Europe a new form of abandonment: parents could give unwanted children to the church. Most of these human "gifts" were not only raised by religious orders but raised to join those orders.[10] Oblation was Christianity's alternative to infanticide and anonymous abandonment, its gift to families whose fertility exceeded their resources. Christianity had begun taking in some portion of abandoned children at least as early as the eighth century.[11] By the medieval period the church allowed families to honorably donate excess children to the church via monasteries and convents. For most of the second millennium, oblation was not only the most common family solution to excess fertility, but since the vast majority of children donated to the church joined the celibate orders and therefore did not reproduce, oblation also served to lower general fertility.[12] At the same time, oblation was not without costs. While oblation was not generally limited to the rich, who practiced it frequently, it was not available to the poorest, who were unable to send with the child even the generally modest dower required by the poorer religious orders.[13]

By the end of the medieval period church-established foundling hospitals began to spread northward from Italy. In Catholic areas unwed mothers were not only forced to surrender their children to foundling hospitals (who also took in many born in wedlock) but were also often forced to wet-nurse other children—never their own—for a year at such foundling hospitals, as punishment for their sins. By the early modern period a unique feature of these foundling hospitals was the *tour* (French) or *ruota* (Italian), a horizontal wheel located on the outside of the hospital building into which the infant could be placed. The wheel could be turned until the child was inside, at which time the abandoner, before leaving unseen, could ring a bell to call the wheelwatcher to discover the child.[14] Foundling hospitals were distinctly Catholic; Protestants were more likely to press for men's economic responsibility for their illegitimate children and for punishments for unwed mothers, but to leave the children to be raised by, and stigmatized with, their mothers. Protestants lacked the celibate religious orders on which Catholicism relied for care of abandoned children. Though some few of the foundling hospitals' survival rates approached that of the general population, the vast majority of infants committed to the foundling hospitals were dead within months.

Hundreds of years of official documents and literature referring to abandonment and exposure give some testimony, in the general absence of statistics, as to its high incidence. While some hospices for the sick and dying did accept abandoned infants, some did not. One which did not, the hospice at Troyes, France, declared in 1263 that "abandoned children are not accepted at this institution, because if we did accept them there would be such a host of children that our resources would not be sufficient, and because this is not our responsibility, but that of the parish churches."[15] This gives some sense of the general understanding of the incidence of abandonment at the time.

Abandonment not only had all the same advantages as infanticide over contraception and abortion, being less dangerous to women than abortion, more effective than contraception, and allowing for sex selection, but it also was not final. A common theme in ancient and medieval literature was the restoration of foundlings to their (usually higher status) families. Another advantage of abandonment was the lessened burden of guilt, in that it did not require killing, and even after the advent of Christianity was not considered a sin.[16] In fact, much of the literature on abandonment seems gauged to encourage parents to hope that their abandoned children had prospered beyond the level of their birthright, though the facts suggest that through the end of the Roman Empire most were reared in slavery. In the medieval period most were reared to be celibate religious, and in the early modern period most died in foundling hospitals. In the late modern period, states took over most foundling hospitals from the church, and advances in medicine and nutrition cut deaths somewhat, though death and sickness rates for foundlings continued at many times the rate for other children.

Given this historical record, it becomes clear why there were for so long no major discourses on contraception and abortion within the church: these were not the most common birth limitation practices. The primary pastoral battles until well into the second millennium were around infanticide, the banning of which undoubtedly raised the incidence of abandonment. By the early modern period, abandonment had reached epidemic proportions. Boswell suggests that the reason that regulation of abandonment figures so heavily in successive Roman codes and hardly at all in the codes of the Germans and the Celts is that these northern European peoples practiced infanticide; the "civilizing" of these peoples by Rome, both Empire and Church, entailed getting them to practice abandonment in place of infanticide.[17] This seems to have been the general Catholic position: to ban all methods of general fertility control, especially infanticide yet including contraception and abortion, but to offer families the option of abandonment whether through oblation or foundling hospitals. For the most part this pastoral position was effective.

At least two interrelated historical changes began to disrupt this church position beginning in the late eighteenth century. One change was the demographic transition that reached its midpoint[18] in Europe in the nineteenth century, one impact of which was a tremendous increase in the numbers of abandoned children.[19] As the death rate dropped, more and more children survived infancy, placing tremendous economic burdens on families in all classes.[20] Abandonment rates soared; care of the abandoned rested with institutions, sometimes still church institutions though increasingly governmental institutions, both of which were commonly fatal to the abandoned infants.

A second challenge to the religious status quo on reproduction—which was certainly a response to the first—was the growing use of contraception. The French upper classes seem to have been the original innovators in European contraceptive use, despite the strength of Catholicism among these classes. Beginning in the late seventeenth century and continuing through the late nineteenth, France showed the earliest and strongest fertility declines in the world. French historian Philippe Aries writes that by the mid-eighteenth century respectable middle-class Catholic couples were so convinced of the propriety of contraception in reaching family limitation goals that they no longer confessed it despite church teaching to the contrary.[21] Among the more comfortably off, writes Aries, women had great incentive to limit their children because of both new economic pressures for more and longer education and supervision of children, as well as modern French redefinitions of motherhood to include closer relationships with children and more domestic presence.

Much of the evidence for methods of contraception among the French middle and upper classes of the late eighteenth and nineteenth centuries comes from physicians who refer to the use of vaginal sponges and pessaries and rubber condoms/sheaths in addition to coitus interruptus, the most historically ubiquitous method.[22] Petchesky supports the general agreement that, except for coitus interruptus and under some circumstances breast-feeding, these methods and the private physicians who distributed them were not available to the poor, who nonetheless accounted for the bulk of the marked and persistent drop in French fertility between the late eighteenth and the early twentieth centuries. Petchesky infers coitus interruptus, abortion, and infanticide as the birth limitation methods of the poor. Abortion was more likely than infanticide, because though both were illegal as well as proclaimed sinful, abortion was less likely to be detected and therefore punished.[23]

In the last half of the eighteenth century there were 20 to 40 foundlings for every 100 births in Paris, with 40,000 abandoned French babies every year.[24] There were a variety of reasons that the French lower classes desired fewer children. French laws and customs regarded both poor married and poor unmarried women as responsible for providing food, clothing, and shelter for children, rather than fathers.[25] Female domestic servants and factory workers did not make enough money to support children, and the conditions of their labor did not allow them to raise children even if they were respectably married. Nor did the working conditions of most employed women allow them to extend breast-feeding of children in order to decrease fertility.

Rural areas of France, Britain, and the United States had initiated a major decline in fertility before contemporary scientific methods of contraception and abortion became available.[26] Thus, the initial lowering of fertility in the West does not seem to have been primarily the result of new scientific techniques. Nor has it been a direct response to industrialization—the other dominant theory. Clearly, in France, the shift to lower fertility began in advance of industrialization and did not correlate with the geography of the industrialization process within France.

Church Teaching and Practice on Contraception and Abortion

Church teaching on contraception and abortion developed before the late modern era has been consistently negative, though by no means uniform. Both contraception and abortion were generally forbidden. The only licit means of decreasing fertility were sexual abstinence and breast-feeding. No direct method of abortion was permitted after the fetus received a soul, the timing of which event was accounted to happen at various times ranging from 40 days after conception to early in the fifth month. Indirect abortion was allowed; that is, when measures that would ordinarily be undertaken to save the mother's life result in the death/expulsion of the fetus, they may be done even though the death of the fetus can be expected to result (e.g., removal of cancerous uteri or ruptured fallopian tubes in tubal pregnancies). This is not the same as allowing abortion to save a mother's life. No direct attack on the fetus is allowed for any reason (e.g., no craniotomy to save a mother bleeding to death who is unable to deliver a large-headed fetus).

In terms of church practice this lack of uniformity has been glaring. Noonan provides a chart depicting the penances confessors were to assign to those who confessed contraception or abortion according to various penitential books written for confessors between the sixth and the eleventh centuries.[27] Nine of the eighteen penitential books in the chart list penances for abortion, three for contraceptive potions, and two for coitus interruptus. These penitential books also state sanctions for other sexual practices that are not (or were not thought to be) open to reproduction: for anal intercourse nine of the eighteen books list penances; for oral intercourse, five; and for dorsal intercourse (female-mounted, like animals), six. While the penitential books that mentioned abortion varied a great deal in the penances to follow its confession (from a high of 10 years fasting on bread and water to a low of 40 days), the range for homicide in these same sources was significantly higher (fasting for seven years to life). It should not be assumed that silence on any of these particular practices signified approval; four of the penitential books do not assign penances for homicide, but we assume they found it sinful.

In the later medieval and Renaissance periods, contraception and abortion continue to be condemned, often in connection with sorcery or witchcraft, but without any consistency regarding the severity of these offenses. Often there was no distinction made between contraception and abortion; both were treated as homicide. For example, Gregory IX wrote in the Decretals of 1230: "He who does magic or gives potions of sterility is a [doer of] homicide. If anyone to satisfy his lust or in meditated hatred does something to a man or a woman or gives something to drink so that he cannot generate, or she conceive, or offspring be born, let him be held a homicide."[28] Within some of the penitentials the discrepancies between penances for the various offenses are difficult to understand. That of Pseudo-Bede (ca. 750), for example, demands seven years of fasting on bread and water for a layman who commits homicide, one year for performing an abortion, but seven years for contraception.[29]

The connections between contraception and abortion, on the one hand, and these with sorcery and magic, on the other, persisted into the Renaissance. Innocent VIII wrote in *Summis Desiderantes* in 1484:

> It has recently come to our ears . . . that many persons of both sexes,
> heedless of their own salvation and forsaking their Catholic faith,
> give themselves over to devils male and female and by their incanta-

tions, charms, and conjurings, and by other abominable superstitions and sortileges, offenses, crimes and misdeeds, ruin and cause
to perish the offspring of women, the foal of animals, the products
of the earth, the grapes of vines, and the fruits of trees, as well as
men and women, cattle and flocks and herds and animals, and
hinder men from begetting and women from conceiving, and prevent all consummation of marriage.[30]

Sixtus V in 1588 further insisted on classifying both contraception and
abortion under homicide, whether these be achieved through *maleficia* or by
"cursed medicines," and thereby increased the penalty to excommunication.
But three years later his successor, Gregory XIV, disturbed by the decree's
conflict with both pastoral practice and theology on ensoulment, issued a new
teaching that "where no homicide or animated fetus is involved," priests were
"not to punish more strictly than the sacred canons or civil legislation does."[31]
Thus, Gregory was affirming delayed hominization without specifying which
method of calculating how the time of hominization is to be determined.

By the nineteenth century references to contraception as magic and sorcery
disappeared, and contraception and abortion were no longer treated as the
same sin. By 1930 *Casti Connubii*, Pius XI's marriage encyclical, treats contraception and sterilization as sins against nature, and abortion as a sin against
life.[32]

The Desire for Fertility Control and Contextual Change

One of the most constant aspects of Catholic teaching on contraception and
abortion until very recently has been its assumption about the motivation for
desiring fertility control. Because the church taught that the primary blessing
of marriage was offspring and the primary purpose of sex in marriage was
offspring, ideally only those who desired children were supposed to marry.
Desire for fertility control was consequently assumed to characterize only for-
nicators, adulterers, and prostitutes—all of whom were serious sinners. The
covertness of fertility control practices tended not to be explained in terms of
their being both illegal and condemned by the church, but rather in terms of
their resulting from sin and being intended as sin. For example, St. John
Chrysostom wrote:

> Why do you sow where the field is eager to destroy the fruit?
> Where there are medicines of sterility? Where there is murder be-
> fore birth? You do not even let a harlot remain only a harlot, but you

make her a murderess as well. Do you see that from drunkenness comes fornication, from fornication adultery, and from adultery murder? Indeed it is something worse than murder and I do not know what to call it; for she does not kill what is formed but prevents its formation. What then? Do you condemn the gift of God, and fight with His laws? What is a curse, do you seek as though it were a blessing? Do you make the anteroom of birth the anteroom of slaughter? Do you teach the woman who is given to you for the procreation of offspring to perpetrate killing? That she may always be beautiful and lovable to her lovers, and that she may rake in more money, she does not refuse to do this, heaping fire on your head; and even if the crime is hers, you are the cause. Hence also arise idolatries to look pretty; many of these women use incantations, libations, philtres, potions, and innumerable other things.[33]

It was not always assumed that contraception and abortion were sins committed on one's own body. Many of the references to contraceptive potions (*maleficia*) assumed that witches were slipping potions into the food and drink of both men and women (and their animals) against whom they had grudges in order to cause sterility, impotence, or abortion.[34] When women were caught consulting with these "witches" and "sorcerers" out of desire to control their own fertility, the midwives and herbal healers were condemned to penances at least as severe, and often more severe, than those given the women who sought them out. Lesser penalties for clients was especially the case for poor women, who a number of church authorities recognized had understandable, if not acceptable, economic motives for their sin. But no such mitigation was understood to lessen the sin of women who practiced the (magical) contraceptive arts.[35]

Today, it is incontrovertible that most of the demand for fertility control is neither for purposes of concealing fornication, adultery, or prostitution, nor is it a pursuit of magical witchcraft. Married couples with clear economic, social, ecological, medical, and personal motivations constitute by far the largest contraceptive user group around the world. Nor is it appropriate to describe desire for smaller families as selfish, as many twentieth-century church texts do, any more than nineteenth- and early-twentieth-century commendations of large families as generous were appropriate.[36] Farm families had economic incentives to increase income by growing more laborers; urban families have economic incentives to decrease expenses by growing fewer. Both respond to economic incentives. In the past, large families often had social benefits, as in North America where labor was scarce until the twentieth century. In the midst of our ecological/population/consumption crisis today, having fewer children confers benefits on families and society. It is simply insane to describe as "selfish" whatever confers any benefit on one's self or group; to do so is to define virtue in terms of self-hatred and self-destruction and to deny the possibility of a common good in which one shares.

While it is clear that the growing rates of employed married women have also supported a decrease in fertility, both trends—employment for women and decreased fertility—are responses to economic pressures. It is unrealistic of church officials to assume that men work of necessity and women work for selfish whims. Likewise, it is unjust to call men and women to radically unequal levels of labor as did John XXIII:

> But even if the economic independence of women brings certain advantages, it also results in many, many problems with regard to their fundamental mission of forming new creatures! Hence we have new situations that are serious and urgent, and that call for preparation and for a spirit of adaptability and self-sacrifice. These arise in the area of family life: in the care and education of youngsters, in homes that are left without the presence of someone that they need so much; in the loss or disturbance of rest resulting from the assumption of new responsibilities; and above all in keeping feast days holy, and, in general, in fulfilling those religious duties which are the only thing that can make the mother's work of training her children really fruitful.
>
> Everyone knows that outside work, as you might naturally expect, makes a person tired and may even dull the personality; sometimes it is humiliating and mortifying besides. When a man comes back to his home after being away for long hours and sometimes after having completely spent his energies, is he going to find in it a refuge and a source for restoring his energies and the reward that will make up for the dry, mechanical nature of the things that have surrounded him?
>
> Here again, there is a great task waiting for women: let them promise themselves that they will not let their contacts with the harsh realities of outside work dry up the richness of their inner life, the resources of their sensitivity, of their open and delicate spirit; that they will not forget those spiritual values that are the only defense of their nobility; last of all, that they will not fail to go to the fonts of prayer and sacramental life for the strength to maintain themselves on a level with their matchless mission.

They are called to an effort perhaps greater than that of men, if you take into consideration women's natural frailty in certain respects and the fact that more is being asked of them. At all times and in all circumstances they are the ones who have to be wise enough to find the resources to face their duties as wives and mothers calmly and with their eyes wide open; to make their homes warm and peaceful after the tiring labors of daily work, and not to shrink from the responsibility in raising children.[37]

It is extremely unlikely that a contemporary pope would make such a statement. The Vatican is aware that much of the world has begun to look for justice within the relationship of men and women and would question why it is that when both spouses work in the harsh public world of paid employment, it is only the wife who must come home and make a warm refuge for her spouse and children. Who creates a refuge for her? But the quote does illustrate the extent to which church teaching constructed women's role and gave it priority over the personhood of women. Men and children were here treated as having needs emanating from who they are and the circumstances into which they are placed. Women were understood as having *duties* based on the needs of men and children and the circumstances in which women find themselves.

Today, Catholic theological teachings are moving beyond either blaming women's selfishness for the decrease in fertility or calling women to sacrifice themselves for larger and larger numbers of children.[38] Though the change has been slow to come, perhaps the final straw that broke the back of pronatalism in the church was that by the 1990s the church began to recognize the seriousness of the environmental crisis facing the world.[39] In the sixties and seventies the Catholic hierarchy in the person of the pope, as well as various bishops around the world, had repeatedly rejected analysis depicting the world as imminently overpopulated.[40] That analysis was largely focused on food resources, and the Vatican response was to deny that there was insufficient food and to insist that more equity in the sharing of resources was all that was needed. Couples who wanted or needed to have fewer children due to individual circumstances were allowed to use "natural means" (abstinence) to reach that end.[41] Allowed circumstances for limiting fertility were initially focused on the health of the mother, but moved steadily toward including lack of socioeconomic resources, and have come to include environmental health. Recent evidence of environmental crisis has challenged earlier church refusal to see overpopulation as a problem by insisting that consumption levels among the rich—long a target of Catholic social teaching—combine with overall population levels to produce environmental crisis.

Today the areas of environmental crisis on which there is the strongest agreement begin with global warming and breaks in the ozone layer and include the destruction of wetlands, jungles, and forests and the extinction of their animal and plant species, and various kinds and degrees of polluted air, soil, and water from chemical, nuclear, biological, and simple compound waste. Lowering consumption among the rich peoples of the earth would help tremendously, since each child born in the United States consumes in a lifetime, for example, 24 times the energy, 3 times the water, and 2.5 times the cropland used for food of an African, as well as producing 22 times the number of tons of CO_2 emissions.[42] But given population projections for the next two centuries, even drastic lowering of excess consumption among the rich will not be sufficient to save the already stressed biosphere if we accede to Catholic social teaching's insistence that the majority poor of the world need to *increase* consumption levels. Catholic social teaching centers on justice, and so it calls for the poor to consume more—more food, more shelter, more health care, more education, more technology. It is this justice message in Catholic social teaching that mandates that the church accept the need for limiting and even reducing the human population if it is serious about sustaining the environment not merely as God's gift to be consumed by future humans but as also expressing God's goodness and creativity and therefore as requiring preservation for its own sake. We are in crisis now—we cannot increase numbers while the poor majority increases consumption, even if the rich minority does decrease consumption—of which there is no sign yet. Since 70 percent of the U.S. population increase of 2.3 million persons a year is from natural increase (not immigration), and given the disproportionate ecological burden of a human life in the United States reducing the fertility rate here is at least as important as reducing it in poor nations.

The Contemporary Catholic Church on Contraception

Many of the long-standing arguments as to why contraception is wrong have been gradually dropped even by the hierarchy in the church so that though a contraceptive ban still remains, it is now solely a ban on use of unnatural means.[43] No longer is contraceptive intent, or contraceptive result, understood as sinful. When Pius XII approved the rhythm method[44] in his 1954 address to midwives, he approved both contraceptive intent and results. What remains sinful is the use of illegitimate means, into which category both barrier and chemical methods are understood to fall. Disputes exist concerning the classification of banned methods that could be understood either as contraceptive or as abortifacient because they prevent implantation of the fertilized ovum. Only abstinence during fertility is deemed natural. The basis of this conclusion is an understanding that God's intention in sex is procreation. For some decades now the hierarchical church has recognized other divine purposes in sexual intercourse as well, but procreation has been understood as a permanent, central divine purpose. Papal arguments insist that while humans can make use of the natural infertile time to engage in sexual intercourse for unitive purposes, it is wrong to use God's gift of sexuality while thwarting the divine intentions for the act.

Catholic opponents of the ban on the use of artificial contraception argue that (1) this view is physicalist in that it interprets human nature (and God's intention for it) only in biological terms while ignoring the psychological, sociological, and spiritual dimensions of humans that support sex without fertility, and (2) this is a static view of human nature that ignores biological evolution.[45] Furthermore, say critics, the ban ignores the larger picture in Christian revelation in which human welfare takes precedence over specific formulations of law because of God's love for creation. Just as Jesus taught that "The Sabbath was made for man, not man for the Sabbath,"[46] so sex and procreation were given as life-creating and -enhancing capacities of humans, not as chains meant to cause suffering and/or the destruction of creation.

Many of the critics of the ban on artificial contraception point out that it is a relic of a context in which women were understood as having been created solely for the purpose of reproduction, for as Augustine stated and Thomas Aquinas seconded, the term *helpmate* in Genesis could not have meant anything but reproduction, "for in any other task a man would be better helped by another man."[47] Thus, one of the things that had made contraception unnatural was that contraceptive sex was a misuse of women, as in the Chrysostom quotation above. The severe asceticism in the Catholic church with regard to sex until the twentieth century focused on sexual pleasure as the moral problem in sex. This was why Augustine found that marital sex even for the purpose of procreation always included at least some venial sin: because it was virtually impossible to avoid pleasure in the sexual act.[48] (A very male perspective! One can only wonder how open wives were with their confessors on sexual matters, and how many women's confessions Augustine heard!)

Historically, these two attitudes have been linked. One reason that sexual pleasure has such a negative moral connotation is that the status of women was so low that it was believed impossible to have mutual—much less equal—relationships between men and women. Sex was understood for the most part as lustful (male) use of the (female) body. The most sexually open of the churchmen (e.g., Clement) had seen themselves as redeeming marital sex from the sin of lust by focusing it on the one activity that men and women could collaborate in: the making and rearing of children. By ruling out lust, they sought to dignify the marital relationship. For many other churchmen, holiness for the married came from renouncing sex and adopting what were called Josephite marriages, in which spouses mutually agreed to permanent sexual abstinence.

The gradual acceptance in the modern West of the equality of women combined with the related shift toward marriages based on love and arranged by the couple themselves transformed secular attitudes toward sex and made mutuality in sex not only possible but increasingly common, desirable, and expected. Couples engaging in love-based, consensual, mutually pleasurable sex came to see this sex as both expressing and creating love. For example, in the 1980s Catholic theologians commissioned by the bishops' conference of the United States proposed loving marital sex as the experience of the laity that most closely approximated the love expressed within the Trinity, and insisted that one of the chief pastoral tasks of the church was to keep sexual desire alive.[49] Such a theological understanding of sex in effect radically reconstitutes one of Augustine's blessings of marriage, the sacramental bond, by insisting that sex is not an obstacle to this bond of love, but is a part of its construction and maintenance. Shared mutual pleasure bonds persons together, just as do parenting and the myriad tasks and experiences of shared daily life. The intention that mutual love be life-giving, then, need not be limited to shared physical sex, but can be lived out in all aspects of shared life as it unfolds. A couple who is raising a child, caring for the aged, disabled, or abandoned, helping to maintain the health of their neighborhood, their church, their community, and their environment does not need each act of intercourse to bind them to responsibility for giving and maintaining life.

Contemporary Catholic Teaching on Abortion

There is no clear and continuous Christian tradition on abortion beginning in the early church and extending to present times. John Connery places the beginning of such a tradition in the thirteenth century; Dan Maguire, in the fifteenth.[50] Before that time the record is inconsistent in two ways. One type of inconsistency results from the fact that until the late nineteenth century human life was not understood to begin at conception. One reason that the penitential books assigned such varied penances to abortion is that ignorance prevailed around the processes of generation.[51] The dominant, but not the only, *theological* position was adopted from Aristotle and championed by Thomas

Aquinas, who counted ensoulment of the fetus as occurring 40–80 days after conception, depending on the sex of the fetus. The dominant *pastoral* position—obviously because it was more practical and obvious—was that ensoulment occurred at quickening, when the fetus could first be felt moving in the mother's womb, usually early in the fifth month. Before ensoulment the fetus was not understood as a person. This was the reason the Catholic church did not baptize miscarriages or stillbirths. As we have seen, abortion has not been the birth limitation practice of choice because it was, until well into the twentieth century, so extremely dangerous to the mother, as well as not allowing for sex discrimination. Treatment of abortion in church teaching tended, then, to be undeveloped.

The nineteenth-century discovery of the ovum and the process of fertilization, together with the rudimentary science of genetics, were almost immediately seized upon in the Catholic church as evidence that completely individuated human life—a person—is present from fertilization of the ovum. The church therefore decreed that human life begins at the "moment" of conception. This has led to some irreconcilable differences with later scientific discoveries, especially the discoveries that fertilization, and therefore conception, is an extended process, not a moment, and that individuation is not necessarily complete for weeks (since identical twins may not separate for 12–14 days after conception and genetic material from the mother continues to be absorbed into the blastocyst/embryo for many weeks after fertilization).

Christianity originally developed out of Judaism, which recognizes a person as existing from birth and not before. All traditions change and develop over time; there is no general reason that Christianity or any other religion could not legitimately become anti-abortion over time even if it began from an understanding of the fetus as prehuman. But it should have to present a compelling case for adopting a moral position that significantly broadens the obligations and narrows the bodily freedom of (female) humans. Yet even Catholic defenders of the hierarchical church ban on abortion are not in agreement with each other. Some argue the Vatican's position that all direct abortions are immoral; others argue that all direct abortions except those to save the mother's life are immoral; yet others argue that all direct abortions are immoral except in cases of rape and to save a mother's life.[52] A few would even include severe genetic deformity as a justification for abortion. This failure to agree is the best evidence that the Catholic position is not set in stone and is, rather, in development.

Prospects for Change in Hierarchical Church Teaching

Despite the consistent tendency of the hierarchical church to oppose the use of contraception and abortion, it is impossible to simply conclude that therefore opposition to contraception and abortion can never be acceptable practices for Catholics, for a number of reasons. One reason is that, as we have already seen, the explanations given for the negative judgments vary a great deal. For example, until the late modern period contraception was generally treated as homicide. This teaching clearly changed in the modern period, thus raising the question as to whether other teachings can or should be changed.

Many of the most frequent historical reasons given for the condemnations of contraception and abortion either are no longer factually true or are no longer recognized in the church as sacred truths, such as contraception as sorcery. But the larger reason that we cannot simply assume that negative past judgments still have force is that the whole ecclesial context for contraception and abortion has changed in two ways. First, Christians can no longer assume that we stand under the Genesis imperative to increase and multiply, since to continue to do so in today's fragile biosphere undermines the divine call to human stewardship over creation also revealed in Genesis. Second, the Roman Catholic Church (and Christianity in general) has in the last century drastically rethought the meaning of marriage, the dignity and worth of women, the relationship between the body and the soul, and the role of bodily pleasure in Christian life, all of which together have revolutionary implications for church teaching on sexuality and reproduction.[53] In effect, the foundations of the old bans have been razed and their replacements will not support the walls of the traditional ban.

Nor is a refusal to simply accept historical church opposition to contraception and abortion as still binding based solely on historical theological analysis. The fact that the church ban on contraception has been rejected by the majority of Catholics around the world, and in many places by priests and bishops as well, for two generations speaks to a sense of the faithful on this matter. And in Catholic teaching, the sense of the faithful carries some authority of its own, and must be consulted by ecclesial authorities.

Nor is widespread lay repudiation of the ban on contraception limited to "Protestant" lands such as the United States or even to developed nations. Latin America, the most historically Catholic continent in the world, illustrates the tremendous drift of Catholics from the hierarchical magisterium. In no nation of South America is the non-Catholic population greater than 30 percent. Yet despite the hierarchical church ban on contraception, and the church's success in legally banning both abortion and sterilization in many nations, the average fertility per woman has dropped from slightly over six children per woman in 1960 to just over three today.[54] It is difficult to believe that fertility was cut in half through voluntary abstinence from sex. A recent statistical study was done of fertility in Brazil, where the average woman has 2.8 children and 80 percent of the population is Catholic.[55] Using 1989 census data, this study found that even when controlling for income (necessary because in Latin America Protestants tend to be poorer, and the poor to have more children) Brazilian Catholics have 0.14 fewer children than Protestants.[56] There is also evidence that Catholics in Brazil are ignoring the Catholic ban on abortion, too. A 1996 study in three maternity hospitals in northeastern Brazil found that of 2,074 women admitted in a single year for life-threatening complications following self-admitted (illegal) abortions, 91.6 percent were Catholic, a rate significantly higher than the presence of Catholics in the population.[57]

Theologians also exercise authority in the church, and at times their magisterium has been understood to rival that of the hierarchy. Today, in the face of divergent theological opinion, the Catholic laity has clearly chosen to implement traditional Catholic moral probabilism.[58] Probabilism is a traditional Catholic practice under which, given theological doubt about the application of a moral law, one may follow any probable opinion of a theological expert. On contraception, opposition by moral theologians to the hierarchical teaching is so widespread that dissenting laity could claim to be practicing the stricter probabiliorism,[59] which requires that one follow the law unless it is more probable that one's action is not subject to the law.

Nor is the hierarchy of the church at all monolithic on the questions of contraception. When *Humanae Vitae*, the papal encyclical retaining the ban on artificial contraception was issued in 1968, the episcopal conferences of 14 different nations issued pastoral letters assuring their laity that those who could not in good faith accept this teaching were not sinners.[60] Underneath all these movements of dissent from the Catholic Church's hierarchical ban on artificial contraception is a venerable tradition of respect for individual conscience within the church. Catholic teaching on conscience understands that conscience is a potential in all persons, which must be formed in virtue and faith community in order to be reliable. In most of us, conscience will not speak often, because it has not been formed in many areas of life. At the same time, not every prompting of conscience in every individual is a reliable guide to moral good. But Catholic theologians and bishops have repeatedly affirmed that the voice of conscience must be obeyed. All Christians have an obligation to pursue the good as they see it, Many Catholics do not know this aspect of their tradition. "They have been led to believe," says Catholic moral theologian

Timothy O'Connell, "that in any situation of conflict between conscience and church authority, they ought always to follow authority. . . . But in the present context it still ought to be pointed out that this understanding is not the authentic tradition of the Catholic Church."[61]

The situation of opposition to abortion within Roman Catholicism is different from opposition to contraception for a variety of reasons. While Catholic recourse to abortion where it is legal has often been as high as non-Catholic (e.g., in the United States and Poland), theological attacks on the church ban on abortion have not been as common. Opposition to the church's teaching on abortion has not had the same opportunity to develop that opposition to the teaching on contraception has had in that abortion is still illegal in many places. Where it is legal it has only become so in the last generation, and where abortion is illegal it is much more difficult for popular reflection and discourse to occur. Where abortion is legal today—and in much of the world it is still not legal[62]—the morality of abortion has not yet been a matter of popular reflection and discourse. Church disciplining of theologians who do question the abortion teaching has been swift and severe, unlike church response to contraception dissent. Abortion has been made one of the major touchstones of orthodoxy by the present pope (along with the ordination of women). Theologians, priests, and religious who questioned the teaching have been fired, silenced, censured, and forced to recant on threat of expulsion.[63] Anti-abortion has been made the center of the church's diplomacy, especially with the United Nations and other multilateral agencies, as well as the center of national churches' legislative agendas for over two decades now. Yet popular reflection on—and political opposition to—civil and church bans on abortion grows; changes in civil abortion bans are only now beginning to be proposed and debated in many nations of Catholic Latin America.

Conclusion

At the time that Christianity began, infanticide was by far the leading method of global fertility limitation. Christianity, in conjunction with the mores of the pre-Christian Roman Empire, played a major and morally benevolent role in the European shift from infanticide to abandonment, and developed what came to be the most common, as well as the most humane, form of abandonment, oblation, in which the church as institution accepted and raised excess children.

In the modern period Christianity also played a role, but a more unconscious role, in the shift from abandonment to contraception and abortion as

methods of population management. The church ended the practice of oblation, which had been the safety valve for many nations since oblation cared for
excess children while preventing them from reproducing. The church also,
sometimes from coercion and sometimes voluntarily, surrendered control of
most foundling hospitals to the states, which gradually, due to dramatic expansion of the number of foundlings under demographic transition pressures,
penalized abandoners, thus reducing abandonment. Yet as the safety valves
for surplus population were dismantled, the church began to press more
strongly than in the past its opposition to contraception in response to contraceptive options becoming more effective and accessible. Church hierarchical
teaching on abortion became even more restrictive with the nineteenth-century
insistence that human life began at the "moment" of conception.

Morally optimal contraception today would be so effective that nonthera-
peutic abortion was never desired, and so convenient that populations would
voluntarily utilize it to achieve a fertility rate at replacement level. But all methods of contraception have failure rates, which raise demand for abortion. For
a variety of reasons ranging from medical to moral, it seems better to use
abortion as a back-up for contraception rather than as a primary method of
birth control. This is the reason that today in those parts of the world where
abortion has been, largely for economic reasons, the primary method of fertility
limitation it is now giving way to contraception. In most Eastern European
nations under communism, abortion was the primary method of fertility management because it was a free service provided by the government, while few
effective contraceptive methods were made available, most with fees. Oral contraceptives not only had to be imported from the West and were expensive but
also had been depicted by communist propaganda as dangerous. Condoms
were low quality with high failure rates. Since the fall of communism in 1989,
however, the introduction of contraceptive methods has proceeded apace,
though slowed by the need to reverse negative propaganda and to educate
physicians in available drugs and techniques.[64] In Japan, traditional use of
abortion multiplied in the wake of the Second World War and rebuilding. In
later decades gynecologists leery of the effect on their livelihoods of shifting to
contraceptive methods blocked acceptance of the oral contraceptive, which was
first approved for use in Japan in June 1999. The oral contraceptive is expected
to quickly become the dominant method of fertility control in Japan.[65]

It is likely that within a generation or two, given the need for development
in poor nations and the inevitable augmentation of present ecological pressures
from such development, that Catholic hierarchical teaching will change to encourage contraception in marriage and to allow early abortion under some
circumstances. This change has already occurred among Catholic theologians.

The hierarchy will follow because as they confront the reality of a biosphere gasping for survival around its teeming human inhabitants they will discern the will of God and the presence of the Spirit in the choices of those who choose to share responsibility for the lives and health and prosperity of future generations without reproducing themselves, even if that choice involves artificial contraception and early abortion.

NOTES

1. John T. Noonan, *Contraception: A History of Its Treatment by Catholic Theologians and Canonists* (Cambridge, Mass.: Harvard University Press, 1965), 1–29; Rosalind Petchesky, *Abortion and Women's Choice*, rev. ed. (Boston: Northeastern University Press, 1990), 25–35; Linda Gordon, *Women's Body, Women's Right: Birth Control in America.* Rev. ed. (New York: Penguin, 1990), 35–46.

2. Petchesky, *Abortion and Women's Choice*, 30.

3. Gordon, *Birth Control*, 40.

4. Anne Llewellyn Barstow, *Witchcraze: A New History of the European Witch Hunts* (San Francisco: HarperCollins, 1994), 113–114.

5. Gordon, *Birth Control*, 32–35.

6. David L. Kertzer, *Sacrificed for Honor: Italian Infant Abandonment and the Politics of Reproductive Control* (Boston: Beacon, 1993), 29–36.

7. Kertzer, *Sacrificed for Honor*, 29.

8. John Boswell, *The Kindness of Strangers: The Abandonment of Children in Western Europe from Late Antiquity to the Renaissance* (New Haven: Yale University Press, 1988), 39–45.

9. Boswell, *Kindness of Strangers*, 45.

10. The medieval theologian Thomas Aquinas, for example, was a younger son in a large family who was sent as an oblate to Monte Cassino in 1230 at age five. (Elizabeth Clark and Herbert Richardson, eds., *Women and Religion: A Feminist Sourcebook of Christian Thought* [New York: Harper, 1977], 79).

11. Boswell, *Kindness of Strangers*, 219.

12. In the late medieval and early modern periods a remarkably high percentage, between 10 and 15 percent of the European population, was celibate. S. Ryan Johansson, "The Moral Imperatives of Christian Marriage: Their Biological, Economic, and Demographic Implications in Changing Historical Contexts," in John A. Coleman, ed., *One Hundred Years of Catholic Social Thought* (Maryknoll, N.Y.: Orbis, 1991), 136.

13. Dower was a common English term used not only for a marriage portion but also for the entrance fee to the order.

14. David L. Kertzer, *Sacrificed For Honor*, 102–104.

15. Boswell, *Kindness of Strangers*, 361.

16. This does not imply that it was never condemned by individual documents or theologians. Lactanius, in "The True Religion" in the sixth book of the *Divine Institutes*, written about 300 C.E., speaks of a Christian who is too poor to raise a large

family, but condemns abortion, infanticide, and child abandonment as solutions no Christian could accept. The only solution is complete continence (6.20.25 *Corpus scriptorum ecclesiasticorum latinorum* [Vienna, 1866] 19: 559).

17. Boswell, *Kindness of Strangers*, 209–210.

18. The midpoint of demographic transition is where the death rate has dropped dramatically but the birth rate has remained stationary or even increased (with improved maternal health). Demographic transition ends when the birth rate has dropped to the level of the death rate, so that the population is in equilibrium.

19. Kertzer writes: "By the early nineteenth century babies were being abandoned in vast numbers in France, Belgium, and Portugal, and the situation was even worse in Spain, Ireland, Poland, and in most of the Austrian provinces. In Madrid, Dublin, and Warsaw up to a fifth of all babies were being abandoned, while Milan had reached a third, and Vienna a half. What made the dimensions of abandonment especially shocking was the contrast to countries such as Prussia, England, Switzerland, and the United States, where newborns were seldom abandoned. In all, at midcentury, more than 100,000 babies were being abandoned every year in Europe, and most were taken in by a formal governmental system for their care, a system which proved to be so inept that most of the children perished within a few months" (Kertzer, *Sacrificed for Honor*, 10).

20. But especially among the richest and the poorest. Since among the upper classes there were a limited number of income-producing positions that did not require property ownership, an increase in the number of surviving children meant not only more dowries for daughters but that additional male children had to be given income-producing property, which divided the family estates and diluted its power. Among the poorest, of course, the basic issue was food, clothing, and shelter.

21. Philippe Aries, "Interpretation pour une Histoire Mentalites," *in La Prevention des Naissances dans la Famille*, ed. Helene Bergues (Paris: Institut National d'Etudes Demographiques, 1960), 318–319.

22. Interestingly, Noonan found that despite having the biblical story of Onan in Genesis 38 as a foundation for condemning coitus interruptus, coitus interruptus is not mentioned in either the Irish or the British penitentials. It appears in one French penitential, circa 813: that of Bishop Theodulphus of Orleans (161).

23. Petchesky, *Abortion and Women's Choice*, 50.

24. Olwen H. Hufton, *The Poor of Eighteenth-Century France* (Oxford: Clarendon Press, 1974), 318.

25. Petchesky, *Abortion and Women's Choice*, 47.

26. Petchesky, *Abortion and Women's Choice*, 30.

27. Noonan, *Contraception*, 164.

28. Quoted in Maureen Fielder and Linda Rabben, eds., *Rome Has Spoken* (New York: Crossroad, 1998), 149–150.

29. Noonan, *Contraception*, 164.

30. Quoted from Fielder and Rabben, *Rome Has Spoken*, 150.

31. Quoted from Fielder and Rabben, *Rome Has Spoken*, 150.

32. Pius XI, *Casti connubii*, para. 314–347 in *Papal Teachings: Matrimony* (Boston: Daughters of St. Paul, 1963).

33. St. John Chrysostom, *Homily 24 on the Epistle to the Romans, Patrologia graeca*, ed. J. P. Migne (Paris, 1857–66), 626–627.

34. Noonan, *Contraception*, 159–161.

35. Noonan, *Contraception*, 159–160.

36. See, for example, the speeches of Pius XII, the last Catholic pope to be unreservedly pronatalist, in *Papal Teachings: Woman in the Modern World* (Boston: Daughters of St. Paul, 1959), pp. 73, 82–84.

37. John XXIII, "Ci e gradito," *Osservatore Romano*, December 8, 1960; translation: *The Pope Speaks* 7:172–173.

38. Pius XXII was the church leader who most romanticized large families in the last few centuries, though it was a common theme for other popes and bishops. See my *Catholic Social Teaching on Liberation Themes* (Washington, D.C.: University Press of America, 1980), chap. 5.

39. See John Paul II, "The Ecological Crisis: A Common Responsibility," January 1, 1990 (Publication No. 332–9, United States Catholic Conference).

40. John XXIII, "Mater et Magistra," para. 186–199, and Paul VI, "Humanae Vitae" (July 25, 1968), para. 2, in Joseph Gremillion, ed., *The Gospel of Peace and Justice* (Maryknoll, N.Y.: Orbis, 1976).

41. *Catechism of the Catholic Church* (United States Catholic Conference, 1994) 1652–1654, 2366–2372.

42. Population and Resources Supplement, *National Geographic Magazine* (Washington, D.C.: National Geographic Society, October 1998).

43. "Humanae Vitae," para 14, and *Catechism of the Catholic Church*, 1652–1654.

44. Rhythm is the use of sexual abstinence in the fertile period, and has been refined into a number of types differentiated by the method by which the fertile period in the female cycle is discerned. The rhythm method is usually called Natural Family Planning within Catholic circles.

45. That is, that we know God's will by discerning it within creation, which has, under God's will, undergone and still undergoes a process of evolution in which human sexuality has significantly changed. Originally, sexual activity was, as in apes, limited to the period of female estrus—the fertile period. But human females, as well as males, now have the desire and ability to engage in sexual activity at all times. Does God then have less procreative intent for human sex since this change? How should we understand the meaning of this change, given Catholic traditions of natural law discernment?

46. Mk. 2: 27.

47. Thomas Aquinas, *Summa Theologiae*, 1: 92, 1.

48. Augustine, *Dei Civitate Dei*, 14, 24; *De Nupt, et concup.* I: 6–7, 21, 33.

49. Charles Gallagher, George A. Maloney, Mary F. Rousseau, and Paul F. Wilczak, *Embodied in Love: Sacramental Spirituality and Sexual Intimacy* (New York: Crossroad, 1986) 15–16, 49.

50. Daniel C. Maguire and James T. Burtchaell, "The Catholic Legacy and Abortion," in Stephen E. Lammers and Allen Verhey, eds., *On Moral Medicine*, 2nd. ed. (Grand Rapids, Mich.: Eerdmans Publishing Co., 1998), pp. 586–599.

51. The existence of the female ovum was not discovered until the nineteenth century.

52. For example, John Connery (*Abortion: The Development of the Roman Catholic Perspective* [Loyola, 1977]) takes the official position; James T. Burtchaell, C.S.C., in "The Catholic Legacy and Abortion: A Debate" (with Dan Maguire), in *Commonweal* 126 (Nov. 20, 1987): 657–672, argues for the mother's life exception, and many Catholics in the Right to Life Movement include rape as justification because they feel that without this there is no hope of majority support.

53. Among many other texts, see my *Body, Sex and Pleasure: Reconstructing Christian Sexual Ethics* (Cleveland, Ohio: Pilgrim Press, 1994).

54. Population Reference Bureau, *1996 World Population Data Sheet* (Washington, D.C.: Population Reference Bureau, 1996.

55. Population Reference Bureau, *1996 World Population Data Sheet.*

56. Christine E. Gudorf, "Religion and Fertility in Brazil: The PNAD Data." Unpublished, 2000.

57. Walter Fonseca, Chiyuru Misago, Luciano L. Correia, Joao Parente, and Francisco Oliveira, "Determinants of Induced Abortion Among Poor Women Admitted to Hospitals in a Locality of Northeastern Brazil," *Rev Saude Publica* 30. 11 (1996): 13–28.

58. Donald A. McKim, *Westminster Dictionary of Theological Terms* (Louisville, Ky.: Westminster/John Knox Press, 1996), 222.

59. McKim, *Westminster Dictionary of Theological Terms,* 222.

60. Charles Curran et al., *Dissent in and for the Church* (Franklin, Wisc.: Sheed and Ward, 1969).

61. Timothy E. O'Connell, *Principles for a Catholic Morality* (New York: Seabury Press, 1978), 92–93.

62. According to the Center for Reproductive Law and Policy, Chile and El Salvador prohibit abortion even to save the mother's life, 52 nations (25% of world population) allow it only to save the mother's life, 23 nations (10% of world population) allow abortion to save the mother's life or physical health, 20 nations, 4% of world population allow abortion to save the mother's life, physical health, or mental health. On the other hand, 6 nations with 20% of the world's population also allow abortion for socioeconomic reasons, and 49 nations with 41% of the world's population do not require any of these reasons to allow abortion. Catholic nations including Brazil, Guatemala, Haiti, Ireland, Nicaragua, Panama, Paraguay, Philippines, and Venezuela all allow abortion only to save the mother's life and health. Remaining majority Catholic nations fall either into the category of allowing abortion only to save life and physical health (Argentina, Bolivia, Costa Rica, Ecuador, Peru, Poland) or the category that adds the mother's mental health to these reasons (Spain and Switzerland). *The World's Abortion Laws 1998* (poster), The Center for Reproductive Law and Policy, 120 Wall Street, New York, New York 10005.

63. In the United States the best known examples were the priests and religious who were forced to recant their signatures on the *New York Times* ad calling for open discussion of abortion in the church, on pain of being forced out of religious life. In

Latin America, the best known case is that of Ivonne Gebara, a Brazilian nun silenced and sent to Europe for a year of theological study for opining that for the poorest of women in the favela in which she worked, moral culpability for abortion was questionable.

64. "Women in Catholic Church Politics in Eastern Europe," *Journal of Feminist Studies in Religion* 2 (1995): 101–116.

65. Sheryl WuDunn, "Japanese Officials Move to Lift Ban on the Pill," *New York Times*, June 6, 1999, sec. 4, WK2(N), col. 1.

3

Contraception and Abortion Within Protestant Christianity

GLORIA H. ALBRECHT

Protestantism Defined

Protestantism is most honestly defined with the admission that, except for some broad generalities, its pluralism defies definition. Therefore, the best way to define how the term currently is employed is by defining the negative, what it is not. Protestantism refers to any form of Christianity that does not recognize itself to be under the authority of the Roman Catholic Church or within the communion of those churches loyal to Eastern Orthodox Christianity. Historically, Protestant Christianity began with protests that arose within western Catholic Christianity in the early modern period of European history. These religious protests were part of the rapid changes in economics, politics, and culture that transformed western Europe in the sixteenth century. The growth of nation-states and a sense of nationalism, the Renaissance emphasis on the individual and individual expression, and concern over what were seen as abuses within the existing structure of western Catholic Christianity all played a part in fueling these protests. Whether or not the reformers, as they are now called within Protestantism, intended to stir renewal within the existing western Christian church centered on the Bishop of Rome, the ultimate result of their actions was the development of separate, institutionalized traditions, later called "denominations."

Four distinct Protestant expressions took form out of the ferment of the sixteenth century, a time in European history now referred to as the Reformation. The earliest, arising in German-speaking areas, was the Lutheran tradition connected to the reform activities and theology of an Augustinian monk, Martin Luther (1483–1546). At nearly the same time, what are now known as the "Reformed" churches developed out of the movements associated with the leadership of Ulrich Zwingli (1484–1531) in Zurich, Switzerland, and John Calvin (1509–1564), a Frenchman who had fled the persecutions of Protestants in France to settle in Geneva, Switzerland. Both the Lutheran and Reformed traditions continued the practice of infant baptism and formed themselves around the traditional medieval assumption that everyone who lived in a given area would be members of the denomination established by law there. Therefore, both maintained close and cooperative ties with the state. A third and quite different tradition arose primarily among the rural peasantry. Known as Anabaptists for their rejection of infant baptism, often pacifist, and typically emphatic about the individuality of faith, this tradition believed in churches composed only of those who had experienced a sincere conversion of faith. Suspicious of the unconverted world and of its secular governments, Anabaptists tended to withdraw from society into communities of their own. Anabaptists disagreed with, and were opposed by, those loyal to Roman Catholicism, as well as those loyal to the developing Lutheran and Reformed traditions. Finally, the mixture of rising national sentiments, economic dislocation, dissatisfaction with practices within Roman Catholicism, and the consequent desire to return to the practices of the first Christian century also led to protests on the other side of the English Channel and, ultimately, to the creation of the Church of England and Anglicanism (1534). For almost all of the three centuries that followed, from 1500 to 1750, the interconnection of political, economic, and cultural turmoil spawned religious persecutions and war in Europe. Protestants of various sorts, as well as Catholics, flowed over borders seeking safety and a place to practice their religion. As part of that process, representatives of these four broad Protestant strands emigrated to North America, established their churches, and often repeated the process of internal dissent that ends in reform or separation and the establishment of a new denomination.[1]

The success of Protestantism at this point in European history may be accounted for, at least partially, by the resonance it had with new developments in Western culture arising to replace the culture of the Middle Ages: Renaissance humanism, Christian humanism, and the beginnings of scientific theory and method. It is possible to talk about some general characteristics of European Protestantism in terms of this resonance. First, the reformers found their justification for attempting to bring about changes in the western Catholic

Church by returning to those texts understood as the Christian classics, the Bible. Protestants generally saw themselves as returning to the one authentic source of Christian belief and practice undistorted by centuries of human embellishments. Each denomination attempted to adopt what they believed had been the teachings and practices of Christians in the first century of the Christian calendar. This desire to return to the roots of Christianity, and the conveniently timed invention of the printing press, placed the Bible in the center of Protestant deliberations. *Sola Scriptura* is Luther's Latin phrase for the principle that expresses the Protestant claim that the Bible is the primarily guide for authentic faith and faithful living. As students of Christian humanism, however, both Luther and Calvin stressed the necessity of studying these texts with the same historical and linguistic scholarship applied to the literary classics of Greece and Rome. *Sola Scriptura* is still recognized as a central characteristic of Protestantism. However, continuing developments in the study of linguistics, in theories of interpretation, and in the global expansion of Protestantism make for much diversity among Protestants in determining what the Bible says and how the Bible functions as authority. Consequently, while the Bible remains the one authentic witness for Protestant faith, disagreements over its use and interpretation are not an insignificant source of Protestant interdenominational and intradenominational tensions.[2]

Second, the right of the reformers to question established structures of authority was justified by their appropriation, on religious grounds, of the growing secular emphasis on individual rights and responsibilities. Martin Luther's often repeated defense, now popularized as "Here I stand, I can do no other," symbolizes this personal burden of authenticity. Generally, Protestant denominations emphasize the duty of each person to develop his or her religious knowledge (especially of the Bible) and to take responsibility for his or her own spiritual relationship with God. This latter expectation, sometimes referred to as "the priesthood of all believers," explains the Protestant emphasis on "faith" as a more subjective experience of the sacred, rather than an intellectual adherence to tradition or prescribed beliefs.

Third, in what might appear to be a contradiction, Protestantism tends to approach all religious systems of belief and practice with suspicion. Theologically, this "Protestant Principle" warns against the absolutizing of anything that is created. It is a recognition of the human tendency to turn our own ideas and creations into idols. That is, having originated in resistance to one historical expression of Christianity, and having simultaneously originated in a condition of pluralism, Protestantism recognizes the limits of human ability to know the mind and will of God even as humans are compelled, by love and gratitude, to serve God faithfully. Thus, much Protestant theology emphasizes the importance of God's gifts of grace and forgiveness to humans who are by definition finite, if not also sinful. In some instances the combination of individualism with the recognition of human frailty has led to a variety of democratically influenced forms of church government. Latourette argues that the logical conclusion of Protestant theologies (salvation by faith and the priesthood of all believers), although not the preference of the reformers themselves, implies government in which each has a voice, rights, and responsibilities. This possibility is seen, for example, in the descendants of the Anabaptists: Independents, Baptists, and Quakers.[3]

From its roots in Europe and North America, Protestantism spread by the vehicle of European conquest and by missionary zeal to every part of the world. Today, Protestants, defined in the broadest sense, account for not quite a fourth of the approximately two billion Christians worldwide.[4] They represent slightly more than 50 percent of the population of the United States. The Baptists, one of the descendants of the Anabaptists, are the largest Protestant denomination in the United States. But there are also a million Baptists in Nigeria. About 90 percent of the populations of Scandinavian countries are Lutheran, as is 50 percent of the population of Namibia. There are about two million Lutherans in Indonesia, while about 25 percent of the population of South Korea is Protestant, primarily Presbyterian. In fact there are now more Presbyterians in South Korea than there are in the United States.

It is important to note that wherever Protestantism has spread, it has taken on new life and produced new forms. In the United States, Methodism arose out of the Episcopal Church and both thrived. The Anabaptist strand, with its emphasis on local church autonomy, has proliferated into several larger denominations and a multitude of smaller groups and independent churches. Of particular importance in the United States was the development by African-American slaves of religious cultures, and ultimately denominations, separate from the white Christianity of slave owners.[5] Black and womanist theologies, as they are known today, continue to develop out of the interlocking experiences of racism, sexism, and class oppression that have characterized African-American life. Included in this work is the important analysis of how political loyalties, economic needs, and social commitments ground hermeneutical principles and practices.[6] Similarly, cultures around the world have appropriated and changed what European and North American Protestants represented. Kwok Pui-lan, a Chinese Christian, has described the Asian experience in which Christian missionaries understood themselves to be bringing the Word of God to heathens lost in a culture of idolatry and superstition. Kwok identifies and challenges the cultural embeddedness of Christianity in western perspectives. She writes: "If other people can only define truth according to the western perspective, then Christianization really means westernization."[7] The term *Protestantism*, then, no longer means only those Christian denominations with European roots, or even their direct offspring. Everywhere indigenous Christianities are emerging. The fastest growing segments of Protestant Christianity are in the southern hemisphere, especially in Africa. In 1900, Christianity was primarily the religion of Europeans and their descendants. In 2000, only 45 percent of the world's Christians are European or of European descent.[8]

Obviously, this diversity makes it impossible to provide a scholarly account of contraception and abortion that is representative of all the groups that fall under the label "Protestant." For purposes of this chapter, then, I will restrict my discussion to the European-generated denominations and their direct heirs that are typically called the "mainline" Protestant denominations. I will argue, as Beverly Harrison has argued, that with the Reformation these European-generated denominations set themselves upon a trajectory leading away from hierarchical forms of doctrinal control. By the implication of their theologies, and by the ongoing experiences of history, this trajectory continues to lead toward the development of communities where theological discourse is grounded in the embodied experiences of all of the community's people, and others. This reading of the Protestant experience takes note of the impact on issues of contraception and abortion of admitting new voices: first, married men; later, women and ex-slaves. Today, the economically poor and lesbian, gay, bisexual, and transgendered persons add their struggle for inclusion to the as yet incomplete inclusion of white women and people of color. This reading of Protestant history argues that the clear movement of Protestantism has been in the direction of accepting the importance of family planning and the use of contraceptives, as well as, in the twentieth century, support for legal access to abortion, although with qualifications regarding the moral justification of specific acts of abortion. The hope of reformation is that out of inclusive communities of embodied discourse a shared discernment of a truth might arise that is more inclusive and more just and more akin to the will of God.[9]

Protestant Fundamentalism

However smooth and inevitable this historical process might appear with hindsight, the historical reality then, as now, was one of struggle, conflict, and tension. New voices have been admitted into the discourse only after prolonged struggle. As they become part of the discourse, new voices often bring a critical reading of established thought. Today the official positions taken by the mainline Protestant denominations continue to develop in a direction that affirms and protects reproductive choice. However, strong resistance to this direction continues. To understand the current state of these issues within Protestantism, then, requires an analysis of Christian Fundamentalism and what I argue is its historical resistance to the Reformation tradition, in general, and to reproductive choice, in particular.

The terms *fundamentalism* and *traditionalism* are unfortunately interchanged in common discourse. For the purposes of this chapter it is important to make a clear distinction between them. Traditionalism, as I use the term here, involves a strong and positive relationship with one's religious tradition: its rituals, its narratives, its way of interpreting experience, its practices of moral and theological discernment. Traditionalism, as it is expressed in Protestantism, is capable of preserving the central characteristics of Protestantism that developed in the European context of struggle against hierarchical authority. Traditionalism need not become fundamentalist.

Fundamentalism, on the other hand, is inimical to that heritage. As a reaction against modern worldviews, fundamentalism is itself an outgrowth of modernity. The development of both the social and physical sciences, as well as growing cross-cultural experiences that revealed the existence of large, ancient, complex, alternative religions, presented a challenge to all Christian denominations in the late nineteenth and early twentieth centuries.[10] The "liberal" Protestant response emphasized confidence in human reason and its new knowledges with the expectation that reason and faith need not be adversarial. The fundamentalist response that developed near the end of the nineteenth century was, and is, a reaction of fear as modernity produced multiple alternative knowledge sources that challenged any narrowly defined religious control over how people will understand their world. As I described earlier, a central characteristic of the Protestant Reformation was the recognition that all things human, including the human experience of religion, were finite and fallible. The reformers argued that no guarantee of absolute truth could reside in the magisterium of the western church, nor in its traditions. The fear that drives fundamentalism, however, requires the reimposition of an absolute truth that will stand, unchanging, against all contending sources of knowledge. In the mid-nineteenth century, the need to counter the knowledge claims of modern science with an unquestionable source of religious truth led to a new theology of biblical inerrancy.[11] Although the reformers made no claim to biblical inerrancy, nor would they given their schooling in Christian humanism, certainly the temptation of such a claim can be traced to the way in which they tied their claims to biblical texts.[12] Protestants, in denying the simple authority of tradition or of a church hierarchy, are left with the unending task of relating a culturally based scripture with always new, culturally produced texts—the texts of the social and physical sciences and of all the cultures of the world. In doing so, Protestants face over and over again the temptation to freeze the theological truth of this moment. Protestants are continually faced with the temptation to stop being Protestants. Here arises the temptation for biblical idolatry: to claim the power (politics) to name theological truth, to control the limits of change, to permanently set the boundaries of religious community.[13] Fundamentalism, at heart, is the desire to stop the process of re-formation. As Beverly Harrison has written: "Fundamentalism is, at root, always a rejection of increased openness, inclusiveness and religious neighborliness within Christian community and between Christians and other religio-cultural groups."[14]

In the late twentieth century, the changing roles of women in the United States, initiated as much by structural economic transformations as by women's struggles for equal civil and economic rights, have become the lightning rod for a renewed fundamentalism. Fundamentalist Protestants in the United States clearly intend a rejection of women's progress toward equal status with men in both public and private spaces. Beverly LaHaye writes: "Unless we accept the Bible's teaching that woman was created for man, we cannot begin to follow God's plan for happy marriages. Denial of this foundational truth may be the first step of a rebellion against God's plan for happiness in marriage. . . . A man's role as leader is threatened when the woman refuses to give him the support he needs in the challenging task of undertaking godly leadership."[15] The patriarchal language of fundamentalism, justified by its claim of biblical inerrancy, has profoundly shaped the Protestant debates of the last century over contraception and abortion. Its rhetoric is as virulent at the end of the twentieth century and the opening of the twenty-first as it was at the end of the nineteenth.[16] Fundamentalist resistance to family planning, to new forms of contraception, and to safe, surgical abortion as a form of birth control need to be read for what they are most deeply—resistance to women's full and equal standing in public places, in private places, and in the church. As such it is also a rejection of what I argue is the heart of the Protestant project begun in the sixteenth century.

The Development of Protestant Positions on Contraception and Abortion: The Reformation

Views on contraception and abortion are inevitably rooted in cultural understandings of human sexuality, generally, and of women's sexuality, in particular, as it is related to men and the family. The reformers, and I am particularly focused on Luther and Calvin here, inherited views about sexuality that had become dominant within the western Catholic Church over a period of fifteen hundred years. Thus, we must go back and look at that development. I do so with some provisos about the turn to history that feminists in many fields of inquiry have developed.

Fortunately, the feminist reconstruction of this history was impressively accomplished by Harrison almost 20 years ago. It is to her groundbreaking book *Our Right to Choose* that I now turn for historical guidance.[17] First, when researching a question of Christian ethics, one must deal with the question of what constitutes "history." Typically, scholars have assumed that relevant history is found in the intellectual writings of those theologians whose views are consistent with current dogma and who are now revered as central to the development of orthodox Christian faith and practice. There are at least two problems with this approach. One is that theologians of equal or greater stature in their own time, whose views may differ, are overlooked. Yet theologians not particularly influential in their own age may be given eminence in hindsight. Moreover, even their writings that express other views on the same topic are likely to be ignored. In other words, it is quite typical for a direct line of orthodoxy to be drawn from the contemporary dogma back into the past, ignoring the presence of a much more complex and nuanced intellectual heritage. The second problem is that this almost total focus on intellectual history erases from consideration what were the actual moral practices of the people of faith. This is especially problematic when the issues under consideration are those that profoundly shaped the lives of women. A history drawn from a male, intellectual discourse is simply incomplete. It may be more proscriptive or prescriptive than descriptive. A second issue in ethical history is the tendency to lift rules (prescriptions and prohibitions) out of their historical and cultural context. Without analyzing the reasons and the context for the rule, the rule is made to appear as an unchanging and unquestioned moral dictum. What may be missed are variations in the sort of acts being proscribed, as well as the values that were informing the motivation and intentions of the proscription. With these cautions in mind, Harrison sets about to disprove what has become a commonsensical assumption about the history of Christian ethics on abortion: that the life of the fetus has, in Noonan's words, "an almost absolute value in Christian history."[18]

Contrary to the impression given by many recitations of early Christian texts on abortion,[19] Harrison notes that these antiabortion texts are both few in number and fragmentary in context. Given the existence of large numbers of Christian writings from the first six centuries of the Christian calendar, the overall silence of these writings on the issue of abortion is most compelling.

Harrison concludes, "How can this be the case if Christianity were truly involved in the effort to foil morally inferior forces so cavalier toward human life? The answer, I believe, is that concern about abortion constitutes a minor, episodic matter in Christian discussion until the late nineteenth century. Furthermore, I find no evidence until the modern period that compassion for the presumed 'child' in the womb was a generating source of Christian moral opposition to abortion."[20] If not concern for the fetus, then what was reason behind the negative texts that do exist? Harrison argues that in almost all of the texts abortion is one act along a continuum of acts that were denounced as murder because they blocked the only, divinely given, reason for sexual intercourse: procreation. The primary issue, then, was the development and imposition of a strongly negative and fearful view of sexuality. Margaret Farley argues that Stoicism had the greatest impact on the development of early Christian thought. The Stoic belief in the necessity of humans to control emotions with reason led to their teaching that sexual desire must be regulated by a rational purpose. Their norm for sexual ethics, then, was procreation. Farley writes that this norm was adopted as the Christian sexual ethic in order to avoid the two extremes of Gnosticism. In one Gnostic position, procreation was a vehicle for evil forces and celibacy was the norm. In the other, any sexual experience was advocated as long as it was not procreative. The justification of sexual intercourse for procreation allowed Christian theologians to avoid a doctrine that sex was bad while providing a rigorous standard for its goodness. With the addition of Augustine's arguments against the Manichaeans, the tenor of the Christian sexual ethic was set until the sixteenth century.[21] Vern and Bonnie Bullough also suggest that resistance to Gnosticism contributed to the development of Christian sexual asceticism—a hostility to sex, they note, that was actually more similar to the Gnostics than to the Jewish tradition of Christian origins.[22] Timmerman connects the growing antisex asceticism of the early Christian centuries to Christian appropriation of the dualism of the Greco-Roman world. When salvation of a nonmaterial soul is the goal of religion, the earth and the body, especially the female body that provides the material stuff that imprisons the soul, becomes a source of feared desires.[23] The consequence was the solidification of a dualistic theology of sexuality that was antisex and antifemale. In the hierarchy of virtues, martyrdom, virginity, and celibacy led the way. Marriage that was committed to sexual abstinence was more holy than marriage in which spouses had intercourse for the sake of procreation. There was no good simply in the pleasure of sex.[24] Thus, sex outside marriage and the use of contraception within were denounced as murderous. All nonprocreative sex was murderous. The value of fetal life did not need to be discussed; it was assumed as the God-given product of sexual activity, activity that is designed only for the production of this product.[25] In fact, the scattered condemnations of abortion that appear in Christian writings through the sixth century were primarily aimed at women who were assumed to be hiding the result of illicit, that is, nonprocreative, sex. The Councils of Elvira and Ancyra outlined (differently) penalties for abortion which applied only to women who had committed a sexual crime of adultery or prostitution.[26] As there was no agreement among the theologians as to penalties for abortion, there was also no agreement as to whether early abortions—of an "unformed" embryo—were in fact murder. In the twelfth century this debate was settled for the next four centuries when Gratian set the work of Ivo of Chartes into his compilation of canon law: abortion of the unformed fetus is not murder.[27] By the sixteenth century, therefore, the shape of Christian sexual ethics inherited by the reformers was based on the fear of sexuality, fear of women as the source of sexual temptation, and the need to confine sexuality to its one good purpose: procreation. Contraception and abortion were both impediments to the appropriate use of sex. Both were murderous. But, as we have seen, in the prevailing Roman Catholic tradition, abortion became murder only after formation.[28]

The reformers generally accepted the sexual ethics they inherited. With regard to abortion, they actually took a more conservative stance than their Roman Catholic counterparts. However, the issue they addressed was not abortion, per se. The issue for Luther was his understanding that original sin affected the totality of each person: mind, body, and spirit. The issue for Calvin was predestination: that from before time, each individual was destined to be saved or damned. Each theological position led, for consistency's sake, to a revival of the early traducian view that both body and soul merged at conception. Thus, theological concerns caused them to argue, in fragmentary passages, for the full humanity of the fetus from its earliest stage.[29] And it is likely that this unexamined acceptance of the proscription against abortion has been part of the reason that change in this issue has been slower than change regarding contraception and family planning. Yet, as Harrison points out, neither Luther nor Calvin actually paid much attention to the question of abortion and neither reasoned about it directly. In Geneva, where Calvin exerted extensive direct influence on the laws of the city, one would expect to find civil law on abortions just as one finds laws related to the duties of parents. However, the civil laws of Calvin's Geneva are silent about abortion.[30]

The early reformers also accepted the prevailing view that sexuality was procreative in purpose.[31] However, they were also aware that the ideal presented by Roman Catholic tradition was not the norm of actual lives. Cahill reports that marriage and family life were in a state of crisis in the early sixteenth century due to the incongruity of ideals of virginity that demeaned married people with the sexual scandals surrounding clergy and the variety of ecclesiastical impediments to marriage that could be overcome with the purchase of a dispensation.[32] Economic strains were another source of family crisis. In the fifteenth century, Augsburg, like other cities, ran a brothel to regulate a "necessary evil." A significant number of young men, serving as journeymen and apprentices, could not marry until they became masters. Yet they were facing restricted opportunities to become masters and form their own households. The city provided supervised prostitutes, who had an accepted place in society, and, by doing so, presumably kept men from worse offenses against "respectable" women.[33] Luther became convinced that through humanity's fall into sin, men's sexual urge had been debased into lust. He taught, therefore, that all should marry as it was God's intention for men and women, and that almost all must marry to avoid the sins of lust.[34] But he also held that the purposes of marriage were "to live together, to be fruitful, to beget children, to nourish them, and to bring them up to the glory of God." John Calvin considered marriage to be a covenantal relationship but procreation was still the purpose of sexuality. He called coitus interruptus "doubly monstrous." The *Encyclopedia of Bioethics* attributes the reformers' acceptance of procreation as the purpose of sex to be due to both their reliance on Catholic predecessors and the demographic reality that shifts in population affected the religious composition of the country and its political control.[35]

Yet it should be emphasized that the reformers had departed significantly from the Roman Catholic valuation of ascetic sexual practices. Indeed, in a distinct rejection of Roman Catholic teaching, they regarded marriage as the normal condition for adults, including ministers. No longer would marriage be unlawful for clergy. Protestants repudiated monasticism for men and women, and the great majority of clergy, even bishops, married. Sex, of course, remained under suspicion. The brothels as well as the monasteries were closed. While Luther could celebrate marriage as a divine gift, he also saw marriage as a necessity due to the strength of sexual urges. While Calvin saw marriage to be primarily a companionate relationship, he maintained traditional suspicions about sex. Yet, these changes, small though they were, were the beginning of the Protestant move in the direction of valuing sexual intercourse in marriage for reasons other than procreation. Equally or more important, however, is the shift in Christian life this represented. Protestant attitudes toward sexuality would arise from beliefs that placed the family as the basic unit of society. Luther's doctrine of the three estates names ministry, marriage, and magistracy as the three Christian vocations. Marriage is a divinely ordered institution of society under the authority of the state for the chief purpose of raising children and bringing them to a saving faith. Parents are, in fact, "apostles, bishops, and priests to their children, for it is they who make them acquainted with the gospel."[36] Calvin, on the other hand, was most positive about the possibility of establishing a Christian society. In Geneva, all of social life was to be transformed into a covenant community, a "holy commonwealth." The important point is to notice how the emphasis of Christian life shifted in the Reformation from the church and its sacraments and rituals to the congregation, the Christian community, and its families. Marriage and family had become the new moral norm for Protestants. Cahill's description of Luther's personal experience makes clear the embodied learning that clerical marriage made possible: "He was a sympathetic husband who left remarkably concrete observations about the tribulations of pregnancy and deeply mourned the loss of two daughters among their six children. He writes of their shared grief: 'The force of our natural love is so great that we are . . . crying and grieving in our hearts.' Luther made Catherine the executrix of his will, an unusual step in the culture and legal system of his time."[37]

The Christian teachings about sexuality, women, and procreation inherited by the reformers had developed in centuries characterized by the deliberate separation of male clergy from women, their experiences, their well-being, and their moral issues. Since ancient times, women, faced with the blessing and the curse of fertility, had practiced a variety of methods by which to effect some control over their procreative capacities, including the use of contraceptives and early-term abortifacients.[38] With the Reformation, the impact of both the blessings of children and the curse of uncontrolled reproductive fertility, fertility that is too many and too often, became the daily, embodied experience of Protestant clergy who were now husbands, fathers, and breadwinners. The impact of this lived-world experience in covenantal relationships with mothers, wives, and daughters cannot be overstated. I do not want to imply by this that Protestant families met the twenty-first-century ideal of egalitarian marriages. Cultural patriarchal standards shaped Protestant families, as well as the biblical teachings concerning male heads of households, the Household Codes, and so forth. The sixteenth and seventeenth centuries were also centuries of the witchcraft craze. Midwives and their knowledge of birth control, both contraceptive and abortive, were often the target.[39] However, Protestant theologies were less likely to blame misfortune on the devil and "his" female recruits. Barstow argues that the new Protestant teachings had the effect of moderating the witch hunts in most Protestant lands.[40] For the first time, the male experience of marriage, parenthood, and family responsibilities was able to inform theology as well as practical, pastoral responses.

The Protestant colonies in America were primarily influenced by the views of the Church of England and its reformers. By the mid-sixteenth century, the

English Puritans had come to an understanding that companionship was the primary aim of marriage.[41] The family was not a democracy, but a small commonwealth ruled by the husband and father. Male rule and female subordination were an order to be maintained for the good of the society and for a lasting relationship of (unequal) companions. Respectable and good sexuality, even pleasurable sexual union, was a blessing of marriage. According to Gudorf, "the Calvinist tradition brought to New England by the Puritans additionally understood sex as an important manner of cherishing and loving the spouse. . . . Few married couples were warned away from sex, or interrogated about it by clergy, as continued to occur among Catholics."[42] One does not find among Protestants the admonitions to procreate, nor the warnings about avoiding procreation. Sexual relations between engaged couples could be tolerated in light of the marriage to come, but heavy penalties awaited the woman who gave birth outside of marriage. Once married, high infant and child mortality rates encouraged frequent pregnancies. D'Emilio and Freedman argue that it is unlikely that married couples (with the possible exception of the aristocracy) used contraception to limit fertility until the seventeenth century.[43] Nelson points out that as this companionate view of marriage became the dominant Protestant interpretation (by the eighteenth century), it subordinated the importance of both procreation and the control of sexual lust as reasons for the marriage state (the emphases of the reformers). With Protestantism's turn to Scripture, it encountered the Jewish view that the full humanity of a person occurred only at birth. This, together with the ideal of companionate marriage, laid the basis for developing Protestant views that would justify abortion in those contexts where the life of the woman was at risk.[44] By the end of the eighteenth century, historians find evidence in England and the United States of the use of contraception by married couples to limit the size of families.[45] The relationship between sexuality and procreation had changed for Protestants.

The Development of Protestant Positions on Contraception and Abortion: The Nineteenth and Twentieth Centuries

It was not until the nineteenth century that the household, as a unit of personal, economic, and political relations, comprised of parents, children, and, if property owning, apprentices and servants, became what modern Europeans and North Americans would recognize as "the family."[46] Occurring in different places at different times, the development of industrial capitalism and urbanization reconfigured the family unit and gender roles in ways that affected cultural understandings of sexuality. The general trend was to smaller families among urban middle-income families. Holland, in 1882, was the home of the first birth-control clinic. In Germany contraception was so widely practiced that it was common to speak about a "birth strike." Factors that influenced this trend included the reduced availability of land with which the next generation could get an economic start, the greater economic investment that families had to make in children in order for them to get skilled jobs, the need to limit the number of children in order to maintain a middle-level social status, the growing Protestant understanding that to take responsibility for one's own future was an expression of faith, and the growing power of middle-level women to wield some influence over the governance of the home.[47]

In the United States reproduction rates fell from an average of about 7 children per married woman in 1800 to an average of only 4.24 in 1880.[48] Information about contraception and abortion circulated widely in the nineteenth-century United States in books, marital advice literature, advertisements, almanacs, circulars, and with itinerant lecturers. Women's letters show a rather open willingness to share contraception knowledge with other women relatives and friends. Historians estimate that the incidence of abortion also increased significantly in the nineteenth century. However, women leave little direct evidence of this. The evidence comes from physicians and public health agencies. In the first half of the century, states followed the tradition of English common law and retained the quickening doctrine. State laws passed between 1820 and 1840 were intended to protect women from being coerced into having an abortion. Yet, by the end of the century, the U.S. Congress had passed a law that outlawed the circulation of contraception information and devices through the U.S. mail, and almost all of the states had passed anti-abortion laws. This dramatic change needs to be explained.

Part of the explanation lies in the development of a new gender identity for women who, with industrialization, found themselves confined to the domestic sphere and defined as being, in some natural sense, domestic. In this middle- and upper-income ideology, women were defined by their capacity to nurture and men by their capacity for aggression.[49] The good wife of colonial days, good because she was equally essential in the economic activities of the family unit, gave way to the good bourgeois wife: docile, domestic, and reproductive. She was also pure, and responsible for the moral upbringing of her children. However, this latter aspect of what is now called "the Cult of True Womanhood" was used by Protestant women to justify their sense of a calling to step out of the home of the nuclear family and into the "home" of society. Women began to organize for political equality, especially for suffrage, in order to reform the evils of society. In the second half of the nineteenth century,

Protestant women developed expanded roles in home and foreign missionary societies and deaconess orders. They were socially active in their own countries, bringing the gospel to poor and immigrant women, and they were teachers, evangelists, and even, by the end of the century, physicians on every continent. Accepting the role of mothers as the center of social order and moral purity, Protestant women organized to nurture the world.[50] As their social work brought them into contact with poor women and prostitutes, they were not necessarily in agreement about the widespread availability of contraception and abortion. Some argued that contraception played into the hands of male irresponsibility and the male double standard by which men engaged in illicit sex, but women paid the price. These women argued instead for "voluntary motherhood" by which they meant that wives should submit to marital intercourse only when they wanted to since they bore the burden of motherhood. Opposition to contraception was not opposition to family planning.[51]

Yet, even as "domestic" women were making the world their home, another significant event contributed greatly to the change in social attitudes toward contraception and abortion in Protestant countries. This was the rise of a new, male-dominated medical profession, struggling to replace healers, often women, who were not trained in the new science of medicine. As the scientific experts, in an age awed by modern science, doctors began to supplant clergymen as the male authorities in sexual matters. Involvement in social reform was one activity by which nascent medical associations enhanced their drive toward prestige. Male doctors, particularly in the new specialty of gynecology, provided a scientific definition of women's health and wholeness. According to one Dr. Horatio Storer, in 1871, woman is "what she is in health, in character, in her charms, alike of body, mind and soul because of her womb alone."[52] Certainly, this can be seen as part of a reaction against women's growing public activism and demand for equal civil rights. In the United States it can also be seen as part of the fear that the established white population felt due to lowering white birth rates in the face of much higher birth rates among the waves of foreign immigrants as well as local populations of people of color.[53] With regard to contraception, however, this U-turn in the Protestant trajectory was short-lived.

Early in the twentieth century, Protestant ministers joined with others in the campaign to reverse the laws against contraception.[54] Again, their role as husbands and fathers, and their role as pastors to families experiencing growing economic instability, enabled them to recognize the nonprocreative benefits of marital intercourse, as well as the disruption to families of too many children. Support for legalizing abortion would come more slowly. Yet, most western European countries, as well as Canada and the United States, began to legalize abortion after 1950. By the 1970s in the United States, major main-line Protestant denominations would endorse, not abortion per se, but the need for women to be able to exercise the freedom of their own consciences in the difficult decisions necessitated by unwanted pregnancies.

However, it must be confessed that Protestant support for family planning and legalized abortion has not always been for commendable reasons. The eugenics movement of the early twentieth century traded on race-based and class-elitist fears.[55] In the United States, the history of African-American women's reproductive lives has been marked by the denial of reproductive freedom, from compulsory motherhood in slavery to compulsory sterilization in the 1960s and 1970s, to family caps in welfare reform. The misuse of perspectives that enable the life choices of more affluent white women while curtailing the choices of less affluent women of color needs to be exposed.[56] The role that contraception and legalized abortion may play in facilitating male irresponsibility in societies that refuse to support those conditions that would enable women to gain economic and political equality also needs to be ana-lyzed. And the use of birth control as a weapon of the so-called First World in its scapegoating of the world's poor in the population and environmental crises needs to be acknowledged.[57]

Nonetheless, the mainline Protestant denominations have been instru-mental in promoting the connection between women's well-being, in families and in the work world, and a woman's need to determine if, when, and how often she will use her procreative capacity.

Protestant Affirmations of Reproductive Choice

Since the 1970s, mainline Protestant denominations in the United States have issued, and in many cases reissued, theologically argued positions that affirm "a woman's right to follow her own conscience concerning child-bearing, abor-tion and sterilization . . . free of coercion."[58] Several theological themes are common to these statements. One such theme reiterates, now for women in regard to reproductive decisions, the classical Protestant emphasis on the ne-cessity of each person of faith to live with integrity before God. The statement of the American Baptist Churches, USA (1988) is an example of this:

> Recognizing that each person is ultimately responsible to God, we
> encourage women and men in these circumstances [of unplanned
> pregnancy] to seek spiritual counsel as they prayerfully and consci-
> entiously consider their decision.

Similar in emphasis is the statement of the Young Women's Christian Association (USA):

> The position of the YWCA is not "pro-abortion." It is a position supporting a woman's right to make an individual decision based upon her own religious and ethical beliefs and her physician's guidance. (YWCA, National Convention, 1970, 1973, 1988)

A second theme recognizes and urges respect for the diversity of views expressed by people of faith. This theme resonates with the historical Protestant recognition of human finitude and its unease with mandating absolute moral rules. Moreover, in a pluralistic democracy, the concept of civil liberties makes imperative the neutral role of government with regard to religion. In this case that neutrality must be expressed by protecting women's legal access to the abortion services she may choose. Protestant statements typically include a reference to freedom from government interference. Some go further and advocate positive steps that government must take to implement such neutrality for all women:

> The church's position on public policy concerning abortion should reflect respect for other religious traditions and advocacy for full exercise of religious liberty. The Presbyterian Church exists within a very pluralistic environment. Its own members hold a variety of views. It is exactly this pluralism of beliefs which leads us to the conviction that the decision regarding abortion must remain with the individual, to be made on the basis of conscience and personal religious principles, and free of government interference. (Presbyterian Church [USA] General Assembly, 1983 [reaffirmed 1985, 1987, 1988, 1989])

> To prohibit or severely limit the use of public funds to pay for abortions abridges and denies the right to an abortion and discriminates especially against low income, young and minority women. (Episcopal Women's Caucus, Annual Meeting, 1978)

> Members of the Presbyterian Church are urged . . . to model the just and compassionate community by: . . . Opposing adoption of all measures which would serve to restrict full and equal access to contraception and abortion services to all women, regardless of race, age, and economic standing. (Presbyterian Church [USA])

While Protestant statements vary in the way in which they refer to the fetus, they all agree that the sacredness of life includes fetal life and, therefore, they express the seriousness of any decision to terminate life. What is common to all is the unwillingness to ascribe absolute value to fetal life. Valuing the sacredness of life must include not only valuing the physical existence of a fetus and a woman (as in those instances in which the existence of one jeopardizes the existence of the other) but also regard for "fully developed personhood, particularly when the physical, mental, and emotional health of the pregnant woman and her family show reason to be seriously threatened by the new life just forming" (United Methodist Church, General Conference, 1988). The recognition that there are circumstances in life that make an unintended pregnancy threatening to the well-being of a woman causes some statements to call attention to the issues of social justice:

> WHEREAS the incidence of abortion could be greatly reduced with social and cultural changes for which we all have responsibility, including complete and accurate sex education, adequate and available contraception, responsible non-coercive sexuality, health care, child care, parental leave, and other social support; . . . BE IT FURTHER RESOLVED that the Lutheran Women's Caucus call upon our various church bodies to work actively for the social and cultural changes that will reduce the incidence of abortion and stop scapegoating women who have abortions. (Lutheran Women's Caucus, Convocation Gathering, 1990)

The concern for social justice is also expressed in the concern for how abortion debates are unacknowledged debates about women and women's sexuality. Thus, the Presbyterian Statement "recognizes that negative social attitudes toward women cast doubt on women's ability to make moral decisions and urges ministers and congregations to work to counter these underlying social attitudes and affirm the dignity of women." The Lutheran Women's Caucus states that "abortion has become the symbol for ambivalent feelings about female sexuality and female self-determination." Yet, that suspicion about women's sexuality still appears in the form of statements that reject abortion if it is used, in effect, frivolously:

> We emphatically oppose abortion as a means of birth control, family planning, sex selection or any reason of mere convenience. (Episcopal Church, General Convention, 1988)

> We denounce irresponsible sexual behavior. (American Baptist Churches, USA, General Board, 1988)

For a brief 30 years most mainline Protestant denominations have supported the view that a woman's choice to terminate her pregnancy may be a
moral decision in her context and that she should be the final determiner of
that decision. To safeguard this appeal to the freedom of individual conscience,
Protestants have supported a public policy that makes medical abortion services
legal and accessible to all women. However, many of these statements admit
the serious conflict within their own gatherings over these positions. Paradoxically, the resultant support of women's moral agency seems at times to depend
on the existence of this unreconciled, internal controversy. Respect for
women's moral agency as a condition of social justice itself seems less secure.
Recognition of the structural nature of women's inequality seems less clear.
And, therefore, the commitment to a common, public good, a society structured to enable women to control our procreative power, seems less than secure.

The New Battle Within Protestantism Over Abortion

It remains to be seen whether Protestantism in the United States will continue
to follow the trajectory set by the Reformation. A number of social conditions
have led to increased activity on the part of the fundamentalist Christian Right
and the construction of a backlash against changing gender roles and women's
economic and political gains. The climate of U.S. society at the beginning of
the twenty-first century bears remarkable resemblance to the tensions that
existed at the end of the nineteenth. Structural economic changes are creating
economic instability for most while the disparity between rich and poor keeps
growing. Most women are in the workforce because their families need the
income. Most mothers of preschool-age children are in the workforce because
their families need the income. Racial disparities in well-being are much as
they were a half-century ago. Poor women, disproportionately women of color,
continue to be denied medical coverage for the legal abortion services they
might choose, but Medicaid programs cover up to 90 percent of the cost of
sterilization. Welfare has been replaced by a mandate to get a job and/or get
married. Surveys continue to reveal the fears that many white males have about
competing in a workforce that is increasingly diverse by gender and race. The
response of the Protestant fundamentalists has been to target as heretics those
who work for political/economic change—change in the power dynamics of
society. Pat Robertson declared that support of the Equal Rights Amendment
was a "socialist, anti-family political movement that encourages women to leave

their husbands, kill their children, practice witchcraft, destroy capitalism and become lesbians."[59] Fundamentalist rhetoric ties together women's actual social equality with the murder of children and the demise of family and capitalism. Opposition to abortion is central to the success of the fundamentalist agenda.

One fundamentalist strategy has been to try to gain legitimation within the African-American community by equating the moral duty to oppose abortion with the nineteenth-century moral duty to oppose slavery. In a stunning misappropriation, Ralph Reed distributed in 1995 a Christian Coalition pledge based on the pledge written by Dr. Martin Luther King, Jr., for the Southern Christian Leadership Convention.[60] This strategy is a callous attempt to exploit what is assumed to be an ambivalence among African Americans about abortion, given the history of forced sterilization and birth control by whites upon poor black women in the twentieth century.[61] A second highly successful strategy has been to personalize the fetus from its earliest formation. Aided by the development of sonograms and the publication of biographies and "autobiographies" of unborn children, the fetus is affirmed as a fully human person with thoughts and feelings.[62] Any moral analysis of the fetus is rendered suspect in this celebration of the innocent child. What has become invisible again is the woman, willingly or unwillingly pregnant, and her well-being and personhood. A third strategy is a remarkable return to the language of women's weakness and men's need to reclaim their lost masculinity. Tony Evans of the Promise Keepers tells men to take back their leadership of the family: "Unfortunately there can be no compromise here. If you're going to lead you must lead. Be sensitive. Listen. Treat the lady gently and lovingly. But *lead!*"[63] Stu Weber describes wives as "weaker vessels," not only physically but due to the depression and irritability produced by premenstrual syndrome (PMS).[64] Essentially, fundamentalism intends to reduce the biblical vision of justice, as it would apply to racism, to sexism, and to the pillorying of the poor, to an ethic of personal love judged solely on the basis of (white) men's subjective intent to love those they lead.

On the other hand, the "seamless garment" argument arose from somewhat liberal Roman Catholic sources attempting to link opposition to various forms of "violence," such as capital punishment and abortion (but not war). It has found receptive ears among some liberal Protestants. While making an erroneous claim to an unbroken history of antiviolence Christianity, it has the appeal of a simplistic and pure morality that is based on ignoring the reality of violence in women's lives and the violence of imposing an absolutist moral standard on women that is not imposed in their ethical approach to men's war or economic practices. Finally, in the face of clinic bombings and the murder of physicians who provided family planning that included abortion, further violence to women arises as doctors choose not to become involved in providing the abortion services some women need.

In her strongly written book *Body, Sex, and Pleasure: Reconstructing Christian Sexual Ethics*, Christine Gudorf charges: "Traditional Christian sexual ethics is not only inadequate in that it fails to reflect God's reign of justice and love which Jesus died announcing, but its legalistic, apologetic approach is also incompatible with central Judaic and Christian affirmations of creation, life, and an incarnate messiah."[65] She rightly points out that even as Protestantism elevated marriage and rejected celibacy, even as it valued the experiences of individuals in their relationship with God, it never reexamined its theology of sexuality, its theology of the body, its theology of pleasure, and, I would name for emphasis, its theology of women.[66] The result today is that Protestantism is in danger of embracing an idolatry of familism—the belief that "saving" the heterosexual, two-parent family solves most, if not all, of our social problems and a rejection of the challenge to embrace different forms of family and the social policies necessary to sustain the common good of all. There is another option. We can claim the less-than-perfect courage of the Reformers, and continue the trajectory they set of increased openness to the realities of human experiences, increased inclusiveness of those with differing experiences, and increased response to those who bear the burdens of our social sins. We can see what new truth lies in *our* reformation.

NOTES

This essay was prepared with enormous assistance from Beverly Harrison, in terms both of her published works and of her willingness to share an unpublished manuscript on this topic. While I take responsibility for what is written here, I want to acknowledge Harrison as the scholar whose original thinking stands behind so much of our (Protestant feminist) work.

1. A classic history of this European period is Kenneth Scott Latourette, *A History of Christianity, Vol. 2, Reformation to the Present*, rev. ed. (New York: Harper and Row, 1975).

2. For a history of Christian methods of biblical interpretation and of struggles in the Reformed tradition, especially over this issue, see Jack B. Rogers and Donald K. McKim, *The Authority and Interpretation of the Bible: An Historical Approach* (San Francisco: Harper and Row, 1979).

3. Latourette, 977–978.

4. For global statistics on religions, see David B. Barrett, George T. Kurian, and Todd M. Johnson, eds. *World Christian Encyclopedia* (New York: Oxford University Press, 2001). Some statistics are also available at www.adherents.com. The data used in this chapter are taken from these sources.

5. Important sources for this development include Cheryl Townsend Gilkes, *If It Wasn't for the Women . . . : Black Women's Experience and Womanist Culture in Church and Community* (Maryknoll, N.Y.: Orbis, 2000); Gayraud S. Wilmore, *Black Religion and Black Radicalism: An Interpretation of the Religious History of African Americans* (Maryknoll: Orbis, 1998), and *African American Religious Studies: An Interdisciplinary Anthology* (Durham: Duke University Press, 1989); Albert J. Raboteau, *A Fire in the Bones: Reflections on African American Religious History* (Boston: Beacon Press, 1996), and *Slave Religion: The Invisible Institution in the Antebellum South* (New York: Oxford University Press, 1980); Evelyn Brooks Higginbotham, *Righteous Discontent: The Women's Movement in Black Baptist Church, 1880–1920* (Cambridge: Harvard University Press, 1994).

6. See Katie Cannon, *Black Womanist Ethics* (Atlanta: Scholars Press, 1988).

7. Kwok Pui-lan, "Discovering the Bible in the Non-Biblical World," in *Lift Every Voice: Constructing Christian Theologies from the Underside*, ed. Susan Brooks Thistlethwaite and Mary Potter Engel (San Francisco: Harper and Row, 1990), 273.

8. Richard N. Ostling, "Book Counts World's Religions," *Detroit News*, 16 March 2001, available at www.detroitnews.com/2001/religion.

9. Beverly Harrison, *Making the Connections* (Boston: Beacon Press, 1985), 1–21.

10. For a description of this development in U.S. church history, see Robert T. Handy, *A History of the Churches in the United States and Canada* (New York: Oxford University Press, 1976), 286–294.

11. Rogers and McKim trace the first recorded usage in English of the term "inerrant" to a 1652 scientific work. It is under the impetus of the promise of science to allow humans to describe the workings of nature with a mechanical precision that theologians developed a mechanical model of biblical interpretation. That is, words in the Bible could be treated like facts of nature: a simple, direct intake of objective knowledge (see p. 235). For the claim that the theology of biblical inerrancy was a new development in the nineteenth century, McKim and Rogers quote Ernest R. Sandeen, *The Roots of Fundamentalism* (Chicago: University of Chicago Press, 1970), 106:

> Most twentieth-century Fundamentalists and many twentieth-century historians have mistakenly assumed that Protestantism possesses a strong, fully integrated theology of biblical authority which was attacked by advocates of the higher criticism. As we shall see, no such theology existed before 1850. . . . A systematic theology of biblical authority which defended the common evangelical faith in the infallibility of the Bible had to be created in the midst of the nineteenth-century controversy. The formation of this theology in association with the growth of the millenarian movement determined the character of Fundamentalism. (314, n.89)

12. Both Luther and Calvin had a strong sense of God's accommodation to human finitude; that is, the divine message had to be adapted to the capacities of its hearers. Luther writes: "When discrepancies occur in the Holy Scriptures and we cannot harmonize them, let it pass, it does not endanger the articles of the Christian faith" (qtd. in McKim and Rogers, 87). Likewise, Calvin understood the need to inter-

pret context and intent that goes beyond the literal words. For example, the responsible exegete must "inquire how far interpretation ought to overstep the limits of the words themselves so that it may be seen to be, not an appendix added to the divine law from men's glosses, but the Lawgiver's pure and authentic meaning faithfully rendered." John Calvin, *Institutes of the Christian Religion*, ed. John T. McNeill, trans. Ford Lewis Battles (Philadelphia: Westminster Press, 1960) 2: viii, 8.

13. For a discussion and critique of the fundmentalists' claim of biblical errancy, see Daniel Maguire, *The New Subversives: Anti-Americanism of the Religious Right* (New York: Continuum, 1982), esp. ch. 3.

14. Beverly Harrison, unpublished manuscript.

15. Beverly LaHaye, *The Desires of a Woman's Heart* (Wheaton, Ill: Tyndale, 1993), 116. Beverly LaHaye is the founder of Concerned Women for America. Tim LaHaye, her husband, was a member of the original board of the Moral Majority and the founder of the American Coalition for Traditional Values.

16. See, for example, Karen Armstrong, *The Battle for God* (New York: Knopf, 2000); Anne Bathurst Gilson, *The Battle for America's Families* (Cleveland: The Pilgrim Press, 1999); Linda Kintz, *Between Jesus and the Market: The Emotions That Matter in Right-Wing America* (Durham: Duke University Press, 1997).

17. Beverly Harrison, *Our Right to Choose: Toward a New Ethic of Abortion* (Boston: Beacon Press, 1983), esp. ch. 5.

18. John T. Noonan, "An Almost Absolute Value in History," in *The Morality of Abortion: Legal and Historical Perspectives*, John T. Noonan, ed. (Cambridge: Harvard University Press, 1970), 1–39, cited in Harrison, *Our Right to Choose*, 125.

19. For example, see James T. Burtchaell, "Condemnation of Abortion and Infanticide in the Early Church," in *Abortion*, Lloyd Steffen, ed. (Cleveland: The Pilgrim Press, 1996), 94–104.

20. Harrison, *Our Right to Choose*, 131.

21. Margaret Farley, "Sexual Ethics," in *Sexuality and the Sacred: Sources for Theological Reflection*, James B. Nelson and Sandra P. Longfellow, eds. (Louisville: Westminster/John Knox Press, 1994), 59–62.

22. Vern Bullough and Bonnie Bullough, *Sin, Sickness, and Sanity: A History of Sexual Attitudes* (New York: New American Library, 1977), 18–20.

23. Joan Timmerman, *The Mardi Gras Syndrome: Rethinking Christian Sexuality* (New York: Crossroad, 1984), 35–38.

24. James B. Nelson, *Embodiment: An Approach to Sexuality and Christian Theology* (Minneapolis: Augsburg Publishing House, 1978), 52–53.

25. Harrison, *Our Right to Choose*, 132.

26. Kristin Luker, *Abortion and the Politics of Motherhood* (Berkeley: University of California Press, 1984), 12–13.

27. Luker, *Abortion*, 12–13; Harrison, *Our Right to Choose*, 138–144.

28. Luker, *Abortion*, 13. Luker points out that this was held to happen at 40 days for males and 80 days for females. However, where there was ambiguity, the embryo was considered female. Fetuses continue to appear female to the naked eye until the fourth month. Consequently, in practical terms, first trimester abortions were not treated as murder until the nineteenth century.

29. James B. Nelson, "Protestant Attitudes Toward Abortion," in *Abortion*, Lloyd Steffen, ed., 138–139.

30. Harrison, *Our Right to Choose*, 146–147.

31. Nelson, *Embodiment*, 54–56.

32. Lisa Sowle Cahill, *Family: A Christian Social Perspective* (Minneapolis: Fortress Press, 2000), 61.

33. Rosemary Radford Ruether, *Christianity and the Making of the Modern Family* (Boston: Beacon Press, 2000), 67.

34. Ibid., 74.

35. John T. Noonan, Jr., "Contraception," in *Encyclopedia of Bioethics*, Vol. 1, Warren T. Reich, ed. (New York: Free Press, 1978), 209.

36. Martin Luther, "The Estate of Marriage," *Luther's Works* (Philadelphia: Fortress Press, 1962) 45:46 as cited in Cahill, *Family*, 66.

37. Cahill, *Family*, 64.

38. John M. Riddle, J. Worth Estes, and Josiah C. Russell, "Ever Since Eve: Birth Control in the Ancient World," *Archaeology*, March/April 1994: 29–35.

39. Anne Llewellyn Barstow, *Witchcraze: A New History of the European Witch Hunts* (San Francisco: Pandora, 1994), 129–135.

40. Ibid., 60.

41. The Church of England did not require the end of celibacy for its clergy as did the continental reformers. In 1547, the *Book of Homilies*, a collection of sermons to be read in all parishes, was first published. It had no sermon on marriage, and maintained the traditional praise of celibacy. In 1549 celibacy became an option for clergy. In 1563, when the *Book of Homilies* was reissued, it advocated marriage as a "friendly fellowship." Rosemary Radford Ruether and Rosemary Skinner Keller, eds. *Women and Religion in America*, Vol. 2, *The Colonial and Revolutionary Periods* (San Francisco: Harper and Row, 1983), 134.

42. Christine E. Gudorf, *Body, Sex, and Pleasure: Reconstructing Christian Sexual Ethics* (Cleveland: The Pilgrim Press, 1994), 208.

43. John D'Emilio and Estelle B. Freedman, *Intimate Matters: A History of Sexuality in America* (New York: Harper and Row, 1988), 4–6.

44. Nelson, "Protestant Attitudes Toward Abortion," 139. Harrison points out that the question of therapeutic abortions had arisen sporadically since the thirteenth century in Roman Catholicism and that toward the end of the seventeenth century the distinction between a direct and an indirect abortion (the principle of double effect) began to be developed. Harrison, *Our Right to Choose*, 144.

45. D'Emilio and Freedman, *Intimate Matters*, 48.

46. See Stephanie Coontz, *The Social Origins of Private Life* (New York: Verso, 1988), ch. 4.

47. Linda Gordon, *Woman's Body, Woman's Right: A Social History of Birth Control in America* (New York: Penguin Books, 1977, 1986, reprint ed.), 172.

48. D'Emilio and Freedman, *Intimate matters*, 58. The discussion that follows is taken from chapter 4. These aggregate rates mask class, race, and regional differences. Higher rates existed among immigrant groups, frontier communities, the

southern black population, and southern whites. Therefore, the drop in aggregate rates marks a sharp decline in urban, white, married, middle-level families.

49. Class location makes women's experiences quite different in all societies. Poor and working-class women often had to work outside the home in factories and/ or use domestic work as a way to increase the family's income, as in taking in borders, laundry, etc. In the U.S., race also separated women's experiences of gender and sexuality. The gentility and fragility attached to middle- and upper-class white women was in opposition to dominant white views of black women as sexually permissive and as manual laborers.

50. Rosemary Radford Ruether and Rosemary Skinner Keller, eds. *Women and Religion in America*, Vol. 1, *The Nineteenth Century, A Documentary History* (San Francisco: Harper and Row, 1983), 242–253.

51. D'Emilio and Freedman, *Intimate Matters*, 154–155.

52. Cited in ibid. 146.

53. See Gordon, *Woman's Body, Woman's Right*, ch. 7.

54. Ibid., 256.

55. Ibid., 274–290; Dorothy Roberts, *Killing the Black Body: Race, Reproduction, and the Meaning of Liberty* (New York: Pantheon Books, 1997), ch. 2.

56. See Roberts, *Killing the Black Body*. Roberts argues convincingly that the experiences of black women challenge in fundamental ways the dominant notion of reproductive freedom in liberal societies, specifically its emphasis on individualism and freedom from government intervention, and its narrow focus on the right to abortion.

57. See, for example, Betsy Hartmann, *Reproductive Rights and Wrongs: The Global Politics of Population Control* (Boston: South End Press, 1995).

58. American Friends Service Committee 1970 (reaffirmed 1989). All of the following statements are available from the Religious Coalition for Reproductive Choice at www.rcrc.org/religion/weaffirm.

59. Cited in Barstow, *Witchcraze*, xiii–xiv.

60. Kintz, *Between Jesus and the Market*, 24.

61. In fact, the 1991 "Women of Color Reproductive Health Poll" found that 83 percent of African-American women believe that a woman should be able to make her own decision about abortion; 76 percent rejected the idea that abortion is a white plot against the survival of people of color. Linda Villarosa, ed. *Body and Soul: The Black Women's Guide to Physical Health and Emotional Well-Being* (New York: HarperCollins, 1994), 186.

62. Kintz, *Between Jesus and the Market*, 266–269

63. Tony Evans, "Sexual Purity," *Seven Promises of a Promise Keeper* (Colorado Springs: Focus on the Family, 1994), 73, cited in Kintz, *Between Jesus and the Market*, 129. (Emphasis in the original.)

64. Stu Weber, *Tender Warrior: God's Intention for a Man* (Sisters, Ore.: Multnomah, 1994), 123, cited in Kintz, *Between Jesus and the Market*, 129.

65. Gudorf, *Body, Sex, and Pleasure*, 2.

66. Ibid., 209.

4

Family Planning, Contraception, and Abortion in Islam

Undertaking Khilafah

SA'DIYYA SHAIKH

In the buildup to the 1994 United Nations International Conference of Population and Development held in Cairo, many Muslim
communities and leaders expressed suspicion toward the UN initiatives for family planning and population control.[1] The Saudi Arabian "Council of Ulama," that nation's highest body of religious authorities, condemned the Cairo conference as a "ferocious assault
on Islamic society" and forbade Muslims to attend.[2] Sudan, Leba-
non, and Iraq then joined Saudi Arabia in announcing that they
would not send delegates to Cairo. Among other things, the conference agenda specifically relating to issues of family planning and
birth control was seen as an imposition of western values on the
Muslim people and an attempt to revive "colonial and imperial am-
bition."[3] While this by no means represented the whole spectrum
of Muslim voices in the debate, since there were many Muslim participants who were involved and committed to the goals of the conference, the voices of resistance were loud and well documented by
the media.

This type of vociferous antipathy to family planning in some
Muslim communities presents a fairly sharp contrast to the way in
which Muslims have historically addressed the issue. Even a cur-
sory investigation into the Islamic intellectual legacy will demonstrate that eight out of nine classical legal schools permitted the
practice of contraception and that the Islamic legal positions on

abortion range from allowing various levels of permissibility of abortion under 120 days, to prohibition.[4] In addition, medieval Muslim physicians had documented detailed and extended lists of birth control practices including abortifacients, commenting on their relative effectiveness and prevalence while the Arabic Islamic erotica literature provided detailed descriptions of popular understandings of contraceptive techniques.[5] These facts illustrate the level of incongruity between the Islamic legacy where family planning was widely permitted and even encouraged in certain contexts, and some prevailing Muslim perspectives that reject family planning as contrary to Islam.

However, in order to understand some of the contemporary Muslim resistance to this topic, one needs to contextualize the debate within the present matrix of postcolonial power relations. Over the past several centuries the shift in the balance of power between Islam and western powers has contributed to the prevalence of a polarized "Islam vs. the West" schema.[6] The historical colonial presence in many Muslim countries has shaped some of the forms of political and cultural resistance to western presence. In the current era this is exacerbated by the fact that Euro-American cultural forms, through the processes of globalization, are perceived as encroaching and increasingly threatening to Muslim societies.[7] Within this context family planning, contraceptive usage, and access to abortion are regularly framed as either a conspiracy by western powers to limit the growth and power of the Muslim world or as a reflection of the permissive sexual mores of western society.[8] Thus, the issues relating to birth control are submerged within a larger minefield of political and cultural polemics.

As a result, many Muslims have assumed a defensive posture in these debates contributing to a particular myopia in significant pockets of the Muslim world. The need to resist what is perceived as a colonizing western discourse has ironically resulted in the reality that Muslims are being defined, albeit oppositionally, by that very discourse. In allowing perceptions of western narratives on family planning to assume a defining place in one's own stance to an issue, even if that stance is antithetical, implies that one's own positioning is determined largely by the perspectives of one's perceived adversary. Contemporary Muslim rejection of family planning endeavors becomes particularly salient in light of an investigation into the Islamic historical legacy, which is characterized by rich diversity and a remarkable openness to issues of family planning. In fact, scholar Norman Daniel shows how medieval churchmen found the Islamic permissiveness regarding contraception as another of the sexual "horrors" of Islam![9]

In this chapter I will draw on a number of traditional Islamic resources in delineating a more "self-referential" and what I consider a less defensive

Islamic approach to the questions of family planning, contraception, and abortion. I will demonstrate the reality of a diverse Islamic legacy with a number of different approaches to the questions related to family planning.

In order to explore an Islamic perspective on family planning, contraception, and abortion, it is necessary to have a broader grasp of some of the fundamentals of Islam, which inform such thinking. In this chapter I will begin by discussing some of the essential Islamic teachings about God and humanity, which form the basis for an Islamic approach to addressing ethical concerns and contemporary challenges of population growth, family planning, and human well-being. I will argue that the central Islamic concept of human moral agency (*khilafah*) in Islam demands that one address these challenges holistically. This includes a response to structural injustices relating to economic and gender hierarchies, as well as an informed approach to particulars of family planning.

God and Humanity: *Tauhid, Fitrah,* and *Khilafah*

The belief in the oneness or unity of God, known to Muslims as the principle of Tauhid, is the center from which the rest of Islam radiates. It is a foundational ontological principle anchored within the deepest spiritual roots of the religion suffusing different areas of Islamic learning that includes theology, mysticism, law, and ethics in varying ways. While transience, finitude, and dependence define everything else, God is the only independent source of being.[10] As such, God is primary to our understandings of the very meaning of reality and is constitutive of the ultimate integrity of human beings.[11]

According to the Qur'an, human beings are uniquely imbued with the spirit of God and in their created nature have been granted privileged knowledge and understanding of reality.[12] Human weakness, on the other hand, is presented primarily as the tendency to be heedless and forgetful of these realities. God's revelations through the various prophets in history are an additional mercy intended to remind one about what is already ingrained at the deepest level of one's humanity. Mediating between faith and heedlessness is the human capacity for volition and freedom of choice. This uniquely endowed human constitution with an inborn capacity for discernment is called the *fitrah*.

Within Islam, therefore, while humanity is primed for goodness, our moral agency is bound to the freedom of choice and the active assumption of responsibilities that ensue from such agency. This understanding of human purpose and potential is reflected in a pervasive Qur'anic concept called *khilafah* that can be translated as trusteeship, moral agency, or vicegerency, where the subject of this activity, the human being, is referred to as the *khalifah*, that is, the trustee, the moral agent, or the vicegerent. This core Qur'anic concept provides the spiritual basis for understanding ethical action in Islam. Within this framework, each individual, as well as every community, is responsible for the realization of a just and moral social order in harmony with God's will.[13] In Islam, enacting one's moral agency is intrinsic to a right relationship with God.

Social and Ethical Implications

One of the crucial secondary principles that flow from the Tauhidic view that God is one and that all human beings are God's *khalifah* is the notion of the "metaphysical sameness of all humans as creatures of God."[14] Each person, irrespective of gender, race, and nationality, possesses the birthright to be God's *khalifah* in this world. According to the Qur'an, the only real criterion for distinction among human beings is that of *taqwa*, which can be translated as God-consciousness and righteousness.[15]

Moreover, the Qur'an repeatedly describes the true believer as one who enacts the moral imperative for justice in the world.[16] Within the Qur'anic worldview the belief in the unity of God explicitly relates to the striving for the unity of humanity, for which justice is a prerequisite.[17] Thus, the theological concepts of *tauhid* and *khilafah* explicitly intersect—bearing witness to God's absolute oneness in Islam is intrinsically related to an enactment of that awareness into the world for the purposes of justice and human well-being.

As foundational Islamic constructs, they have an overarching relevance to the Islamic approach to family planning since the concept of *khilafah* is replete with the importance of human moral agency, the distillation of one's inner conscience, freedom of choice, and the striving for an ethically alive social order. I would argue that in working toward an ethical order, particularly in addressing the challenges of population growth, it is imperative to look at the question holistically, situating it within the relevant social, economic, and political forces of today. To this end I will focus on, first, poverty and economic justice and, second, sexism and gender justice as concerns that are structurally implicated in the concern for family planning.

Poverty and Economic Justice

In addressing the state of human well-being globally, the issues of poverty, resources, and wealth distribution are paramount. The introduction to this volume has already clearly pointed out that contemporary concerns with population growth and sustainable resources are intimately connected with the inequitable distribution of wealth. Frequently, the multiple levels of sociopolitical inequity in the world are connected to questions of how wealth and resources are controlled.[18]

An Islamic response to these economic realities begins with the Qur'anic view that wealth is part of the beneficence and bounty of God and in reality belongs to God—it is entrusted to human beings to be used wisely and with a responsibility to the well-being of all.[19] The poor, the orphaned, and the needy have a right to a portion of one's wealth and Muslims are obligated to pay a welfare tax called *zakat*. The root meaning of the term *zakat* is "to purify" or "to grow," which is particularly relevant since wealth is also a means through which God tests humanity.[20] Wealth sharing purifies the individual from greed and material attachment while simultaneously increasing the giver's good deeds and spiritual wealth.

The circulation of wealth among all segments of a society is seen as a duty placed on the individual *khalifah* and the larger Muslim community.[21] Not only does the Qur'an encourage one to share wealth but it also categorically condemns greed and selfish hoarding.[22] There is an explicit link between those who decline to pay the poor their due and the idolaters.[23] Given that the belief in God's oneness (*Tauhid*) is so central in Islam, this association between idolatry and miserliness is among the harshest criticisms of the concentration of wealth among the few at the expense of the rest. It speaks to the incongruity between genuine belief in God and a disregard for the needs of others, and to the inextricability of an individual's well-being from the well-being of others. In terms of this ideal it is unacceptable to have a society characterized by the coexistence of extreme wealth and poverty, and Muslims are urged to work toward generating systems of socioeconomic justice that foster the common good.

These ethics of wealth sharing and socioeconomic concern for the economically marginalized have a pressing urgency in a world characterized by huge economic disparities between nation-states.[24] The reality that economic marginalization occurs most brutally at the nexus of race, nationality, and gender hierarchies is illustrated by the fact that women, primarily in the poorer nations, constitute 70 percent of the world's 1.3 billion poorest, own less than 1 percent of the world's property but work two-thirds of the world's working hours.[25] Even within a heart of capitalist wealth like the United States one finds significant pockets of poverty and neglect in the inner city, generally divided along racial lines.

These realities reflect a paradigm that is contrary to *Tauhidic* teaching, where human lives are not equally valued but rather are prioritized on the basis of race, nationality, gender, and class stratification. The lives of those who do not belong to privileged groups or nations are removed from the radar screen of social concern and moral responsibility. Here the Qur'anic critique points us to the reality that economic injustice, a lack of appreciation of lives outside the centers of power and privilege, and the maldistribution of wealth reflect a failure of human beings to carry out their trusteeship (khilafah) from God. In addressing human well-being in the world, transforming systems of economic injustice and exploitation and establishing a more equitable distribution of wealth are as crucial spiritual and ethical concerns as are issues of family planning and population management.

Sexism and Gender Justice

Another pivotal area of concern relates to Islamic perspectives on gender relations and marriage, and their implications for family planning. The notion that God's unity is reflected in the equality and unity of humankind provides a basis for a strong critique of sexism and gender hierarchy. The Qur'an explicitly asserts the fundamental equal worth of male and female believers, as well as the fact that gender relations are intended to be cooperative and mutually enriching.[26] This ethos of reciprocity between women and men is further reinforced in the Islamic understanding of marital relationships.

The Qur'an presents marriage and children as a gift from God to be cherished and enjoyed.[27] As such, marriage is valued and encouraged in most Muslim cultures. Despite this incentive to have a family, neither marriage nor children are considered obligatory in the life of a Muslim man or woman. In fact, the Qur'an also warns the believer that if she or he does not approach marriage and parenting with the right attitude and awareness, these too can have a negative impact in one's life.[28] If one fears such a possibility and does not have the wherewithal for marriage, the Qur'an even permits one to remain unmarried.[29]

Al-Ghazzali (d. 1111), one of most renowned Islamic intellectuals, discusses some of the potential disadvantages of marriage. Among these he includes the possibility of excessive financial burden of a family or that one may get ensconced within the enjoyment and needs of the family, thereby becoming distracted from the true purpose of life, which is the individual's journey to Allah.[30] Thus, within Islam, marriage, like many lawful things in Islam, if approached correctly is an opportunity for growing closer to God. However, if it is approached as an end in itself, it can become destructive.

I would argue that one of the instances in which marriage becomes an obstacle instead of an aid to God-consciousness occurs when the notion of male superiority or privilege emerges as a defining aspect of the relationship. Systems of patriarchy and sexism that place male human beings above female human beings solely on the basis of their gender is a denial of the essential equality of humanity, thereby constituting a negation of the reality of *Tauhid*. While this position is not uncontested, there is certainly a strong Qur'anic basis for developing a hermeneutic of gender justice in marriage and in society more broadly.[31]

A number of contemporary Muslim scholars have argued that the Qur'anic view of the inviolable sanctity of every human being, both male and female, implies a duty to protect each person's physical, emotional, psychological, so- cial, and intellectual integrity.[32] This implies that the whole range of explicit violations of women's personhood, including physical violence against women, honor killings, and clitoridectomy, constitute a transgression of the spiritual sanctity of the individual and therefore a disregard for the principle of *Tauhid*.

At the more insidious level, socialization processes and cultural ideals of womanhood in many Muslim communities are premised on male-centered norms. Social ideals that promote women's silence and subordination to men, that deny or limit women's access to education, that restrict their mobility and agency in the world, that define women primarily in terms of their sexuality, or that fix women's roles or value *solely* as mother and wife constitute structural violence to women's full humanity.

These types of sociocultural constructs also often reinforce structural eco- nomic inequities where resources, skills, and education are dominated by men, thereby perpetuating patriarchal power relations. It is no coincidence that the world's poorest are women—patriarchy and classism are structural injustices that intersect and reinforce one another to create the most brutally impover- ishing conditions for many women in the world, including some Muslim women. Within this context, the burden of numerous pregnancies and chil- dren may be fundamentally debilitating, threatening one's very survival and well-being. Moreover, in conditions of poverty, undernourished and weak off- spring are more a source of anxiety and stress than the "comfort" or "allurement" of the parents' eyes as the Qur'an intends.[33]

These varying levels of systematic injustice operating against women vio- late the essential Tauhidic notion of the equality of human beings. This in- cludes the reality that poor women often do not have access to information and education around issues of family planning, including religious rights and medical information. Moreover, the fact that many women are deprived of educational, intellectual, social, and economic opportunities often traps them into accepting notions that they are obliged to reproduce and serve their husbands. The fact that in many Muslim societies the important roles of wife and mother are presented to the exclusion of other avenues of women's intellectual and spiritual development constitutes a violation of our access to the fullness of moral agency or *khilafah*. While Islam encourages marriage and family life for both men and women, no Muslim is obligated to marry or reproduce. However, every Muslim woman, like her male counterpart, is obligated to undertake her *khilafah*, which includes realizing one's full potential for intellectual, economic, and social agency in the world.

In articulating a relevant Islamic response to contemporary challenges, including the realities of population growth, it is imperative to focus on addressing the problems of economic and gender injustice. In our context, it is inadequate, if not irresponsible, for any religious or ethical framework to address questions of human well-being, family planning, and birth control without looking at the related systems of socioeconomic injustice that directly restrict human agency and freedom and exacerbate human misery in the world. An Islamic ethical vision needs to address the issues of social justice as an organic component of family planning and population control. This, nonetheless, has to be coupled with a responsible and informed approach to the specifics of family planning.

Family Planning

In addressing the question of family planning from an Islamic perspective, it is necessary to consult the various sources of guidance within the religious tradition. These include the Qur'anic revelation and the prophetic traditions, as well as an one's inner moral capacities of discernment. In addition, it is valuable to inform oneself of the relevant aspects of the Islamic legal legacy, as well as all the contemporary advances in knowledge on the subject.

The Qur'an and prophetic traditions, both considered primary sources of authority in Islam, do not have unambiguous and explicit teachings relating to family planning. Within Islamic legal philosophy, issues that require independent intellectual exertion and moral circumspection in light of a changing context and varying individual circumstances are called *ijtihadi* issues. *Ijtihad* is based on the assumption that in dealing with issues that are not explicitly addressed in the primary sources, jurists, informed by the spirit of the Qur'an, use their moral capacities for creative reasoning and judgment to arrive at relevant legal solutions.[34] Thus, this opens up the possibilities for more dynamic Islamic approaches to understanding the issues of family planning in the current context.

Proponents and opponents of family planning both derive their positions from their understandings of what constitutes "the good" and interpret broader Qur'anic injunctions to inform and support their respective positions. The possibility to sustain contrary readings of the divine text speaks to the reality that exegesis is a hermeneutical enterprise informed by the varied human capacities for understanding and moral reasoning. All readings are not equally convincing or legitimate, and in reviewing the arguments provided for both, it is my contention that family planning is in fact a legitimate and important Islamic priority.

Opponents of family planning often base their rejection of both contraception and abortion on their reading of the following verse:[35] "Kill not your children, on a plea of want, we provide sustenance for you and for them" (Q 6:151).

It is important to look at the context of revelation of this verse. This verse was a response to the pre-Islamic Arab custom of burying female children alive.[36] It was therefore a condemnation of infanticide and of the deep misogyny of that culture. Proponents of family planning have argued that the interpretation of these Qur'anic verses to counter all family planning initiatives is therefore a misreading of the text.

Furthermore, opponents of family planning base their resistance to it on the basis that it constitutes a lack of trust in God and in God's sustenance and that it is an assertion of one's own will vis-à-vis God's will.[37] The verses that they use to support this position are the following:

> There is no creature on earth, but its sustenance depends on God.
> He knows its habitation and its preservation. (Q 11:6)

> And whosoever is conscious of God, He will find a way out (of difficulty) for him, and He will provide for him in a manner beyond all expectations, and for every one that places their trust in God, He alone is sufficient. (Q65: 2–3)

Indeed trust in God and in God's sustenance is an integral dimension of Islam. These verses speak to the reality that in Islam ultimately the outcome of all things resides with God, for God is, without doubt, the Sustainer, the All-Powerful. I do, however, disagree with the conclusion that this absolves human beings from any responsibility for agency in the world. On the contrary, I would argue that this type of reasoning is contrary to the very fundamental

Islamic notion of human *khilafah*. We have established that *khilafah* implies that humanity is entrusted with moral agency that demands a God-conscious, active and responsible attitude to oneself, to fellow human beings, and to the world. It includes using the faculties of reason, judgment, and God-consciousness that are part of our *fitrah*, to plan one's life, to seek out sustenance, and to strive actively for the well-being of self and society in relation to the challenges of our age. In the current context of living in a world characterized by increasing populations with limited access to resources, being a *khalifah* includes responding constructively to these difficulties instead of further taxing the overburdened resources of the world. While we trust that ultimately all lies within the power of Allah, human agency is intrinsic to the Qur'anic worldview and the prophetic teachings.

The Qur'anic narrative of Joseph's planning and preservation of food in anticipation of the famine describes an act of agency that does not demonstrate a lack of trust in God's sustenance. Similarly, there are prophetic traditions that address the combination of human agency with trust in God as is reflected in the Prophet's advice to a man to tie up his camel and then trust in God; or the caliph Umar's statement that reliance on God means to plant the seeds in the earth, then trust in God for a good crop.[38] Family planning, including contraceptive usage, may be seen as extension of the human capacity to plan, to respond to, and to actively make choices in terms of contextual needs and emerging realities.

Contraception

Contraception has a long history in Islam that needs to be situated in relation to the broader Islamic ethos of marriage and sexuality. In Islam if one chooses to marry, this is not automatically linked to procreation. Within the Islamic view of marriage, an individual has the right to sexual pleasure within marriage, which is independent of one's choice to have children.[39] This type of approach to sexuality is compatible with a more tolerant approach to contraception and family planning.

Historically, the various Islamic legal schools with an overwhelming majority have permitted coitus interruptus, called *azl*, as a method of contraception.[40] This was a contraceptive technique practiced by pre-Islamic Arabs and continued to be used during the time of the Prophet with his knowledge and without his prohibition.[41] The only condition the Prophet attached to acceptability of this practice, which was reiterated by Muslim jurists, was that the husband was to secure the permission of the wife before practicing withdrawal.

Since the male sexual partner initiates this technique, there needs to be consensual agreement about its use by both partners for two primary reasons. First, the wife is entitled to full sexual pleasure and coitus interruptus may diminish her pleasure. Second, she has the right to offspring if she so desires.[42] These requirements speak to the priority given in Islam to mutual sexual fulfillment as well as consultative decision making between a married couple in terms of family planning.

As early as the ninth century female contraceptive techniques such as intravaginal suppositories and tampons were also a part of both medical and judicial discussions in Islam.[43] While medical manuals listed the different female contraceptive options and their relative effectiveness, legal positions differed around whether the consent of the husband was necessary or not with the use of female contraceptives. In classical Islamic law, which informs contemporary Islamic jurisprudence law, the majority position in eight out of the nine legal schools permits contraception.[44]

Due to this broad-based legal permissibility of contraception in Islamic law, Muslim physicians in the medieval period conducted in-depth investigations into the medical dimension of birth control, which were unparalleled in European medicine until the nineteenth century.[45] Ibn Sina in his *Qanun* lists 20 birth control substances, and physician Abu Bakr al-Razi in his *Hawi* lists 176 birth control substances.[46] The permissibility of contraceptive practice in Islamic history at the level of both theory and practice is abundantly evident in both its medical and legal legacies.

While different legal scholars discussed the acceptability or reprehensibility of particular individual motives for using contraceptives, this discussion did not contest the overarching permissibility of contraceptive practice. Al-Ghazzali supported the use of contraceptive practice for a number of different reasons, including when a large number of dependents would impose financial and psychological hardship on the family.[47] He reasoned that a large family may cause one to resort to unlawful means to support these excessive responsibilities. Fewer material burdens, he adds, are an aid to religion.

He also supported the decision to use contraception in order to protect the life of the wife, given the possible physical dangers that childbirth posed to the life of the mother. In addition, he considered the need for the wife to preserve her beauty and attractiveness for the enjoyment of the marriage as a reasonable justification for contraception.[48]

While the last-mentioned rationale may characterize a patriarchal emphasis on the primacy of the wife's appearance to the enjoyment of the marriage, it nonetheless simultaneously illustrates the high levels of tolerance for contraceptive practices in the Islamic legacy. This is reflected in the fact that there are many other influential jurists and theologians in different historical periods who discussed the permissibility of contraception (*azl*) for similar and additional reasons.[49]

In the present context there are a number of considerations that speak to the urgent need for family planning in Muslim societies. At the national level, physician and demographer Professor Abdel Rahim Omran demonstrates through population statistics that the population in the Muslim world is growing at a rate that is not matched by economic and service development. Due to these realities he states that:

> Muslim countries have been forced to acquire debt, import food and rely on foreign aid to cope with the needs of growing populations. The result is a vicious cycle of poverty, ill health, illiteracy, overpopulation and unemployment being compounded with social frustration, extremism and social unrest.[50]

There are significant internal social and economic reasons to focus on family planning in the Muslim world. Thus, arguments by religious scholars who see family planning as an external western conspiracy aimed at curtailing the growth and strength of the Muslim world appear to be uninformed of both the sociopolitical and demographic realities in many Muslim countries, as well as the historical permissibility of contraception within the Islamic legacy.[51] In fact, I would argue that, given the profound socioeconomic and political difficulties in various parts of the Muslim world, a lack of family planning and increasing populations would weaken and curtail the strength of Islam.

At the more personal level, the demands of a large family affect the quality of life of all its members, including parents and children. Numerous offspring make it less possible for parents to provide for the full range of their children's needs, including spiritual, emotional, psychological, and financial dimensions, resulting in children's experiencing a reduced quality of life. Similarly, multiple demands on parents generally create the need to work harder to provide for these numerous needs. This in turn often reduces their quality of life and gives them less time and energy for the spiritual and religious introspection also required in Islam.

It is noteworthy that the majority of contemporary Islamic leaders who are well educated in the Islamic legacy and are aware of social needs, with few exceptions, state the religious permissibility of contraception.[52] The fairly widespread encouragement of family planning and the permission to use contraceptive practices are reflected in a number of different conferences and religious publications participated in by leading Islamic scholars in various parts

of the Muslim world.[53] Some of the key arguments in these books and conference publications involve an application of Qur'anic ethical principles to the
perceived needs of the age. The following represent some of the recurring
elements in many of these conferences and publications:[54]

- Islam is a religion of ease and not of hardship. Moderation is the recommended approach to life (Q 2:185; 22:78). Thus, large families in
  the context of a limited access to resources often impose difficulties on
  the provider.
- In Islam there is a prioritization on the quality of life rather than a
  large quantity of lives.
- Planned spacing of pregnancies will allow the mother the time and opportunity to suckle and care for each child. The Qur'an recommends
  that a mother should suckle her child for two years.
- Undernourished and weak offspring are more a source of anxiety and
  struggle than the "comfort" or "allurement" of the parents eyes as the
  Qur'an intends.
- In Muslim countries that are underdeveloped, have limited resources,
  and are overpopulated, an absence of family planning will result in a
  weak multitude enduring more hardships instead of a smaller but
  stronger and healthier population.
- Contemporary contraceptive methods that temporarily avert pregnancy
  are analogous to the Islamically sanctioned practice of coitus interruptus *azl* and are thus permissible.
- Sterilization or any type of contraceptives that would cause permanent
  infertility were impermissible unless there were exceptional reasons.
- People should not be coerced to stop childbearing.

In some Muslim countries, the authorities have emerged with guidelines for
contraception. For example, an official Egyptian manual on family planning
that was compiled by religious scholars included a discussion on the acceptability of various forms of modern contraceptives including condoms, the cer-
vical cap, the loop device, the contraceptive pill, the contraceptive injection, and
the IUD.[55]

A forum that has made some particularly noteworthy and progressive declarations was the International Congress that took place in Aceh, Indonesia,
in 1990. The Aceh Declarations included an emphasis on responsibility that
the present generation owes to the future generations since the lifestyle and
decisions of the former impact the quality of life of future generations. As part
of a family planning program, they also recognized the importance of the em-

powerment of Muslim women, their informed participation in decision-making processes, and the need for improving maternal care and childcare facilities.[56]

It is noteworthy that among the religious scholars who oppose contraception, gender relations and women's rights are also key aspects of the argument, albeit in a different way. For example, Maulana Maududi of Pakistan condemns the entry of women into the public labor force and gender desegregation in society. He argues that in this type of permissive society:

> the last obstacle that may keep a woman from surrendering to a
> man's advances is fear of illegitimate conception. Remove this ob-
> stacle too and provide women with weak character assurance that
> they can safely surrender to their male friends and you will see that
> the society will be plagued by the tide of moral licentiousness.[57]

This type of argumentation is underpinned with a gender ideology that sees women's roles as restricted to the domestic realm under male control. Moreover, women are seen as moral minors whose abstinence from illicit sex is only due to fear of external sanctions and who are easily influenced by the sensual wiles of men. Paradoxically, responsibility for sexual morality of the community is seen to reside with activities of women, for it is their entry into public space that will cause sexual anarchy.[58] These notions are expressly masculinist and patriarchal and counter the very basic Islamic notions of the *khilafah* or full moral agency of every human being, both male and female. Not only is it a violation of the personhood of women but also it considers men as sexual predators who are driven by the needs of their uncontrollable libidos and will at any given opportunity seek out illicit sexual relationships. Accordingly, men too are depicted as lacking in moral agency since their proper conduct is premised on the absence of females in their company. Pervading this argument is the view that sexual morality is dictated from external constraints.

This type of sexual ethos contradicts the very basis of Islamic morality that every human being is endowed with the capacity to be an active moral agent and that no soul bears the burden of another. Moreover, Qur'anically, human morality and ethics are intended to emerge fundamentally from that all-pervasive internal locus of control called *taqwa* or God-consciousness. Accordingly, I would reject Maududi's argument against contraception and family planning as being contrary to some of the very basic premises of an Islamic worldview.

Despite the kind of perspective that Maududi represents, it would appear that the right to family planning is certainly part of the contemporary scholarly Islamic discourse. Based on sociological fieldwork in Morocco, researcher Donna Lee Bowen demonstrates that many of the local religious leaders who oppose contraception have relatively limited education in Islamic scholarship and their views are in sharp contrast with the those who come from the more educated *ulama* class.[59] Given the Islamic scholarly legacy as well as the demands of the current period, I would argue that opponents of family planning are not only inadequately informed but also lacking in judgment and the ability to articulate a dynamic and socially relevant Islamic response to challenges of the time.

In sum, it would appear that the contemporary need for family planning in the Muslim world is premised on the view that smaller families reduce hardships on the family and on national resources and support the conditions for the flourishing of human life. Both of these are authentic and essential Islamic imperatives found in the fundamentals of the Qur'anic worldview.

I would like to reiterate that while the views of the learned scholars may be illuminating and helpful (or not), in Islam the individual believer retains the right to make her own decisions on the basis of being a moral agent (*khalifah*). These decisions need to be informed by the primary sources and the Islamic principles of justice, human well-being, mercy, and compassion, where freedom is always accompanied by moral and spiritual responsibilities.

Abortion

In Islamic scholarship the positions on abortion are more varied and less consensual than the approaches to contraception. Historically, the Muslim legal positions range from unqualified permissibility of an abortion before 120 days into the pregnancy, on the one hand, to categorical prohibition of abortion altogether, on the other. Even within a single legal school the majority position was often accompanied by dissenting minority positions.[60]

Some of the key ethical and legal considerations in addressing the abortion question relate to understanding the nature of the fetus, the process of fetal development, and the point at which the fetus is considered a human being. While scientific inquiry has illuminated the process of fetal development with progressively more clarity, the question of when a fetus is considered a human being is open to varying interpretations. The following Qur'anic verses are central to understanding some of the ways in which Muslim thinkers approach these issues.

> He creates you in the wombs of your mothers
> In stages, one after another
> In three veils of darkness
> Such is Allah, your Lord and Cherisher. (Q 39:6)

> We created the human being from a quintessence of clay
> Then we placed him as semen in a firm receptacle
> Then we formed the semen into a blood-like clot
> Then we formed the clot into a lump of flesh
> Then we made out of that lump, bones
> And clothed the bones with flesh
> Then we developed out of it another creation
> So Blessed is Allah the Best Creator. (Q 23:12–13)

Given these scriptural teachings, Muslim scholars have understood that the fetus undergoes a series of transformations beginning as an organism and becoming a human being. An authenticated prophetic tradition provides a more detailed time frame for understanding the pace of fetal development: "Each of you is constituted in your mother's womb for 40 days as a *nutfa* (semen), then it becomes an *alaqa* (clot) for an equal period, then a *mudgha* (lump of flesh) for another equal period, then the angel is sent and he breathes the *ruh*, (spirit) into it."[61]

Together the Qur'anic verses and the prophetic tradition have been understood to describe a sequential process where the fetus undergoes a series of changes and finally culminates in becoming a full human being when it is "ensouled."[62] According to the Qur'an, this culmination point denotes a significant shift since the fetal organism is transformed into something substantively different from its previous state as is reflected in the verse "then we developed out of it another creation" (i.e., a human being). In the prophetic tradition this same point of transition into a human being is described as the point at which the angel breathes the spirit into the fetus at 120 days.

Medieval Islamic scholars also found support for the Qur'anic position and the prophetic teachings from Greek medicine, which had a corresponding understanding of the stages of fetal development.[63] Contemporary medical technology has developed such that we are able now able to detect vital signs of a fetus like brainwaves and heartbeat. While these advances in medical knowledge are informative and help to illuminate decisions, they still do not provide us with definitive criteria for determining when a fetus becomes fully "another creature," that is, a human person. While science can contribute to a description of the fetal development, it is outside of scientific method to determine the point of spiritual transition into the full human essence. For human beings, any designation of when a fetus constitutes a full human life can be contested since we are unable to know this unambiguously. Thus, revelation and prophetic inspiration remain a crucial way of understanding this issue from an Islamic perspective.

The narratives from the primary Islamic sources provide Muslim thinkers with a way to generate an estimated criterion for establishing personhood during the process of fetal development. This in turn has direct implications for the ethical and legal approaches to the question of abortion in Islam.

The view that the fetus is ensouled at 120 days, thereby becoming a human person and thus a legal personality, was integrated into Islamic jurisprudence.[64] Hence, for example, if someone injures a pregnant woman, causing her to miscarry the fetus, the amount of compensation due to her is based on the stage of fetal development. Causing the miscarriage of an ensouled or what is called a "formed" fetus is considered a criminal and religious offense and the mother needs to be compensated for the full blood money (diya) as though it were a case of a child already born.[65] A lesser remuneration is due if the fetus was considered "unformed." According to Islamic law only a formed fetus that is miscarried or accidentally aborted has the right to inheritance (to pass on to relatives), to be named, and to have a ritual burial.

From this perspective, the abortion of a formed fetus, that is, after 120 days, is considered a criminal offense and prohibited by all Islamic legal schools. Exceptions to this prohibition, however, include situations where the mother's life is in danger, where the pregnancy is harming an already suckling child, or where the fetus is expected to be deformed.[66] Relating to an abortion *prior to the 120-day period*, there are four different positions in classical Islamic, which have been summarized in the following way by Shaykh Jad al-Haq:[67]

1. Unconditional permission to terminate a pregnancy without a justification or fetal defect. This view is adopted by the Zaydi school, and some Hanafi and Shafi'i scholars. The Hanbali school allows abortion through the use of oral abortifacients within 40 days of conception.

2. Conditional permission to abort because of an acceptable justification. If there is an abortion without a valid reason in this period it is considered to be disapproved (makruh) but not forbidden (haram). This is the opinion of the majority of Hanafi and Shafi'i scholars.

3. Abortion is strongly disapproved (makruh). This is the view held by some Maliki jurists.

4. Abortion is unconditionally prohibited (*haram*). This reflects the other Maliki view, as well as the Zahiri, Ibadiyya, and Imamiyya legal schools.[68]

Such diversity in perspectives characterizes the Islamic legal canon, which contains contrary positions where both permissibility and prohibition of abortion are considered legitimate. This range of positions suggests a flexibility to the way in which Muslim societies have historically approached the issue of abortion. Moreover, the extensive discussions of specific types of abortifacients in medical manuals of the classical Islamic world reflect that it was a part of the social reality.

However, the range of approaches in the legal canon is not to be confused with a casual approach to human life—this is evidently not the case as any perusal of the Qur'an and Islamic legal texts will demonstrate. In fact, the minority of classical legal scholars who forbid abortion do not differ with other scholars on the process of fetal development but prohibit abortion because of their religious reverence for the potentiality of human life. Islam teaches the sanctity of human life and shows a profound respect for the potential for human life. Nonetheless, the rightful concern for a fetus needs to be situated in a larger context, juxtaposed and weighted in relation to the broader well-being of the mother, the family, and the society. Islam is a religion of balance and moderation that seeks to maximize the well-being of all elements in a society.

This type of circumspection and balanced judgment characterizes the recent statement of the Grand Shaykh of Al-Azhar, Sayed Tantawi, who supported the *fatwa* (juristic response) that abortion was permissible in the case of rape and that the rape survivor had the rights to privacy about her experience.[69] Last year in Iran, the Ayatollah Ali Khameni issued a *fatwa* in favor of abortion for fetuses under 10 weeks that were tested with a genetic blood disorder of thalassemia.[70] Also in Iran the Grand Ayatollah Yusuf Saanei issued a *fatwa* that permits abortion in the first trimester and not only for reasons of the mother's health or fetal abnormalities. In an interview reported in the *Los Angeles Times* he stated that Islam is a religion of compassion and that in the event of serious problems, abortion is permitted.[71]

In a submission to the South African parliament, the Judicial Committee of Islamic Council of South Africa recognized the right to terminate a pregnancy for a reasonable cause before 120 days. Reasonable causes included, among others, the impairment of the mental capacity or the integrity of the woman, as well as the ability and willingness of the woman to accept the responsibility of parenthood.[72] Finally, contemporary legal scholar Ebrahim

Moosa, drawing on the legal opinions of nineteenth-century Indian Hanafi scholar Abd al-Hayy al-Laknawi, illustrates how some traditional legal thinkers also permitted abortion in the case of pregnancy outside of wedlock.[73] He speculates that al-Laknawi's legal reasoning was possibly informed by the fact that the future prospects of an unwed mother would be radically reduced in his society and thus the Indian jurist recommends the radical act to terminate advanced pregnancies arising from sex out of wedlock. For him it was a case of the lesser of two evils.

It is not surprising that despite the diversity characterizing Islamic legal perspectives on abortion, which even include views of its permissibility, the realities of many contemporary Muslim societies reflect a tendency to adopt a more rigid approach. Part of this motivation, rightfully, is to ensure that people do not adopt an uncritical acceptance of easy abortions since the decision to terminate a potential realization of a human life is a grave decision not be taken lightly or without circumspection. Indeed, the gravity of this whole enterprise bolsters the case for a responsible approach to family planning including reliable contraceptive usage, which would, for the most part, preempt the need for abortion.

In fact, some of the contemporary practices of abortion based on the gender of the fetus are ethically problematic. From the 1980s there has been a growing practice of aborting female fetuses based on ultrasound tests in India, China, and South Korea.[74] This reflects misogyny and constitutes a direct contrast to Qur'anic ethics, which strongly condemns the hatred of "femalehood." Thus, I would propose that from an Islamic ethical perspective aborting a fetus on the basis of gender is unjustifiable.

For more people, however, abortion is not based on the gender of the fetus; neither is it an easy or thoughtless decision—it involves much anguish and internal struggle. In the event that such a decision is deemed necessary, it is important that we remember that the God of the Qur'an is consistently described through the divine qualities of mercy and compassion. In fact, these two portals of God's self-revelation are constantly invoked by Muslims throughout daily activity. It is vital to move from invocation to enactment. The way in which the realities of compassion and mercy manifest in difficult situations requires an awareness of and a response to the suffering and complexity of human lives.

For those that oppose abortion, a compassionate and merciful attitude would include focusing on transforming social structures so that having children does not create hardships for the mother, the family, and the society. This would be a more socially constructive use of energy than the crusade against abortion. A concern for the welfare of the fetus without a concern for its continuing welfare as a human being reflects a limited, if not hypocritical approach.

In Islam, if an individual or a couple are considering the possibility of an abortion it is imperative that they do so with a full awareness of the gravity of such a decision. In this situation, I would present that being a *khilafah*, or moral agent, requires a careful consideration of all the factors, weighing up the different demands and needs of the specific situation, and like in all things, intentionally keeping one's sense of *taqwa*, or God-consciousness, at the forefront. Islamically, the freedom to act as the *khalifah* is intrinsically accompanied by accountability and responsibilities at the personal, social, and religious levels. Often the specifics of a given context determine what the most responsible alternative is. Given these considerations, from within the Islamic perspective there is room for a pro-choice perspective where the individual *khalifah* engages all sources of Islamic guidance—the Qur'an, the prophetic traditions, and the legal positions, as well as his or her own intellectual, moral, and ethical capacities—to inform a decision about abortion.

In conclusion, it is my view that a contemporary Islamic ethical perspective on family planning, contraception, and abortion, requires a holistic vision of the problems of our era. We are confronted with the realities of socio-economic injustice, sexism, overpopulation, and diminishing resources, to name but a few. There is a need for Muslims to assess the needs of the time in terms of an understanding of the political, social, and economic realities of their respective contexts. It is crucial that Muslims move beyond purely defensive posturing and undertake their *khilafah* through adopting a genuinely engaged and informed approach to the world. The Islamic legacy, in its own terms, provides a rich heritage of human agency and creative socially relevant thinking. As a religion, Islam provides its adherents with multiple resources to implement progressive social visions premised on values of human freedom accompanied by responsibility, of human well-being with optimal spiritual development, and of justice tempered with mercy and compassion. It is in the interests of humanity that Muslims bring all these spiritual treasures to the table of discussion on family planning, contraception, and abortion.

NOTES

1. See Greg Noakes, "Cairo Population Conference Still Controversial," *Washington Report on Middle East Affairs*, April/May 1995.

2. Christine Gorman, "Clash of Wills in Cairo," *Time Magazine* (online), Sept. 12, 1994.

3. Noakes, "Cairo Population Conference," pp. 100–101.

4. See Abdel Rahim Omran, *Family Planning in the Legacy of Islam* (London: Routledge, 1992), ch. 8–10.

5. See Basim Musallam, *Sex and Society in Islam* (Cambridge: Cambridge University Press, 1983), ch. 4–5.

6. For a more detailed examination of the issue, see Norman Daniel, *Islam and the West: The Making of an Image* (Edinburgh: Edinburgh University Press, 1960).

7. A collection of essays that looks at the varying relationship between Islam and globalization is edited by Ahmad Akbar and Hastings Donnan, *Islam, Globalization, and Postmodernity* (London: Routledge, 1994).

8. This view is not only reflected at the popular level, as reported by Greg Noakes, "Cairo Population Conference" (pp. 100–101) but also by some Islamic scholars like Maulana Maududi's *Birth Control*, trans. K. Ahmad and M. I. Faruqi (Lahore: Islamic Publications Ltd., 1974), and Abu Zahra's *"Tanzim al Nasl," Liwa al Islam* 1962.

9. Daniel, *Islam and the West*, p. 142.

10. Qur'an 55:26–27.

11. Qur'an 59:19.

12. Qur'an 15:29.

13. See Fazlur Rahman, *Major Themes of the Quran* (Minneapolis: Bibliotheca Islamica, 1980), p. 18.

14. Azizah Al-Hibri, "An Introduction to Muslim Women's Rights," in *Windows of Faith: Muslim Women Scholar-Activists in North America*, ed. Gisela Webb (Syracuse: Syracuse University Press, 2000), p. 52.

15. Qur'an 49:13. Moreover, in situating Qur'anic revelation in the seventh-century Meccan society, this notion of *taqwa* as being the sole criterion for human worth provided a sweeping critique of the very basis of that social formation which was characterized by socioeconomic, gender, and tribal hierarchies.

16. Qur'an 4:135.

17. This synergy is encapsulated by Sufi teacher Shaykh Bawa Muhaiyaddeen, who states, "If we are true believers, we will not see any difference between others and ourselves. We will see only One. We will see Allah, one human race, and one justice for all. That justice and truth is the strength of Islam." *Islam and World Peace: Explanations of a Sufi* (Philadelphia: The Fellowship Press, 1987), p. 6.

18. The realities of structural economic imbalances internationally are borne out by a 1996 UN Development Report which stated that the world's 358 billionaires are wealthier than the combined annual income of countries with 45 percent of the world's population as cited in David Loy, *Religion and the Market* (www.consultation.org/consultation/loy.htm). By 1995 the average CEO of a large U.S. corporation received a compensation packet of more than $3.7 million annually, as reflected in David Korten, *When Corporations Rule the World* (Connecticut: Kumarian Press, 1995), p. 218. This coexists with the reality that there are an estimated 900 million malnourished people in the world, 40 million of which die from hunger and poverty-related causes worldwide, as stated in Clive Ponting, *A Green History of the World* (New York: Penguin Books, 1991), p. 245. Just from these statistics it is clear that equitable wealth distribution and economic justice are urgent human ethical concerns.

19. Qur'an 59:7.

20. Qur'an 64:15–17.

21. Qur'an 59:7. Moreover, it is noteworthy that in defining the believer, the Qur'an repeatedly includes wealth sharing as a criteria of genuine belief in God as reflected in the verses Q 9:71; Q 13:22; and Q 23:1–5. Accordingly, the category of worship (*ibadat*) in Islam is not only restricted to ritual prayers but includes various types of socioeconomic responsibilities like giving charity to the needy, feeding the hungry, and taking care of the orphan. Even the ritual worship (*salat*), which is a duty prescribed to every Muslim to perform five times a day, is itself imbued with various levels of social responsibility. For example, one Qur'anic rationale for *salat* is that it creates a pervasive God-consciousness, thereby enabling people to refrain from injustice; "Establish regular prayer for prayer restrains from shameful and unjust deeds and remembrance of God is the greatest thing in life without doubt. And Allah knows the deeds that you do" (Q 29:45). Furthermore, one's worship is considered spiritually meaningful only when accompanied by ethical behavior in relation to social need: "Do you see the one who gives a lie to the faith? Such a one is he who repulses the orphan and does not encourage the feeding of the indigent, so woe unto the worshippers who are neglectful of worship who only want to be seen but deny the needs of those around them" (Q 107:1–7). Hence, prayer that does not coexist with the worshiper's awareness of the plight of other human beings and related ethical actions is contrary to spiritual truth and thus does not constitute real prayer.

22. Qur'an 47:38; 89:16–26.

23. Qur'an 41:6–7.

24. With the advances of global capitalism, increasing numbers of multinational corporations from richer nations in the world move their factories to poorer countries with the cheapest labor and governments most tolerant of exploitative labor practices in order to retain foreign investment. For a detailed account on impact of the corporate capitalism on the global markets, see William Greider, *One World, Ready or Not: The Manic Logic of Global Capitalism* (New York: Simon and Schuster, 1997).

25. See Daniel Maguire and Larry Rasmussen, *Ethics for a Small Planet: New Horizons on Population, Consumption, and Ecology* (Albany: State University of New York Press, 1997), p. 3.

26. Qur'an 33:35; 16:97; 9:71.

27. Qur'an 16:72; 25:74.

28. Qur'an 64:14–15.

29. Qur'an 24:33.

30. See Madelain Farah, *Marriage and Sexuality in Islam: A Translation of Al-Ghazali's Book on the Etiquette of Marriage from the* Ihya (Salt Lake City: University of Utah Press, 1984), pp. 71–74.

31. Muslims committed to ideals of human equality advocate a holistic reading of the Qur'anic text, which places the different verses on gender in relationship to one another and which historically contextualize the revelation to derive a full picture of the relevant Qur'anic teachings. This is exemplified in the work of contemporary scholar Amina Wadud, *Qur'an and Woman: Rereading the Sacred Text from a Woman's Perspective* (New York: Oxford University Press, 1999). This type of exegetical work

provides a stark contrast to the approach of Muslim patriarchs who interpret and prioritize specific Qur'anic verses in ways that buttress their ideologies of male hegemony.

32. See Riffat Hassan, "Human Rights in the Qur'anic Perspective," in *Windows of Faith*, pp. 241–248; and Amina Wadud, *Quran and Woman*, pp. 94–104.

33. Qur'an 25:74.

34. Ebrahim Moosa, "Prospects for Muslim Law in South Africa: A History and Recent Developments," in *Yearbook of Islamic and Middle Eastern Law*, ed. Eugene Cotrane and Chibli Mallat (London: Kluwer Law International, 1997), p. 140.

35. See, for example, Aboul A'ala Maududi, "Birth Control," trans. and ed. K. Ahmad and M. I. Faruqi (Lahore: Islamic Publications Ltd., 1974), and Abu Zahra's article *"Tanzim al Nasl,"* Liwa al Islam, 1962.

36. See Fazlur Rahman, "The Status of Women in Islam: A Modernist Interpretation," in *Separate Worlds: Studies of Purdah in South Asia*, ed. Hannah Papanek and Gail Minault (New Delhi: South Asia Book, 1982), pp. 286–287.

37. See Omran, *Family Planning*, pp. 89–90.

38. Ibid., p. 91.

39. Islam also recognizes the spiritual dimensions of sexuality as explored by medieval mystical philosopher Ibn Arabi, who stated that in accordance with the spiritual state of the partners, the act of sexual union has the possibilities for unparalleled mystical unveilings and experiences of the divine. See Ibn Al-Arabi, *Bezels of Wisdom*, trans. R. W. J. Austin (Mahwah, N.J.: Paulist Press, 1980), p. 274.

40. See *Islam's Attitude Towards Family Planning* (Cairo: Ministry of Waqfs and Ministry of Information, 1994), pp. 27–34, and Omran, *Family Planning*, pp. 145–182.

41. Omran provides an extensive discussion on the *al-azl* tradition in *Family Planning*, pp. 115–142.

42. Musallam, *Sex and Society*, pp. 31–36.

43. Ibid., pp. 77–88, 37–38.

44. Omran, *Family Planning*, pp. 145–167.

45. Musallam, *Sex and Society*, pp. 60–89.

46. Ibid.

47. Madelain Farah, *Marriage and Sexuality*, p. 111.

48. Ibid.

49. These include Abu Jafar Tahawi (d. 933) in his *Sharh Maani al Athar*, Ibn al Qayyim (d. 1350) in his *Zad al Ma'ad* (d. 1350), Ibn Hajjar Al-Askalani (d. 1449) in his *Fath al Bari*, Al-Shawkani (d. 1830) in his *Nayl al-Awtar*.

50. Omran, *Family Planning*, p. 212.

51. Here again Maulana Maududi's *Birth Control* and Shaykh Abu Zahra's *"Tanzim al Nasl"* exemplify such an approach.

52. See Donna Lee Bowen, "Interpretations of Family Planning: Reconciling Islam and Development," in *The Shaping of an American Islamic Discourse*, ed. Earle Waugh and Fredrick Denny (Atlanta: Scholars Press, 1998), p. 150, and *Islam's Attitude Towards Family Planning*.

53. See Omran, *Family Planning*, pp. 201–224.

54. Ibid. Here I have summarized some of the key arguments found in the dis-

cussions and declarations of these various contemporary conferences and publications.

55. *Islam's Attitude Towards Family Planning*, pp. 34–66.

56. Cited in Omran, *Family Planning*, p. 220.

57. Maududi, *Birth Control*, p. 176.

58. For a discussion on the construction of gender ideology and sexuality, see Sa'diyya Shaikh, "Exegetical Violence: Nushuz in Qur'anic Gender Ideology," *Journal for Islamic Studies* 17 (1997): 49–73.

59. Bowen, *Interpretations of Family Planning*, pp. 150–151.

60. Musallam, *Sex and Society*, pp. 57–59.

61. Muslim, *Book of Qadr*, hadith no. 4781.

62. Ibn Qayyim al-Jawziyya, *Al-Tibyan fi aqsam al-Qur'an* (Cairo, 1933), pp. 374–375.

63. Musallam, *Sex and Society*, p. 54.

64. For detailed legal implications of the religious view of fetal development, see Muhammad Salaam Madkur's *Al-Janin wa Ahkam al-muta'alliqa bihi fi al-fiqh* (Cairo, 1969).

65. Musallam, *Sex and Society*, p. 57.

66. Omran, *Family Planning*, p. 192.

67. Jad al-Haq Ali Had al-Haq, *al-Fatawa al Islamiyya min Dar al-Ifta al-Misriyya*, (Cairo: Wazara al-Awqaf/ al Majlis al-A'la li al Shu'un al-Islamiyya, 1983), vol. 9, pp. 3093–3109.

68. The Zahiri, Ibadiyya, and Imammiyya schools all have a limited following.

69. See Mariz Tadros, "The Shame of It," *Al-Ahram* (weekly online), Dec. 3–9, 1998.

70. "Doctors Refuse Abortion for Blood Disorder," *The Iranian Times* (online), Sept. 18, 2000.

71. See Robin Wright, "Iran, Now a Hotbed of Islamic Reforms," *Los Angeles Times*, Dec. 29, 2000.

72. The Judicial Committee of the Islamic Council of South Africa, *Memorandum on Abortion: Submission to the Parliamentary Committee on Abortion and Sterilisation*, May 1995.

73. See Ebrahim Moosa, *Essays in Islamic Law* (forthcoming).

74. See Celia Dugger, "Abortion in India Is Strongly Tipping Scales Against Girls," *New York Times* (online), April 22, 2000.

5

The Right to Family Planning, Contraception, and Abortion

The Hindu View

SANDHYA JAIN

From the perspective of India, the conception of such a broad and ambitious project as "The Right to Family Planning, Contraception, and Abortion in Ten Major World Religions" poses a formidable challenge but also offers an invaluable opportunity. It is a challenge because India is renowned as a traditional society in which religion plays a large role in defining identity and determining one's personal conduct and belief system, and in which religion and society are believed to be biased in favor of big families and male offspring. The fact that there is a measure of truth in this stereotype only confirms the outsider's impression of a society steeped in tradition and stubbornly resistant to change. This is why the invitation to participate in this project is a welcome opportunity to balance the picture. In India, the ancient religion is as malleable as it is eternal; indeed, religion can be utterly transformed and turned on its head in the name of religion itself. What is more, much in the tradition regards change as nonthreatening and as the "natural" order of things; resistance to change is perceived as an act of ignorance and futility.

India's ancient religion, Hinduism, is properly known as the *Sannatan Dharma*, or the Eternal Tradition. Hinduism has been seen as more of a confederations of religions than a dogmatically unified system, as, for example, is Roman Catholicism. Hinduism is simultaneously a religion and a way of life, and constitutes a unique blend of spirituality and practicality that is inspired by the ideal of universal welfare of all beings, both human and other creatures. *Dharma* can be seen as natural (cosmic) law. It has a formal structure, creed, and ritual but is rarely the captive of absolutism. *Dharma* is not a static notion espousing only the values of a bygone era but is reflective, contextual, and characterized by movement, change, dynamism, and adaptability. It stands for universal values, but is sensitive to the individual and the particular. Thus, in a situation of genuine moral conflict, *dharma* permits, even urges, one to be guided by the demands of the situation. As the goal of *dharma* is emancipation, it is important for one to know one's own *dharma*, or *swadharma*. There are methods for doing this. The *Bhagavad Gita* suggests that when in doubt, one may follow (in descending order) the Vedas, the Smritis (expositions of Vedic wisdom), the conduct of righteous persons, and one's own conscience.

Hinduism, in its quest for the Absolute Reality or Truth, also encompasses a vast unmapped terrain where pure consciousness reigns and knowledge is experienced through intuitive perception. This is a realm about which meaningful verbal communication is impossible, and is best elucidated (to the extent that it can at all be explained) in terms of the Upanishadic "that which is not" or "that which is beyond." This imports a helpful epistemological modesty in the culture informed by these ideas.

This description of its Self in terms of both what *is* and what *is not* is Hinduism's defining quality, and what principally distinguishes it from other major world religions. The distinction is important because it vests Hinduism with the philosophical range and flexibility to face and absorb new challenges and situations with equanimity. At the same time, it protects Hinduism from the dogmatism and rigidity it could have fallen into had the sages "capped" the revelations of the Vedas as final and binding for all times, with no one having the right to discover and experience the Truth for himself or herself.

Arnold Toynbee has observed that the principal monotheistic faiths have grown on the ruins of previously extant civilizations. The *sannatan dharma*, however, is itself a *living civilization* and is also coterminous with the formal religion. It is thus possible to be a good Hindu without subscribing to or practicing any of the known forms in which the religion manifests itself. Hinduism recognizes even the atheist as morally valid, and does not deny the atheist space on the religious-spiritual spectrum.

This is because the *sannatan dharma* is all-encompassing: it is righteousness, it is duty, it is the eternal law that is not fixed (in time or space) but eternally renews itself in response to the changing times and provides for as many paths to salvation as there are individual souls who seek it. The tradition abounds with allusions to *dharma* as a river, which best explain its changing nature and apparent sameness, as also its continuity. Like a river, *dharma* maintains a continuous flow through the ages, constantly renewing and replenishing its waters (contents), and continually altering its course, while giving the appearance of changelessness. This rare ability to combine continuity with what Cromwell Crawford calls dynamic diversity, has saved Hinduism from some of the schisms and ruptures that have often disrupted societies trying to come to terms with change in other parts of the world.

Hindu morality, as Crawford has rightly observed, has an evolutionary character, and this, in turn, imparts contemporary relevance to its fundamental precepts, such as *karma* and *dharma*, whose origins have been lost in the mists of time. Yet they have survived and continue to exert a powerful influence on the minds of their adherents, not *despite* change, as one would be tempted to believe, but *because* of change. In the Hindu worldview, change is the immutable cosmic law (*rta*) that governs the working of the universe. Change cannot be stopped and should not be feared, but rather *experienced*. This extraordinary plasticity of vision of the Vedic seers has bequeathed to Hinduism its incredible capacity to vary its metaphysical and ethical principles in consonance with the social and historical realities of the day, without losing its essential character or sense of identity.

The ultimate goal of *dharma* is one realization of the Self (*Atman*) within, through awareness, self-inquiry, and self-realization. This will release one from the otherwise endless cycle of birth and death, the basis of which lies in one's ignorance of the purpose and goal of one's life. Hinduism *does* believe in the possibility of salvation through grace—the grace of God, or the grace of a Guru. But it rejects the notion of vicarious redemption through the sufferings of another being. Hence, each individual soul must itself aspire to godhead in order to attain *nirvana* (*moksha*, release).

In the *sannatan dharma*, human life is the highest form of life, and is attained after innumerable cycles of birth and rebirth in which the spirit evolves through the densest matter toward forms of consciousness. Human birth, therefore, is a unique gift, and gives the human being the opportunity to realize the Self and merge with the *Atman* (godhead), and end the painful cycle of birth and rebirth. This would imply that every birth bestows human beings with a singular opportunity to work out some of their *karma* (the accumulated effects of their actions, both good and bad), and move toward godhead. In the specific context of our study, however, the question arises that if human birth is so critical to self-realization, can we legitimately interfere with human births, and indeed, should we at all intrude in such a delicate matter?

Fortunately for us, the *sannatan dharma* professes the most uncommon notion of death. In the Hindu view, human birth is not a once-only occurrence but an incessant cycle that affords the individual the chance to negate the effects of his bad *karma* and eventually neutralize both good and bad *karma*. Death is not the end of the story, nor is it equated with sin and suffering. Death is rather a window of opportunity through which an unhappy soul sheds its outer covering and moves on to the next stage of its evolution toward godhead (*Atman*). For the few lucky realized souls, it is the moment of final release (*moksha*) from the bondage of birth and death. Even the dissolution of the universe itself does not imply absolute annihilation, but the beginning of a new stage in the history of the cosmos in which, in the words of S. Radhakrishnan and C. Moore, "the unexhausted potencies of good and evil are provided opportunities of fulfillment." Death is then, in every sense and for every one, a *release* and a new beginning.

Obviously such a concept of death provides enormous comfort, besides holding an immense promise for the individuals who are willing to live their lives with freedom and responsibility. This, then, may be the best place to search for clues as to whether a tradition as holistic as the Hindu civilization can endorse the modern world's exhortation to the individual to limit the size of her family. Can we invoke tradition to frustrate the efforts of a soul seeking reincarnation so that it may work out its *karma*? Can we also set aside the overwhelming corpus of tradition that lays stress on the duties of the householder, particularly the emphasis on childbearing? Surprising as this may seem, we can find the path we seek in the very mainstream of the tradition.

We do not need to search through obscure texts and remote traditions to find the evidence we seek, but can make a promising beginning with the *Mahabharat*, one of the most important and popular Indian epics. The *Mahabharat* is not a fable of a dead or extinct civilization, like the *Iliad* or the *Arabian Nights*, but a part of the living tradition of India. Two of the most popular devotional prayers of the Hindus, the *Bhagavad Gita* and the *Vishnu Sahasranama*, have come down to us from the *Mahabharat*.

The epic begins with the beautiful goddess Ganga (who is also India's most sacred river) assuming a human form and marrying the human king Shantanu, ancestor of the Pandavas, who are the heroes of the epic. According to the story, the goddess contracts to live with the king only until such time as he does not quiz her about her true identity or question any of her actions. She then lives with him in his palace and appears to hold the king in thrall through seven blissful years. Shantanu's happiness, however, is marred by the fact that Ganga gives birth to a son every year and promptly drowns the infant in the river running by the palace. Worse, she does so with a smiling face. When seven infants are thus drowned in cold blood, the anguished king can bear it no more and protests loudly at the proposed murder of his eighth son (who is therefore saved and lives to become the legendary Bhishma).

The goddess now discloses her true identity and explains to the astonished king her mission on earth, which is to give birth to and provide instantaneous release to the eight Vasus (gods) who had incurred the wrath of the great sage Vasisth. Shantanu's objections, she reveals, have the effect of aborting the planned release of the eighth Vasu; hence, his life is spared. Ganga now departs for her heavenly abode after assuring the king that great merit would accrue to him for having fathered the Vasus who had been released from human bondage. The story is truly significant in several respects. Ganga, as divine-and-human mother, conceives, gives birth to, and destroys seven male children. Shantanu, who is unwittingly complicit in this act, incurs great merit for his part of the action. The danger of such a story, of course, is that it would seem to countenance infanticide. It does illustrate the belief that life is not ended by death, a belief that enters into the discussion of abortion.

Later on, the same epic dwells upon the trials and tribulations of the Pandavas, the five sons of Pandu, King of Hastinapur. The Pandavas have, through the ages, served as one of the Hindu prototypes of the ideal family. They are a small, compact, and united family with a deeply ingrained sense of honor, duty, justice, and righteousness. They do not meet the Vedic ideal of 10 sons and are, in fact, the children of two different mothers (Kunti and Madri). Their cousins and enemies, the Kauravas, are the proverbial hundred sons, but they fall far short of the exacting standards of *dharma*.

Contrary to the exhortations of sages and jurists (mainly the writers of the *Dharma sastras*) to have large families, we find that families idealized in the Hindu tradition are all small families. In the epic *Ramayana*, for instance, Lord Rama is the only son of his mother (Kaushalya), although King Dasrath has four sons in all. Even Rama's brother, Bharat, for whose sake he is exiled to the forest for 14 years, is the only son of his mother (Keikayi). This is equally true of other Indian mythological heroes—Krishna, Satyavan, Prahlad—all of whom have profoundly shaped the Hindu moral cosmos. But to return to the Rama story, we find the small family norm continued in the next generation as well. This is evocatively brought out in a beautiful couplet in Tulsidas's *Ram Charit Manas*, one of the most popular versions of the Rama story (written in the sixteenth century), on the children of Sita (Rama's wife) and her three sisters (cousins), who were married to the three brothers of Rama. It may broadly be translated thus:

Two beautiful sons had Sita . . .

Two—two sons did all the mothers give birth to, all beautiful, grace-
ful, and full of virtue. (Uttarkhand, 25th Doha, 6–8 Chaupai)

Surely this is a very powerful legitimation of the small family. Indeed, it
would be observed that in almost all cultures, the Holy Family tends to be a
small family. Large families inevitably breed stress and anxiety and, in our
times at least, also poverty. The question, of course, is whether we can conclude
from this that the small family is conducive to greater spiritual well-being. And
if this is the Big Hint from the cradle of Hindu civilization, how does it square
with the sheer weight given by the cultural tradition to large families? How
does it square with the specific exhortation in the *Dharma sastras* not to practice
abortion, even of the illegitimate child? Which one is the correct position?

Looking briefly at Vedic society, we find that the family was the basic unit
of Aryan society (as the ancient Hindus called themselves). In the Rig Vedic
ideal, marriage is viewed as a sacrament rather than a contract, and is a harmonious union of biological and spiritual elements, wherein the young couple
embark together upon a journey of righteous living. The life of the householder
(*gryhasta ashram*) is regarded as an essential stage in spiritual evolution, and
has been accorded pivotal importance in various ages, from the *Mahabharata*
to Manu and Ramanuja.

The purpose of marriage was to beget children, particularly sons, who
would carry on the lineage in a patriarchal society. However, it may be noted
that often the Vedic word *putra* (literally "son") was a generic term for offspring
and included girls, and that the desire for males did not automatically entail
the devaluation of female children (a latter-day development that has rightly
given Indian society a bad name). The Rig Vedic period lays considerable stress
upon intellectual achievements for both boys and girls, and girls, like boys, are
also expected to go through the *brahmacharya* (bachelor) stage and acquire an
education. The *Atharva Veda* confirms this by pointing out that a *brahmacharini*
has better prospects of marriage than a girl who is uneducated. Women in this
period have a voice in the selection of their husbands, which clearly implies
that they married at a relatively mature age. They have strong marital rights
and are expected to be the mistress in their husband's home. They also have
social rights, move freely in society, participate in public life, and debate in
assemblies.

This state of affairs, of course, does not last, and in the era that follows
there is emphasis on the male child due to the belief that sons alone can enable
the dead to survive in the heavens through the regular offerings of oblations.
This gives sons a ritualistic preeminence over daughters, while the growing

ritual specialization erodes woman's role as an equal religious partner of man. The period of the Upanishads, however, again sees the rise of women, who attain intellectual excellence, are admitted to the highest philosophical groups, and discuss the highest spiritual truths of life, as epitomized in the story of Maitreyi, wife of the sage Yajnavalkya. There are at this time ritual prayers for the birth of a daughter who will achieve the status of a *pandita* (learned woman). Women's education is not limited to household affairs, and they explicitly have the right to study the Vedas in this period, a privilege later denied to them by Shankaracharya.

It must be pointed out that throughout the ancient period, from the time of the Vedas to the Brahmanas and the Upanishads, to the era of the *Dharma Sutras* followed by the *Dharma Sastras*, and beyond, while the status of women may vary, the purpose of marriage is to maintain the continuity of the family. There is, from the beginning, an awareness of the practice of abortion, which is widely condemned in the main body of the tradition, but it is not clear if the aversion to abortion by religious teachers includes the modern-day notion of limiting the size of the family for rational considerations.

It is evident, however, that the apparently implacable aversion to abortion derives from the Hindu theory of conception as the result of a divine act, and hence as holy and worthy of reverence. This is best seen in the description of conception in the renowned medical treatises *Charak Samhita* and *Susruta Samhita*, which proclaim that fertilization is not merely the result of cohabitation, and the intervention of a superior agent is required for the creation of a new life. The *Charak Samhita* states:

> The combination of sperm, ovum and life-principle implanted in the womb is known as embryo.
>
> Embryo is the product of *akasa, vayu, tejas, ap* and *prthvi* being the seat of consciousness. Thus, embryo is the aggregate of the five mahabhutas being the seat of consciousness which is regarded as the sixth constituent of embryo.

Conception is thus simultaneously a unification with the spirit (life-principle, or *Atman*) which abides in the embryo as the embodied soul and provides the unborn life with spiritual continuity. This is in consonance with the Hindu view of the goal of human life as spiritual realization and liberation.

In the Hindu view, therefore, both physical and spiritual life enters the human embryo at the moment of conception itself, and there is never a pure state of matter alone. Conception is the moment when the soul enters the body along with the individual's past *karma* (which determines factors such as the choice of parents), and it is this that gives each embryo its unique identity. The *karmic* inheritance also invests the unborn with moral qualities and entitles it to care and protection. The fetus is thus not merely tissue of the mother's body, but a distinct life with the basic attributes of humanity from the moment of its conception.

The Hindu tradition has from the very beginning placed a high premium on life in the womb and treated abortion as a heinous crime. In fact, it is classified as one of the *mahapatakas* (atrocious acts), and subjected to severe penances and punishments. In the *Atharva Veda*, there are two hymns invoking the goddess Pushan to wipe off "the misdeed upon him that practiseth abortion." The Brahmanas, the second major corpus of Hindu religious literature, also perceive abortion as the basest of sins. This view is continued in the Upanishadic period, wherein abortion is believed to have consequences that *karmically* affect both this life and the next one; mercifully, however, one can be released from its malignant effects through enlightenment. The Hindu juristic schools that follow, Manu, Gautam, Vasistha, Yajnavalkya, and even Charak, all condemn abortion in unequivocal terms, even in the case of illegitimate children.

Hindu thought has, however, traditionally rejected absolutism and is thus intrinsically well equipped to address a scale of competing rights and values. Thus, in pregnancies where the mother risks grave injury or even death, the *Charak Samhita* accords greater weight to the maternal life over the fetus's life. This, in fact, continues to be the Hindu position to this day. Crawford argues that this is because the adult human being is *karmically* more evolved than the unborn child, has existing obligations to family and society, and has far more at stake for her spiritual destiny. Be that as it may, it is a significant instance of putting the life and health of the mother, and by implication her happiness and the integrity of her family, before the esoteric demands of faith.

That this is no accident, but the well-considered position of religious scholars, can be seen from the fact that the *Susruta Samhita* (a treatise mainly devoted to surgery) recommends abortion in difficult cases where the fetus is irreparably damaged or defective, and the chances of a normal delivery are negligible. Susruta suggests that in such instances, the surgeon should not wait for nature to take its course, but should intervene by performing craniotomic operations to remove the fetus.

Hindu thought has ever rejected linear notions of time and morality. The tradition is holistic and varied, and provides for a range of perspectives and needs. Notwithstanding the widely disseminated disapproval of abortion through the ages, there are numerous *Ayurvedic* texts (the ancient medical system) that prescribe methods of avoiding pregnancy (contraception) or getting rid of unwanted pregnancies (abortion). These all attest to the fact that there has always been a human need to control or mitigate the consequences of sexuality, and that this fact was recognized, with sympathy, by at least a section of the religious-medical teachers at various times. It would also appear that some women at least received such services, and this may in turn account for the continuous condemnation of this practice by the majority of teachers/preceptors.

Interestingly, the desire or need to have sexual relationships that were, for whatever reason, free from the fear of pregnancy, figures as early as the *Atharva Veda Samhita*, the fourth and most mystical of the Vedas. It also includes hymns to render certain men or women impotent or barren. For instance: "Thou art listened to, O herb, as the most best of plants; make thou now this man for me impotent *(kliba)*, opaca-wearing."[1]

The commentary does not explain the context in which the invocation is made, nor does it identify the herb that is being addressed. It is possible that this was part of the oral instruction that would have accompanied the written text, as a large volume of learning continued to be imparted orally even after texts began to be written. The *opaca*, however, is a kind of head ornament worn particularly by women. There follow even more violent verses that exult in making a man impotent.

The *Atharva Veda Samhita* also contains invocations to Agni (God of the Sacrificial Fire) against one's enemies: "O Agni, thrust forth my rivals that are born; *thrust back, O Jatavedas, those unborn*; put under the foot those that want to fight (me); may we be guiltless for thee unto Aditi."[2]

The verse makes it amply clear that there was a fervent desire to tackle the unwanted unborn, although in this case in a hostile setting.

There are three other verses in the *Atharva Veda* that appear to be aimed at preventing an enemy's wife or a rival woman from bearing children. However, it is not clear whether the invocations alone are being relied upon to achieve the desired result, or more tangible means (such as a drug administered orally and secretly) are also being utilized.

Overpower away with power (our) other rivals; *thrust back, O Jatavedas, those unborn*; fill this royalty unto good fortune; let all the gods revel after him.[3]

These hundred veins that are thine, and the thousand tubes—of them all of thine I have covered the opening with a stone.[4]

The upper part of thy womb I make the lower; *let there not be progeny to thee*, nor birth; I make thee barren *(asu)*, without progeny; I make a stone thy cover.[5]

I have quoted the verses at length so that the reader may appreciate the profound passion that informed the Hindu view of life through the ages. What is interesting about the verses from the *Atharva Veda Samhita* is the fact that this book ranks among the four Vedas that Hindus regard as the part of Tradition that was "revealed" (literally "heard" by the *rishis* and seers). The inclusion of such verses in the book would suggest that even in this early age, the Hindus were already familiar with practices that could inhibit successful conception. While avoiding the current controversy regarding the dating of Hindu texts, I will only point out that the Vedas are uniformly accepted by scholars as preceding the Common Era by many centuries.

One other point may be made. Throughout Indian history until the modern age, medical ethics and knowledge were part and parcel of the whole body of knowledge in society, and like other branches of knowledge, were conducted under the auspices of religious schools. There was extensive knowledge of the human anatomy; the *Charak Samhita* alone discusses in over a hundred pages diseases of the vaginal tract that can lead to miscarriage or abortion.[6] Although the principal concern of the medical scientists was healthy conception, there is little doubt that the ancient Hindus were acquainted with methods of abortion and used them in times of need. And notwithstanding the formal disapproval of the religious teachers, this knowledge was collected and preserved in texts, indicating that a section of the medical hierarchy provided succor to women in distress. At no stage was this knowledge suppressed.

Classical Ayurveda has, with time, branched off into many schools and sects that have spread out all over the country, with the different regions following their own Ayurveda texts. The *Charak Samhita* and the *Susruta Samhita*, for instance, are popular in north India, though Jaipur and Delhi regions also follow the *Siddhabheshja manimala*, *Rasyagasagar*, and *Bhaisyajyaratnavali*. In the south, the two main classical texts include the *Basavarajeevam* and the *Vaidyachintamani*. Kerala follows the *Ashtanga Samgraham, Ashtangahrydayam*, and the *Sahasrayogam*.

However, almost all the Ayurvedic schools follow the *Yogaratnakar*, an eighteenth-century compilation. The chapter "Yonivogadhikar" (vaginal disorders) specifies eight methods (*upayas*) for inhibiting conception or preventing the fetus from settling in the womb.[7] Similar remedies are also listed in *Cakradatta* and other Ayurvedic treatises.[8] A perusal of these texts, however, shows that much knowledge has been concealed, even though much has been recorded. In most cases, the dosage, frequency, and duration of the medication are not revealed, which implies that these teachings were transmitted orally from teacher to pupil, through apprenticeship, and that this practice continued through the ages.

The concept of liberty lies at the very core of Hinduism. It involves one's freedom to choose one's own path, connect with one's spiritual nature and give meaning to one's life, and thus raise oneself above the level of one's animal nature. Yet Hinduism as a religion seems riddled with taboos; there are a plethora of codes and rules for each and every aspect of life. This often entraps the unwary to live out their lifespans as mere cogs in the wheel, taking little active responsibility for their own welfare and evolution. In the twentieth century, this mental lethargy resulted in the phenomenon of people breeding to the limit, with little realization that science had negated this necessity by drastically lowering the death rate and enhancing longevity. Despite the work of conscious citizens like industrialist J. R. D. Tata, who advocated the need for family planning even before independence, there was for many decades a grievous lack of societal awareness on the issue of population and fertility management. This earned for India the dubious distinction of being one of the most populous countries in the world. Today the population of India has surpassed the one billion population mark.

In such a radically changed environment, it stands to reason that the demands of *dharma* must be appropriate to the demands of the time in which we live. The stability of the social order now necessitates adoption of the small-family norm, and *dharma* includes the notion of public duty and public responsibility. Hence, the small-family norm, achievable through contraception and family planning methods (including abortion in rare or necessary cases), is entirely consistent with, and in no way opposed to, the Hindu concept of *dharma*. As modern Hindus (of all classes, I may add) do not have to worry that their desire to have a good a standard of living and maintain or improve their social status by providing their children with good education and opportunities to move ahead in life may conflict with religious orthodoxy, family planning as a concept is backed by a broad social consensus. The *social* resistance to the small family among lower classes, or the continued insistence in some families on trying for a male child even after the birth of three or four daughters, is not to be confused with a religious opposition. It may, rather, be recognized as an instance of society lagging behind the spirit of the faith.

It may be argued that this is a modern-day rationalization, and that the small family does not really figure on the Hindu religious consciousness. But this would be an incorrect assumption. *Dharma* has to be understood in terms of its inner coherence and functional consistency. Derived from the Sanskrit word *dhr*, it is "that which supports right living" and "that which is conducive to the highest good." That is why what is good for the individual and the society can never be against the tenets of *dharma*. The simple truth of this proposition can be witnessed in the fact that from the time modern India first began debating the rising population (through pioneers like Tata), there has been no religious opposition to family planning or contraception. Not one religious teacher of any stature has raised his voice against the notion. Their silence is not accidental or incidental, but is an informed one, as can be seen from the fact that the Hindu religious fraternity continues to be quite vocal on traditional issues such as cow slaughter.

A point worth noting is that in the nineteenth century a new genre of social reform began in India under the aegis of leaders such as Raja Rammohan Roy. Hitherto, all reforms within the Hindu fold, such as measures to uplift lower caste groups or discard meaningless rituals, were conducted by religious leaders (the centuries-old tradition of the *bhakti* saints) and were formally a part of the religious tradition. Roy, however, was a layman, and he brought evils such as *sati* into the secular sphere and invited ordinary people to think and decide the legitimacy of such matters themselves. Since then, a growing social consciousness has become the barometer for public thought and action in India, and by and large, progressive ideas and movements have not encountered religious opposition. Religion has moved in tandem with society and reformist movements cannot legitimately be opposed only on the ground that they offend an existing orthodoxy. Any such arguments have to be couched in terms of moral validity and righteousness, failing which, customs that are being opposed are slowly uprooted. This can be seen in instances such as eradication of *sati*, promotion of widow remarriage, and Mahatma Gandhi's crusade against Untouchability.

This is in consonance with *dharma*, which places heavy responsibility on the individual to evolve and strive for self-realization (*moksha/nirvana*). This is the secret of how Hindu society can undergo revolutionary changes of the type mentioned above, with little meaningful social or religious resistance. In fact, all such drastic reforms are undertaken in the name of *dharma* itself.

The point is that the Hindu tradition is contemptuous of human beings who refuse to evolve and thus live their lives as "human animals" or *nar-pashu*, as the Bhagavad Gita calls them. This is because while humans are certainly a part of the animal kingdom, they are essentially spiritual beings. Hence, it is their duty to strive to bring their lower selves under the control of the higher Self, and realize their human and spiritual destiny. Human beings who helplessly produce unwanted babies in the manner of rabbits and other animals simply humiliate themselves and lose their self-esteem. Women learn this from experience. Even women from the poorer classes, who are not sufficiently empowered to openly use contraceptives or undergo sterilization, have long been demanding methods of contraception that can be used secretly without the knowledge of their husbands or other members of the family! They want desperately to limit the size of their families, but understandably cannot undertake the risk of open confrontation.

Hinduism, we may conclude, is concerned with a scale of values or a hierarchy of values, rather than absolute values. We have already seen that in cases where the mother's life is at stake, it is given precedence over fetal rights. This concept of compassion (*daya*) is reflected in the modern Indian Medical Termination of Pregnancy Act, 1971, and is invoked to cover cases of rape, incest, and even the mental health of the mother (which may be adversely affected by the birth of an unwanted child). With such broad-ranging provisions, it can easily be seen that in India, provided only that one desires it, abortion is available practically on demand.

Despite all of this, there is no denying that we have not had the expected success with our various family planning programs. Clearly, this is related to sexism and the lack of empowerment of women in many parts of India. However, the goal of bringing total fertility rates to replacement levels is now visible on the horizon, and has been placed by the new National Population Policy at 2010 A.D. Approved by the Union Cabinet in February 2000, the National Population Policy (NPP) seeks to inject political will into policy initiatives taken after the International Conference on Population and Development (ICPD) at Cairo. These included the abolition of method-specific contraceptive targets in April 1996 and the launch of a nationwide Reproductive and Child Health Program in October 1997.

The policy is fairly comprehensive and aims at stabilizing the population in order to promote sustainable development, by addressing "the unmet needs of contraception, health infrastructure, health personnel . . . [and] basic reproductive and child health care." It also aims at making reproductive health care accessible and affordable for all; increasing the provision and outreach of primary and secondary education; extending basic amenities such as sanitation, safe drinking water, and housing; and empowering women by enhancing their employment opportunities. The long-term objective is to achieve a stable population by 2045 A.D. at a level consistent with sustainable economic growth, social development, and environmental protection.

Keeping in mind the unhappy experience during the Emergency (1975–77), when forced sterilizations were sponsored by state power, the NPP has rejected the notion of disincentives, though a series of incentives (called "promotional and motivational measures") are being introduced at both the community and individual level. The policy shows political commitment to the cause of population control by freezing the delimitation of parliamentary constituencies until 2026 A.D., so that the southern states that have made rapid advances in population management are not penalized vis-à-vis north Indian states that had failed to control their burgeoning population.

The population policy has in the main been welcomed by social scientists, women's groups, and planners, for its pro-poor, pro-women approach, though there are reservations about how zero population growth will actually be achieved within the stipulated time period. It has, as one could expect in India, not encountered any religious opposition. While it is yet to be seen what kind of institutional mechanisms are put in place to translate the policy into reality, the government is also planning to amend the already liberal Medical Termination of Pregnancy Act to provide abortion rights to minor girls, under 18 years of age, both married and unmarried, without the consent of their guardians. The draft legislation has been circulated to the state governments, and the purpose of the move is to protect teenaged girls from illegal abortions, which claim several lives every year. Once again, Hindu religious bodies have not expressed any opposition to this move.

NOTES

1. *Atharva Veda* (AV) VI–138.
2. *AV*, VII–34.1; emphasis mine.
3. *AV*, VII–35.1; emphasis mine.
4. *AV*, VII–35.2.
5. *AV*, VII–35.3; emphasis mine.
6. *Charak Samhita*, chap. 30, part 2.
7. See chapter on *"Yonivogadhikar"* (vaginal disorders). The eight methods (*upayas*) for prevention of conception/family planning are expounded in the verses (*slokas*) 50–57, under the heading *garbha nivarnopayah* (or solution against conception/ settling of fetus in womb). The *upayas* are outlined as follows:

(1) Equal quantities of *pippali (Piper longum)* + *vidang (Embelia ribes)* + *tankana (Sodium piroborate)* with milk during menstruation.
(2) Take the flower, *Japa kusuma (Hibiscus rososinensis)* and mix into a paste with *kanji* (preparation of acidic medium). Prescribed with *gur (jaggery)* of one *pala (48 gm approx.)*.
(3) *Saindhawa lavan* (rock salt) processed with *tila taila* (sesamum oil) should be kept in vagina during coitus.
(4) *Tanduliyaka mulam* (root of a shrub) + rice water: make a paste and use internally after *rtu snan* (ritual bath after menstruation) for three days only.
(5) *Yoni dhupana* with *neem* wood can prevent *garbhadhan* (retention of fertilized ovum). Bark of neem is powdered and burnt.
(6) On fourth day of cycle, take one *kasha* (12 gm each approx.) of *Talisa patri*

(Abis webbiana), *Gairika* (haematite, a mineral of iron, red ochre) with *shital jala* (cold water).

(7) Tie the waist with root of *Apamarga (Acyranthes aspara)* (Cilchita plant) during coitus. There will be no pregnancy.

(8) External application with *Apamarga mula sukshmachurna* (fine powder of root) in vagina will prevent pregnancy.

8. *Cakradatta*, LXII–24, 25:

(1) Suppository made of *iksavku* (seeds), *danti, pippali, jaggery, madana*, yeast, *madhuyasti* and *snuhi* latex and kept in vagina induces menstruation.

(2) *Japa* flower mixed with sour gruel or *jyotismati* leaves, both fried, and rice-cake of *durva*—woman taking any of these gains menstruation.

REFERENCES

Atharva Veda Samhita. Trans. with a critical and exegetical commentary by William Dwight Whitney. Vol 1. *Motilal Banarasidass*. Delhi, Varanasi, 1962.

Cakradatta, A Treatise on Principles and Practices of Ayurvedia Medicine. In P. V. Sharma, ed. and trans. *Chaukhamba Orientalia*. Delhi, Varanasi, 1994.

Charak Samhita, Sharma, P., ed. and trans. *Chaukhamba Orientalia*, Delhi, Varanasi, 1981.

Coward, Harold G., Julius J. Lipner, and Katherine K. Young. *Hindu Ethics, Purity, Abortion, and Euthanasia*. Sri Satguru Publications (Indian Books Centre), Delhi, 1991.

Crawford, Cromwell. *Dilemmas of Life and Death, Hindu Ethics in North American Context*. Sri Satguru Publications (Indian Books Centre), Delhi, 1997.

———. The Evolution of Hindu Ethical Ideals. Arnold-Heinemann, Delhi, 1984.

The Dharma Shastra: Hindu Religious Codes. M. N. Dutta, ed. Cosmo Publications, New Delhi, 1978.

Gage, Richard L., ed. *Choose Life, A Dialogue. Arnold Toynbee and Daisaku Ikeda*. Oxford University Press, London, 1976.

Jain, Anrudh, ed. *Do Population Policies Matter? Fertility and Politics in Egypt, India, Kenya, and Mexico*. Population Council, New York, 1998.

Kane, P. V. *History of Dharmasastra (Ancient and Medieval Religious and Civil Law in India)*. Vols. 1–5. Bhandarkar Oriental Research Institute, Poona, India, 1990.

Kaumarabhrtya in Ayurveda (Obstetrics, Gynecology, and Pediatrics). In P. V. Tewari, *Chaukhamba Visvabharati*, Varanasi, Delhi, 1999.

Majumdar, R. C., ed. *History and Culture of the Indian People: The Vedic Age*. Bharatiya Vidya Bhavan, Bombay, 1967.

Ray, Priyadaranjan, Hirendranath Gupta, and Mira Roy, eds. *Susruta Samhita (A Scientific Synopsis)*. Indian National Science Academy, New Delhi, 1993.

Yogaratnakar, Vidyodini Hindi tika sahit. Chaukhamba Sanskrit Sansthan, Delhi, 1999.

Zimmer, Heinrich. *Philosophies of India*, ed. Joseph Campbell. Bollingen Series 26, Pantheon Books, New York, 1953.

6

The Right to Family Planning, Contraception, and Abortion in Thai Buddhism

PARICHART SUWANBUBBHA

This chapter is an effort to present Buddhist teachings and visions to help people make conscientious decisions regarding family planning, contraception, and abortion. The various forms of Buddhism prescribe care for the welfare of all people, whether they are majority or minority, privileged or underprivileged, or men or women. Most often, however, women suffer directly from many kinds of inequality and injustice either in domestic or public domains. In family life, women are facing the call to be good Buddhists and, at the same time, taking the burden of responsibility and guilt in the decision of family planning and abortion. This chapter will explore some important Buddhist teachings in order to define the situation clearly, to give faithful interpretations of Buddhist teaching, and to present some illustrations to support the right to family planning and to express toleration in Buddhism for abortion in particular cases and situations.

Thailand is a Theravada Buddhist country in Southeast Asia whose population is composed of more than 92 percent Buddhists. Thai Buddhism is unique in its characteristics. It is an assimilation and integration of doctrinal Buddhist teaching with some ritualistic Brahmanism and local animistic beliefs. Buddhist monks keep preaching nibbanic[1] Buddhism, which aims at ending rebirth to have nibbana. Most Buddhists believe in kammatic or kammic Buddhism, which leads people to have good kamma: a better life or rebirth such as being born with prosperity, beauty, and wisdom.

But they never expect to attain the highest goal, nibbana. Brahmin or Hindu Gods are also widely worshiped. Propitiating spirits at old big trees or other supernatural places is also a practice seen in Thai society.[2] This practice has increased after the severe economic crisis of 1996. Income distribution gaps between rural and urban areas have not been narrowed. It is estimated that 23 percent of the total population (or 15 million people out of 61 million) are currently below the poverty line (Family Planning and Population Division 1998, 30). This situation causes social and economic injustice. Its effects are changes in employment, family conflicts, crime, the abuse of women and children, prostitution, an increasing number of HIV-infected people, and numerous other social crises. Thailand has been uniquely and severely affected by international economics. The situation is a religious challenge and a challenge to religions. As David Loy (2000, 15) says:

> Our present economic system should also be understood as our religion, because it has come to fulfill a religious function for us. The discipline of economics is less a science than the theology of that religion, and its god, the market, has become a vicious circle of ever-increasing production and consumption by pretending to offer a secular salvation.

This economic religion supplants the traditional roles of religions in encountering the problems related to consumerism, materialism, and modernity. Buddhism as well is so challenged. The many studies on the roles of Buddhism in Thailand indicate that "Buddhism forms an integral, long-lasting, and pervasive part of the Thai value system. Buddhist-based values are not restricted to strictly 'religious' attitudes and actions but influence other sectors of life as well" (Kirsch 1996, 14). In other words, Buddhism is a major participant in shaping the decisions people make in today's society. That is why we read much today about "engaged Buddhism." Therefore, Buddhism, in this aspect, should be "engaged Buddhism," which stresses that Buddhists must address the disturbing problems of daily life and try to help to solve them. As Kraft (1999, 10–11) argues, "Buddhist activists value engagement not only as a potential contribution to the world, but also as a potential instrument of personal development." In this understanding, gender inclusivism on the right of women to family planning and abortion is crucial.

As mentioned previously, popular Buddhism in Thailand is focused on kammic Buddhism, which emphasizes "merit making," such as offering food to monks. The idea of merit making represents a belief in accumulating good kamma (good thoughts, speeches, and actions) and balancing previous bad kamma by the fresh good kamma in order to have a better life with wealth, health, and happiness. Good kamma leads to a prosperous present life and a good rebirth. The popular merit making and the law of kamma are important in Thai Buddhism and play a vital role in shaping the attitudes of Buddhism toward abortion. Together with the doctrine of kamma, the teaching and interpretation of interdependence (Pattica Samuppada) will give a clear picture of Buddhist ethics on family planning and abortion.

It should be clear that this study is supporting family planning and safe and therapeutic abortion when necessary so that people who make abortion decisions may be comforted by Buddhist explanations. However, it is not the effort of this chapter to call for the legalization of all abortions in Thai society. Moreover, this chapter will elaborate the positions that Buddhist teachings support the nonviolent methods of birth control and family planning both in individual and national policy. Secondly, although all abortions are not morally justified, there is still room to justify the deliberate choices of abortion by applying the doctrine of kamma (cetana) and wisdom (panna) including loving-kindness (metta). Thirdly, Buddhist ways of encouraging the empowerment of women in Thai Buddhism will also be discussed.

The Right to Family Planning and Contraception

The Buddha's teachings are applicable both in ending the cycle of rebirth and in living daily life. Marriage and sexuality are accepted by the Buddha for lay people who choose to live in the world. Marriage in Buddhism is not a religious ritual or duty. It can be seen as the gratification of a couple dealing with cravings for sensual pleasure (kama tanha). Monks are always invited to participate in wedding ceremonies in order that a couple would have a chance to make merit with them and to get blessings on their important day. On the one hand, it is clear that early Buddhism aims at getting rid of the attachment of sensual pleasure to escape from the circle of rebirth. Sexuality is considered an obstacle for people wanting to attain nibbana (LaFleur 1992, 19). On the other hand, the Buddha knows the different ability of individuals to attain the highest goals. Therefore, he allows family life because he realizes the nature of human sexuality for both men and women as illustrated in the saying:

> Monks, I know of no other single scent . . .
> savour . . . touch by which a man's heart is
> so enslaved as it is by the scent, savour
> and touch of a woman who obsesses a man's
> heart.

> Monks, I know of no other single form,
> sound, scent, savour and touch by which a
> woman's heart is so enslaved as it is by
> the form, sound, scent, savour and touch of
> a man. Monks, a woman's heart is obsessed
> by these things. (A. 1)[3]

Therefore, it is normal for men and women to have mutual sexual attraction. Passion, sexuality, and reproductivity are respected in Buddhism. As long as sexual misconduct[4] does not occur, marriage and sexuality are positive in the eyes of Buddhism. In addition, there is a right to family planning and contraception. This is morally permissible. Since Buddhism is not a theistic ethics, no plans, wills, and commandments of God are suggested to have pronatalist value. Rather, Buddhism teaches the right to plan for the size of the family as long as methods used do not destroy any life. (How this can be reconciled with abortion we shall see.)

According to Tripitika, life begins at the time of conception when three conditions combine; that is, (1) if mother and father have sexual intercourse, and (2) it is the mother's fertile period, and (3) the "being to be born" (gandhabba) is present (M.I 265–66). Any methods to prevent the process of this conception are welcome as far as no life is destroyed under any circumstances. When life of "a being waiting to be born" is not ended, no immorality takes place. Therefore, it is primarily said that individuals, both a husband and wife, have a right to family planning and contraception.

Does a wife really have a right to family planning? Ideally, it is a positive duty to share the plan between a couple, since the Buddha mentions what is noble and religious in a husband, and also in a wife (Vajiranna 1980, 25). That is, two of a husband's duties to his wife are honor and respect to her.[5] The meaning of "honor" and "respect" implies the treatment of a woman as a person and a companion, not as only a sexual object. The meaningful purpose of sexuality in marriage in human society should be communication and bonding (Searle 1995, 47).[6] However, it is notable that the language of "rights" in Buddhism would refer to the reciprocal duties and obligations between husband and wife. Buddhism stresses an ethics of reciprocity and interdependence that calls for an ethics of responsibility (de Silva 1995, 142). Therefore, it is possible to say that Buddhist teachings allow individuals, including women, to have rights to plan their family according to their own circumstances either related to the size of family or to any methods of safe contraception.

However, it is also part of traditional Buddhist teaching that being born as human beings is a sign of general improvement in the moral state of the universe because only human beings are able to attain the highest goal, nib-bana.[7] This may indirectly encourage population growth in a Buddhist com-munity (Ling 1969, 54).[8] This teaching may have been considered more seri-ously for some people in the past. It should be also noted that in spite of this teaching that being born human is a good thing and a good opportunity, there is no parallel to the "be fruitful and multiply" in Buddhism. As a matter of fact, at the present time, there are many overpopulated countries in the world where social and economic misery result. This is especially true in some Bud-dhist countries. These situations call for Buddhists to realize an important doctrine that emphasizes the middle path: not too much, not too little, not too tight, not too loose. That is to say, moderation in all activities and in every aspect of a life, without extreme austerity or extreme indulgence, is recom-mended (S. vol. 5: 330, S. vol. 5: 421). This implies that having too many citizens who are not satisfied is wrong according to this teaching because it can con-tribute to the economic misery and lower the quality of life of all members in families and in society.

Moreover, the Buddha's teaching (mirroring similar teaching in such di-verse sources as the Jewish Book of Proverbs, Aristotle, and Thomas Aquinas) also states that poverty can become the cause of crimes. When people are provided with opportunities for earning a sufficient income, they will be con-tented and will have no fear or anxiety, and, consequently, the country will be peaceful and free from crime (D: 26). Conversely, wealth and riches are not evil in themselves, but their value depends on the extent to which people are attached to them. In this explanation, it is clear that both too poor, as self-mortification, and too rich, leading to self-indulgence, are not the Buddhist way to survive in this world.

Interdependence and Dependent Origination

Not only is the teaching of moderation important to encourage the possibility of family planning but also the teaching of interdependence reflects the indi-cation of proper population growth. That is, the doctrine of interdependence or dependent origination (Pattica Samuppada)[9] states that whenever certain causes and conditions coexist, there is always an effect. When there is not this, then there is not that; when this ceases, that also ceases (M. vol. 2: 32). Applying this doctrine to population management, when individuals or a small unit of society are unhappy or suffering, it inevitably affects the common good. Since everything is interconnected with everything else, unhappiness in families should influence public policy to solve a number of political, economic, and social problems related to the consequences of an excessive birth rate. That is to say, Buddhist teaching of interdependence should be appropriately considered for covering the related causes and effects of the necessity to have reasonable population management. It should also suggest that the government provide national policy and services to those who want them. Where damaging excesses are tolerated or ignored, Buddhist teaching is offended.

Government's Role in Family Planning

Moreover, the Agganna Sutta of the Digha-nikaya elaborates that rulers should have an obligation to ensure the protection and well-being of the people (Malalasekera 1971, 129). Therefore, according to the doctrine of interdependence and what the teaching in this sutta confirms, it should be a duty of a government or a ruler to bring a justification for provision of services to people. To be sure, the Buddhist attitude toward family planning is certainly positive and allows for a positive enabling role for government. As discussed previously, individuals have rights to use any nonviolent contraception to plan the size of a family and governments should provide access to services for a variety of contraceptive methods. Should a government enforce sterility on an unwilling community or family? Should a government have a role in influencing individuals' desired family sizes? If both answers are "yes," they will not be in accordance with the norms of Buddhist ethics. Such practices will also violate basic human rights, especially those of women. Buddhist ethics considers the appropriate intention, means, and ends of each action as moral decisions. The criterion of all good intention, whether intending means or ends, is the avoidance of actions harmful to oneself or to others and actions that are harmful to both oneself and others. This avoidance is called Kusala Kamma, a skillful action (Atthasalini: 38)

It is one thing for a government to act with a good intention and provide means and services for contraception. But if government forces women to accept experimental methods of contraception, this will be considered an unwholesome means due to the possible mental and physical side effects and suffering of women. Although a government hopes to reduce the economic misery of society by issuing laws to control the desired family size, the consequences may not be acceptable to different individuals. "In this case, birth control is used as an instrument of repression for the realization of ends which are decidedly unfavorable to a section of society" (Malalasekera 1971, 129).

These arguments reflect again the doctrine of kamma, which emphasizes good wholesome intention to perform thoughts, speeches, and actions: "Intention is kamma" (A.II: 82) Whenever there is no intention, there is no kamma—

hence no effects and consequences. At the same time, Buddhist ethics encourages people to think, to reason, and to analyze the consequences of each action by wisdom (Panna). Therefore, people who misuse Buddhist permission to use contraception for sexual enjoyment by developing a promiscuous sexual life are never admired in a Buddhist view. They have insincere and unwholesome intentions to incline to the extremity of self-indulgence. They are not following the middle path, which may cause an increase of unfaithful sexual behavior. More minor wives in society may result because men can use various contraceptive methods to avoid the cultural responsibility for impregnating a number of women.

Family Planning in Thailand

Considering family planning in Thai Buddhist society, it is claimed that Thailand is successful in its family planning program. The fertility rate stands at just below replacement level, 1.9 births per woman. The total population growth rate is now only 1.0 percent. The contraceptive prevalence rate for married women of reproductive age is 72.2 percent (*Mahidol Population Gazette* 2000). The Family Planning and Population Division, Ministry of Public Health of Thailand reports their success partly derives from the tried-and true methods of increasing service utilization and some specific elements to respond to an existing demand for family planning and expanding their services quickly (Family Planning and Population Division 1998, 22). These figures may not directly be a result of Buddhist teachings, but they confirm that Buddhism never prevents people from planning families. Moreover, one of Thailand's most well-established and diverse nongovernmental organizations is the Population and Community Development Association, founded in 1974. This group has gotten some support from Thai government and foreign organizations. Its first active work was the promotion of family planning in urban and rural areas of Thailand, where knowledge and access to such services were scarce. Their popular motto was *"look mak ja yak jon"* ("Too many children will bring poverty to the family"). The concrete activities of this organization have been the distribution of contraceptives to over 16,000 villages, and it has provided free voluntary male sterilization (Population and Community Development Association 1998, 1–8)

However, there are uncomfortable feelings toward contraception in Thai society. There is a sense that it is against the traditional culture of sexual values in Asian countries and may be the cause of widespread premarital sexual intercourse (Ling 1969, 59). There is also the problem of the lack of sexual education for Thai women regarding the proper use of contraceptives. As mentioned above, wives and husbands have mutual duties but Thai women do not know and understand their rights enough.

The Thai ideal for a family calls for sharing and bonding between men and women. This needs to be applied to contraception. According to the Family Planning and Population Division, the figure of male sterilization and condom use are only 1.7 percent and 1.5 percent, respectively. This compares to female sterilization, 22.9 percent; taking oral pills, 24.2 percent; and injection, 18.0 percent (Family Planning and Population Division 1998, 33). As a result, it is necessary to ask for greater male involvement in reproductive health care (Mattiko 1999, 630).

Concerning this, Buddhism offers supporting ideas. According to the doctrine of rebirth, beings have to be born again and again until kamma ceases to bear fruit. Therefore, each being may be born in another human gender and in the process of rebirth, may have already been the other gender. This undercuts the idea of separateness. The whole world is one family as the Buddha said:

> Monks, it is not easy to find a being
> who has not been a mother, a father,
> a brother, a sister, a son, or a daughter
> in this endless repetition of existence. (S. II)

Thus, human beings should be able to share roles as a mother and a father. Childcare can also be provided by a man. Earning money for a family can be performed by a woman. Following this assumption, taking care of and nourishing a family are the duties of both men and women. The best plan for the well-being of a family should be just sharing by both a husband and wife: "It is equally important that all humans including all men, be defined as nurturers and taught nurturing skills, rather than confining this activity to physical mothers" (Searle 1995, 47–48).

In conclusion, it seems clear that the attitudes of Buddhism toward sexuality and family are positive and would encourage women to exercise the right to family planning and contraception. A woman's reproductive right concerning family planning and the use of contraceptives is apparently welcome by Buddhism.

The Right to Abortion

Generally speaking, abortion is referred to as the termination of pregnancy. It is the rules (Vinaya) of monks not being the cause to kill, not to order someone to kill, and not to collaborate to kill any living beings, even an embryo (Sutta-vibhanga: III, 72) For lay people, it is not the commandment but a precept (*sila*) for a normal life to abstain from killing (D.III: 235).[10] This sounds like absolutist ethics and would seem end to all discussion of a just and moral abortion decision. However, what is really absolute is the law of kamma.

What is kamma? The Buddhist kamma covers all the intentional, volitional actions whether verbal and physical. As the Buddha states, "O bhikkhus, it is volition (*cetana*) that I call kamma. Having willed, one acts through body, speech and mind" (Rahula 1988, 590). It is necessary to emphasize that actions can be called kamma when they derive from a doer's volition or intention. Otherwise, they are only "noncausal" acts (*kiriya*) from which there are no effects. Kamma is a neutral term. It functions as a cause, every cause producing every result or retribution or effect (*vipaka*). Roughly speaking, the act of killing will certainly produce retribution.

> Monks, taking life, when pursued,
> Practiced, increased, brings one to kill,
> To an animal's womb, to the peta[11] realm:
> What is the every trifling results of taking
> Life is the shortening of a man's life. (Woodward 1932, 169)

Therefore, according to this teaching, performing abortion would produce a shortening of the performer's life. At this point we must return to the question of when a life begins. As mentioned in the beginning related to the discussion of the right to family planning, life begins at the very moment of conception when there are the combination of the three factors: (1) a mother and father have a sexual union, (2) a mother is in her fertile period, and (3) a being awaiting birth (*gandhabba*) is present. Whenever these three are together, a life begins. The value of the conceptum is the same as a that of a born person although there are no perfect organs yet, since it is already composed of body or matter and mind (S.III: 47) at the very moment of fertilization. This new existence possesses his or her own kamma as well from a past life. In order to understand clearly why Buddhism considers the killing of an embryo unjustified it is necessary to be clear how the mind brings kamma to another existence.

Mind or *mana* in Buddhism is a faculty or organ like eyes, ears, or a nose. The mind not only records all the seeds of actions both good and bad but also carries them from one moment to the next and from the previous life to the present life, and also from the present existence to the next existence. That is, human beings are composed of mind and matter (*namarupa*). Mind is called a thought moment or a stream of consciousness (*vinnana*) kept flowing by the inherent force of kamma (Na-Rangsi 1976, 121). "The changes occurring in a thought moment are (1) The arising of the thought-moment as the preceding one goes into dissolution, (2) Waxing of mind energy to a peak, followed by (3) Waning of mind-energy and (4) Complete dissolution of the thought-moment" (Abeysinghe 1989, 25). Put another way, the mind or the thought moments keep arising and passing away in the one whole life. It may be said that we die and are born innumerable times according to the continuity of the rising, the remaining, and the sinking of thought moments or consciousness. While this repeated process of continuity of thought moments occurs, the kammic energy will transmit to the next thought moment. This process keeps happening in one's own mind and can be applied to explain the rebirth in the next existence. That is, at the point of death, three kinds of thought moments or consciousness are working (Na-Rangsi 1976, 122): *patisandhi-citta*, or consciousness connecting one life with the other; *bhavanga-citta*, or the current of the passive mind; and *cuti-citta*, or consciousness disconnecting from the present life. Now the kammic seeds that have been stored for all one's life will give signs of what is to happen. A dying person will be surrounded with three signs (Aung 1979, 149–50): (1) *Janakakamma*, the past meritorious or demeritorious actions; (2) *Kamma-nimitta*, a symbol of instruments used to perform those past actions, such as flowers or food for good actions, a gun or a knife for bad actions; and (3) *Gati-nimitta*, a sign of the tendencies that are determined by the force of those past actions, such as viewing a beautiful place suggesting rebirth in the good place or heaven. As Na-Rangsi further explains,

> [A]t the point of death the mental activity of a dying man becomes considerably weaker. The patisandhi-citta remains, therefore, in the course of cognition for only five faint thought moments of javana[12] and then sinks down into the bhavanga. At the end of the bhavanga or the passive state of consciousness the cuti-citta arises disconnecting the present life, and then sinks down into the bhavanga. Another patisandhi-consciousness rises up in the next life. (Na-Rangsi 1976, 124)

From such a line of traditional explanation, Buddhists believe that abortion at any time is a killing and unwholesome action because "a being waiting to be born" transmits his or her own kammic energy to be born as a new person. At this point it would appear that the door is shut to allowing a just and moral abortion. However, it is not that simple.

Abortion may not be considered as an act of killing if the following five conditions are not perfectly together: (1) an existing being, (2) knowledge that it is a being, (3) intention of killing, (4) effort of killing, and (5) consequent death (Davids 1958, 128). Certainly, when the act of killing is successful, it produces the retribution. The effects of an abortion done with bad intention is not only a shorter life but also proneness to disease, constant grief caused by separation from loved ones, and constant fear. The intention, however, is key, according to the law of kamma.

As a result, therapeutic abortion, a medical procedure performed by a licensed physician when there is a threat to the life of the mother, may be considered as unsevere kamma as long as this action is not based on the roots of unwholesome or bad intention. They are (1) greed (*lobha*), (2) hatred or anger (*dosa*), and (3) delusion (*moha*) (D.III: 275). This is similar to the Roman Catholic teaching about mortal and venial sins. Abortion with good intentions would be a venial, that is, a forgivable sin, not a mortal sin. In Buddhist terms the retribution, or negative kamma effects, would be less and could even be superseded by the accumulation of good kamma from other good actions. The bad effect would not be the same as for those people who abort a fetus due to a pregnancy related to self-indulgence. The same explanation is applied to cases for the abortion of a fetus resulting from the rape of a woman.

This openness to abortion is reflected in law. It is interesting to note that in Thailand, a very Buddhist country, some abortions are legal. For example, aborting a fetus resulting from rape is legal. Some physicians abort fetuses of women infected with HIV, because of the risk to a safe life. They want to alleviate the suffering of these women and the families, including the unborn babies. This would be considered a good intention and a good means for a mercy killing of fetuses, although these particular cases are illegal in Thailand. According to Thai Buddhist teaching, intention is key. In summary, there is still a morally negative view of abortion, but abortion for good intentions is accepted by many Buddhists, since the persons do not perform such action owing to greed, hate, or delusion.

What about abortion due to economic hardship, unreadiness for child-bearing, and contraceptive failure? Among these cases, it is very difficult to determine absolutely what one should do or should not do. However, applying Buddhist explanation, the doers, especially mothers, will know best what their real intentions and states of minds are when they decide to have an abortion performed. If they hate these fetuses, unwholesome kamma results. They have to weigh the intention and the consequences, then they would know how serious their retribution would be. Obviously, then, an abortion due to contraceptive carelessness and selfishness would be more kammically serious than an abortion due to a contraceptive accident (Hughes and Keown, http:// jbe.la.peu.edu). Not all abortions are morally acceptable in this view. An abortion done for selecting sex of unborn babies, as is often reported in some countries such as India and China, would seem to be one with serious kammic consequences since it seems to involve a hatred of a girl because of preference for a boy.

Not all abortions are morally the same in Thai Buddhism. The killing in some involves more effort and thus more intention. Thus, a later abortion—say, at six months—is more kammically significant than an early abortion. Here is Buddhist teaching on the process of embryo growth:

> At first the *kalala* takes birth, and thence
> The *abbudo*. Therefrom the *pesi* grows,
> Developing as *ghana* in its turn.
> Now in the *ghana* doth appear the hair,
> The down, the nails. And whatsoever food
> And drink the mother of him takes, thereby
> The man in mother's womb doth live and grow. (S.X: 2)

Kalala is the earliest development of life until the being comes to have hair. *Kalala* therefore is the early pregnancy. *Ghana* may be after four weeks, when the hair, nails and other aspects would be developed (Thavaradhammo 1996, 49). Thus, the effort to kill Kalala should be less than killing later in the period of pregnancy. The more effort has to be put forward, the more serious the kammic results. Thus in Thai Buddhism, abortion is viewed with seriousness, but earlier abortions are more easily justified. When the intentions are good, the negative kamma effect is less and may be overcome by good deeds producing good kamma.

A Woman's Right or a Fetus's Right?

At this point a question arises, according to Buddhism: Whose rights should be considered most important, a mother's right or a fetus's right? Generally speaking, the right of every human being, either a man, a woman, or a fetus, is equal in terms that they are still under the same natural law. The point is not whether women's rights are more important than a fetus's rights. However, Buddhist criteria for the ethics of abortion are open to the use of wisdom (Panna) in complex cases, to decide by assessing intentions, means, and ends: "Wisdom is purified by virtue, and virtue is purified by wisdom. Where one is, so is the other" (D.I: 84). Since abortion has a negative quality, the sense of morality and wisdom will determine the different degree of consequences. But, clearly, in Buddhism, abortion is a matter for serious personal responsibility.

By oneself indeed evil is done
By oneself is one defiled
By oneself is evil avoided
By oneself is indeed one purified.
Purity and impurity depend on oneself
No one can purify another. (Dh: 165)

Lapsed Kamma

According to the law of kamma, abortion has consequences and it is true that one is liable to the bad result. However, if one has a strong intention to change and to reduce it, one can do it. There are many kinds of kamma. Some of them may take a long period of time to develop. "According to Buddhism, when one kamma is still bearing its fruit, other kamma with the same or lesser potency do not have the chance to ripen. Only when the kamma currently bearing fruit is weak or exhausted can other kamma have an opportunity to replace it" (Na-Rangsi 1976, 55). In this sense, if one is guilty of bad action, one can change volition to perform only good instead so that the good kamma has more potency than the bad kamma. If you keep sincerely performing good by mind, speech, and action for the sake of good, eventually the bad action has no potency to bear fruit. One day that bad result may become the lapsed kamma (*Ahosi Kamma*)[13] that has exhausted itself because its period for bearing fruit has expired. Therefore, on the one hand, one cannot escape from the result of his or her related action; on the other hand, performing good deeds may reduce or change or even end the potency of the bad result so that the bad result cannot ripen because of its expiration.

In the Buddhist scripture Anguttara-Nikaya, we read that the person who habitually cultivates good thought, speech, and action will avoid bad results easier than the one who habitually commits evil. The Buddha compares a small offense performed by one who "has carefully cultured body, habits and thought" and "has developed insight" (Woodward 1932, 228) to a similar offense performed by one who "is careless in culture of body, habits and thought" and "has not developed insight" (Woodward 1932, 227). A small offense of the former is like throwing a grain of salt into the river Ganges. Due to the mass of water in the big river, the water would not become salty and undrinkable (Woodward 1932, 228), whereas a small offense of the latter is like throwing a grain of salt into a little cup of water: the water would become salty and undrinkable because of the small quantity of water in the cup. The bad action of a good person is insignificant compared to his or her accumulated good actions. Thus, the bad action is too weak to work. For a person who is careless in not performing enough good actions, his or her bad actions have enough potency to ripen since this person seldom accumulates enough good action to counteract the bad kamma. Therefore, we are assured that human beings should take care to perform good in every moment. By way of this explanation, a pregnant woman who has an abortion performed may feel relief and has more hope and encouragement. Her abortion may be only a grain of salt tossed into the Ganges.

To repeat, generally speaking, in Buddhism men, women, and fetuses seem to have equal rights in terms of impossibility to avoid their own kamma. Furthermore, according to Phra Depvethee, a Thai Buddhist monk, the result of killing depends on the size and good contribution of that being (Thepvethee 1993, 30). For example, a father and a mother are considered as precious beings. Killing a mother in order to save a fetus's life kammically refers to more severe and instant retribution than aborting a fetus because a mother is considered as a big animal who can contribute many important and valuable things to her family and society. In other words, a woman would be able to call for her own right as a mother. If there is only one choice, the mother's life would be saved, not the fetus's. By this line of reasoning, one may say that Buddhism encourages indirectly a women's reproductive right.

However, claiming that a woman's body belongs to her may contradict the Dhamma meaning (absolute language). Since everything is no-self (*anatta*),[14] a woman's body is no-self in an absolute sense as well. The idea of "this body belongs to me" is only a concept that arises by the condition of a physical organ and a sensory object reacting interdependently. In reality, nothing exists that one can claim as "mine" (S. III: 47, Taniguchi 1987, 78.) Therefore, according to this teaching, a woman cannot claim her body as her own absolute self. Neither can fetuses. Moreover, there is another argument that Buddhism does not consider the right of woman the same as in western countries. That is, according to the systematic interdependence (Paticca Samuppada), everything and everyone exist only in mutuality—even the fetus. A fetus and a family are involved in the effects of an abortion, not only a pregnant woman alone. Although it is acceptable that a woman has to make a final decision for herself, her decision still affects family and the physicians who are asked to break the law.[15] This reflects the typical values of a relationship in a Thai family. Thai women normally stay with parents until they get married. At the same time, outside their home, they may face temptation of their sexual human nature. When unwanted pregnancy becomes the issue, it affects other people in the family. If teenagers are pregnant, they will have to quit school; otherwise, they become single mothers in Thai society, which is hardly acceptable. Therefore, the decision of an abortion is a crucial issue and involves many people. The right to abortion cannot only be the right of women.

Last, one interesting explanation on human rights in Thai society is "the right to have a life beyond suffering" (Intharakamhaeng 1994, 10). The argument of this definition is trying to link with the ultimate reality in Buddhism, which is nibbana, the end of suffering. That is to say, when people believe that they are exercising "rights" but their lives are still suffering, they do not have the authentic rights. In this way of explanation, women who take responsibility alone for unwanted pregnancies are still far from having authentic "rights." In this argument, more or less, it may be said that the cry for women's rights on abortion will sound louder in Thai society.

Up to this point, the definition of "the right of women" differs from that in the western sense. Although it may also be acceptable for Buddhists to understand that "humans' rights are women's rights," the meanings of "rights" in Buddhism still needs to be related to the law of kamma, the doctrine of Paticca Samuppada, and the doctrine of no-self (*Anatta*) as mentioned earlier. Women may still have hope and encouragement because the Buddha determines everyone to be the boss of his or her own life, when he says:

> In this one-fathom long body along with its
> perceptions and thoughts, do I proclaim the
> world, the origin of the world, the cessation
> of the world and the path leading to the cessation of
>   the world. (S.I: 62)

This saying reminds us of human being as a center to deal with all problems. When women fail in continuing to carry a pregnancy or are suffering, they still have ways out. That is, a woman and associated people who take part in performing abortions would have merit making in various ways, such as giving money to a hospital, supporting children's education, offering food and necessary things to monks, meditating and transferring merit to the dead unborn child, and so on. This is for the purpose of sharing "bun," good merit with them and asking them for forgiveness including blessing them with happiness in the new existence. Thai merit making may be similar to Buddhist memorial services in Japan called *mijuko kuyo*. It is the offering up of prayers for the nourishment (*kuyo* means "to offer and nourish") of the spirit of the aborted or stillborn child (Smith 1985, 73).

However, it is necessary to understand that these merit makings in Thai Buddhism performed by "responsible women" are private, and they seldom welcome other people knowing about it. Although abortion is generally seen as unrightful action, the Buddhist community still sympathizes with suffering women and associated people in family. Buddhism always gives a chance and appreciates anyone who tries to create "a new good kamma" in the present. These merit-making rituals are usually derived from guilt and fear of retribution, yet are also a reflection of love, compassion, and grief of those "responsible mothers" over the loss of the fetus's life. It is believed that the mother's intention of making merits may lead the fetus to a peaceful next existence and enable it to forgive the mothers' action of abortion. The rituals may also give the mother hope that the fetus might be reborn as their child in the proper time and circumstance.

Furthermore, there is another alternative way of thinking to comfort those who have an abortion. That is the doctrine of impermanence (*anicca*). After abortion, the suffering, guilt, and remorse do not last forever:

> Impermanent are all conditioned things
> Their nature it is to rise and pass away
> When they have risen, then again they cease.
> Happiness lies in the tranquilizing of them. (S.I: 158)

Concerning the call for legal abortion, it seems difficult to take place in this Buddhist society. In theory, whenever people perform abortion, unwholesome action takes place. One important reason is that it contradicts the core teaching of Buddhism to avoid two extremes: self-mortification and self-indulgence. It means that it is too risky to allow legal abortion as allowing self-indulgence, on the one hand. On the other hand, we are not supposed to worsen the feeling of a woman with an unwanted pregnancy by punishing her with self-mortification. As a matter of fact, there are a number of illegal abortions performed by a private clinics in Thailand, although it is considered a crime to be punished by law. This is unfortunately the real picture. However, morality and wisdom should go hand in hand as mentioned previously. In Thailand abortion is legal in cases of threat to a mother's life and of rape victims. Why don't we expand the definition of the threat to the mother's life in Thai law to cover more necessary reasons of the present situation, such as contraceptive failure and economic hardship in accordance with Buddhist norms based on "wholesome intention" and "wholesome consequences"? This will testify to the sincerity and responsibility of people in these cases. Although it sounds very clumsy, it would be a good way to help both suffering pregnant women and at the same time uphold Buddhist teachings.

Moreover, government policy should respond to the real picture and situation of widespread illegal abortion. That is, although no legal abortion is established, illegal ones are still performed. It reflects the urgent need to have a center to serve and give advice to public, especially laborers, uneducated women, and teenagers about sex education, family planning, and the process of abortion (Committee for a Woman's Right, n.d. 3).[16] Then let individuals decide because they need to take responsibility for their lives. The point is, they need to have enough information before they make a final decision.

Conclusion

Although abortion is not morally justified according to Buddhism, there is still the possibility for alternative and deliberate choices. I agree with the observation of Pradmasiri de Silva:

> It is thus not merely the availability of norms, precepts and ethical values in Buddhist texts but also need to apply and interpret them with imagination and flexibility to the challenging forms of human rights discourse today. (de Silva 1995, 133–134)

Concerning the issue of an abortion, one knows the Buddhist ethical doctrines; one also attempts to reinterpret them in terms relevant to the new challenges in socioeconomics and women's empowerment. Then a decision to do or not to do depends on applying wisdom and weighing the decision and considering the doctrine of *intention* (*kamma*) and of loving-kindness (*metta*).[17] One has enough freedom to choose the way. Whatever one decides, one has to be brave enough to accept the consequences.

ABBREVIATIONS

A.   Anguttaranikaya
D.   Dighanikaya
Dh.   Dhammapada
M.   Majjhimanikaya
S.   Samyuttanikaya

NOTES

1. In this study, Pali words are used to refer to all Buddhist terms. Therefore one would find "nibbana" in stead of "nirvana," "kamma" instead of "karma," etc.

2. The influences of animistic belief in Thai Buddhism are obvious. One of the reasons is that some parts of animism can work well with some Buddhist understanding. For instance, in Buddhism, anyone who always behaves well and accumulate good kamma but not enough to attain nibbana, may be born in heaven as "Deva"

or "Thevada." Some may live in heaven but others may exist at the big trees. Whenever people propitiate properly, "Thevada" may protect them. The idea of "Thevada"
may fit well with the idea of spirit in animism. However, these "Thevadas" in Buddhism can only provide people psychological support; for spiritual development people have to make effort by themselves. All these "Thevadas" are still under the law of
kamma. They have not reached the stage of nibbana yet. Heaven is not the highest
goal for Buddhists either.

3. The references in this study are to the English translations of the texts that
have been published by or for the Pali Text Society.

4. Sexual misconduct means unfaithfulness to one's spouse and having sexual
activity with ordained persons and with women under protection of their parent. This
meaning does not consider whether homosexual activity is right or wrong.

5. The Buddha suggests a husband minister to his wife in five ways: (1) by
honor, (2) by respect, (3) by faithfulness, (4) by handing over authority to her, and (5)
by giving her ornaments. At the same time, a wife is also compassionate to her husband in five ways: (1) by doing her work well, (2) by hospitality to both her husband's
and her relations' other associates, (3) by faithfulness, (4) by protecting what he earns,
and (5) by skill and diligence in all her duties (D. III: 190).

6. Rick Searle summarized the presentation of Rita Gross on Buddhist Resources for Issues of Population and Consumption in Relationship with the Environment.

7. According to Buddhist cosmology, there are five different realms into which
beings can be reborn: (1) human beings, (2) animals, (3) wandering ghosts, (4) spirits
in hell, and (5) spirits in heaven. Even spirits in heaven (Deva) are still under the law
of kamma, but they are so happy and prosperous that they may not be able to encounter any suffering; therefore, there is no chance to have absolute spiritual liberation in heaven. There is an exception: the Suthavas Deva are able to attain nibbana
without being born as human beings in the world.

8. T. O. Ling refers to the work of Dr. Luang Suriyapongs, 1960, *Buddhism in
the Light of Modern Scientific Ideas* (Bangkok), 303 ff.

9. The doctrine of dependent origination (Pattica Samuppada) originally taught
that the mental process conditions the life process of becoming in the wheel of existence. When there is birth, there is death. As long as the kammic forces survive the
cycle of birth and death (*samsara*) they result in suffering. That is,

(1/2) [From] Dependence on ignorance arise kamma-formations.
(3)   [From] Dependence on kamma-formations arises consciousness.
(4)   [From] Dependence on consciousness arise mind and matter.
(5)   [From] Dependence on mind and matter arise the six sense-bases.
(6)   [From] Dependence on the six sense-bases arises contact.
(7)   [From] Dependence on contact arises feeling.
(8)   [From] Dependence on feeling arises craving.
(9)   [From] Dependence on craving arises clinging.
(10)   [From] Dependence on clinging arises becoming.

(11)   [From] Dependence on becoming arises birth.

(12)   [From] Dependence on birth arise decay and death. There also arise sorrow lamentation, pain, grief and despair. Thus arises this whole mass of suffering. (S.II.1)

10. The Five Precepts for lay people are (1) to abstain from killing, (2) to abstain from stealing, (3) to abstain from sexual misconduct, (4) to abstain from false speech, and (5) to abstain from intoxicants causing heedlessness.

11. Peta is a hungry ghost-being in Buddhist cosmology.

12. Javana is appreciation or impulsion, which is one function of consciousness in Buddhist psychology.

13. Four kinds of kamma are classified according to time of fruition in this lifetime or hereafter:

(1)   *Dittha Dhamma vedaniya*—immediately effective kamma

(2)   *Upapajja vedaniya*—subsequently effective kamma

(3)   *Aparapariya vedaniya kamma*—indefinitely effective kamma in any lifetime within the the repeated cycle of births and death (*samsara*)

(4)   *Ahosi kamma*—lapsed kamma. Where there is no occasion for kamma.

14. Central and unique to Buddhism are the three characteristics inherent in everything:

(1)   *anicca*—impermanency and uncertainty in everything

(2)   *dukkha*—unsatisfactoriness, conflict and suffering in everything

(3)   *anatta*—no-self, insubstantiality, no permanent entity (Dh. 277–79)

15. For more discussion of this point, see Pinit Ratanakul's chapter in *Buddhism and Abortion*, edited by Damien Keown.

16. In Thai society, there are a few emergency homes for women in trouble. One of them is Sathira–Dhammasathan (a Buddhist residence), which provides a community for women who are faced with physical and mental domestic violence. Some pregnant women and abortion cases would be included to live in the home and practice dhamma of simplicity, compassion, and right thought to achieve independence from *Dukkha* (suffering). Other women's organizations are active in protecting the rights of Thai women. They founded "working group for women's rights," composed of 10 women's organizations. A main objective of this group is helping women in the area of sexual abuse, domestic violence, and labor injustice. They generally support "legal abortion."

17. According to Buddhism, a person must cultivate the sublime virtues or divine qualities to be noble (*Brahma Vihara*). They are (1) *metta*, goodwill or compassionate love toward every living thing without any discrimination; (2) *karuna*, kindness and compassion radiated with sympathy to relieve others' griefs; (3) *mudita*, sympathetic joy, sharing the happiness of others and their progress without jealousy; and (4) *upekkha*, equanimity, impartiality, and maintaining harmony without showing any discrimination (A. II).

REFERENCES

Abeysinghe, D. W. 1989. "Souless Rebirth in Buddhism," W. F. B. Review (World Fellowship of Buddhists) 26: 4.

Aung, Shwe San, trans. 1979. *Compendium of Philosophy (Abhidhammattha-Sangaha)*. London: The Pali Text Society.

Committee for a Woman's Right. n.d. "Means To Solve Unwanted Pregnancy."

Davids, Rhys. 1958. *The Expositor (Atthasalini)*, Vol. 1. London: Pali Text Society.

De Silva, Pradmasiri. 1995. "Human Rights in Buddhist Perspectives." In *Human Rights and Religious Values: An Uneasy Relationship*. Ed. Abdullahi A. An-Na'lim et al. Michigan: Eerdmans Publishing Co.

Dhammananda, K. Sri. 1994. *Treasure of the Dhamma*. Taipei: The Corporate Body of the Buddha Educational Foundation.

Family Planning and Population Division. 1998. *Thailand: National Family Planning Programme*. Bangkok: Family Planning and Population Division, Department of Health, Ministry of Public Health.

Hughes, James J., and Keown, Damien. n.d. *Buddhism and Medical Ethics: A Bibliographic Introduction*. http://jbe.la.peu.edu.

Intharakamhaeng, Runjuan. 1994. *Sithisatree vitheebuddha (Women's Rights by Buddhist Ways)*. Bangkok: Gender Press.

Kirsch, A. Thomas. 1996. "Buddhism, Sex Roles, and the Thai Economy." In *Women of Southeast Asia*. Ed. Penny Van Esterik. De Kalb, Ill.: Center for Southeast Asian Studies, Northern Illinois University.

Kittiprapas, Sauwalak. 1999. "Social Impacts of Thai Economic Crisis." In *Social Impacts of the Asian Economic Crisis in Thailand, Indonesia, Malaysia and the Philippines*. Bangkok: Thailand Development Research Institute (TDRI).

Kraft, Kenneth. 1999. *The Wheel of Engaged Buddhism: A New Map of the Path*. New York: Weatherhill.

LaFleur, William R. 1992. *Liquid Life: Abortion and Buddhism in Japan*. Princeton: Princeton University Press.

Ling, T. O. 1969. "Buddhist Factors in Population Growth and Control: A Survey Based on Thailand and Ceylon." *Population Studies* 23, 1: 53–60.

Loy, David. 2000. "The Religion of the Market." In *Visions of a New Earth: Religious Perspectives on Population, Consumption, and Ecology*. Ed. Harold Coward and Daniel C. Maguire. Albany: State University of New York Press.

Mahidol Population Gazette. Distributed by the Institute for Population and Social Research, Mahidol University, Salaya, Nakornpathom, Thailand.

Malalasekera, G. P. 1971. *Encyclopedia of Buddhism*. Vol. 3. Fascicle 1. Ceylon: The Government of Ceylon.

Mattiko, Mullika. 1999. "Family Planning and Motherhood: Whose Determination?" In *Reconstructing the Concept of Women and Health*. Ed. Pimpawun Boonmongkon et al. Bangkok: The Women's Health Advocacy Network, Center for Health Policy Studies, Mahidol University.

Na-Rangsi, Sunthorn. 1976. *The Buddhist Concepts of Karma and Rebirth*. Bangkok: Mahamakut Rajavidyalaya Press.

Population and Community Development Association. 1998. Twenty-five Years of Population and Community Development Association. Bangkok: n.p.

Rahula, W. 1988. *What the Buddha Taught* (Bangkok: How Trai Foundation), quoted in Devamitta Thera, ed. 1929 *Anguttara-nikaya*. Colombo, 590.

Ratanakul, Pinit. 1999. "Abortion among Buddhists in Thailand." In *Buddhism and Abortion*. Ed. Damien Keown. Honolulu: University of Hawaii Press.

Searle, Rick. 1995. *Population Growth, Resource Consumption, and the Environment: Seeking a Common Vision for a Troubled World*. Canada: Center for Studies in Religion and Society, University of Victoria.

Smith, Bardwell. 1985. "Buddhism and Abortion in Contemporary Japan: *Nizuko kuyo* and the Confrontation with Death." In *Gender and Buddhist History*. Ed. José Ignacio Cabezon. Albany: State University of New York Press.

Taniguchi, Shoyo. 1987. *Biomedical Ethics from a Buddhist Perspective*, 3: 75–83.

Thavaradhammo, Phra Samut. 1996. *A Comparative Study on Ethics Relating to Abortion: Theravada Buddhism Viewpoints vis-a-vis Abortion Law*. Bangkok: Mahachulalongkornrajavidhayalaya.

Thepvethee, Phra. 1993. *Tam Tang: Tadsinjaiyangri (Abortion, How Should One Decide?)* Bangkok: Bhuddhadhamma Foundation.

Vajiranna, Medagama. 1980. *Marriage in the Teachings of the Buddha. The Maha Bodhi* 88: 25–28.

Woodward, F. L., trans. 1932. *The Book of the Gradual Sayings (Anguttara-Nikaya) or More-Numbered Suttas*. Vol. I. London: The Pali Text Society.

7

Family Planning and Abortion

Cultural Norms Versus Actual Practices in Nigeria

FUNMI TOGONU-BICKERSTETH

With a population of 122 million in 1998, Nigeria was the world's tenth largest country. By the year 2025, Nigeria is expected to be the world's fifth largest country, with an estimated population of 339 million. Nigeria is also a culturally complex country. There are said to be more than 400 ethnic nations and more than 300 dialects spoken in the country. It is therefore not possible to speak of a "Nigerian tradition" in the sense in which one can speak of a "Protestant tradition." The focus of this chapter will, however, be on the Yoruba tradition. This narrows the scope somewhat. When we speak of a Yoruba tradition, we are speaking of a confederation of cultural traditions, many aspects of which can be called religious. Yoruba is not monolithic. The question can be raised, "Whose Yoruba tradition?" Is it that of the Egbas, the Ijebus, the Oyos, the Ondos, or the Ekiti? For these are all Yoruba subethnic groups with their own unique traditions, depending on which of the various deities they lean on for their interpretation of the essence of human existence and the place of humans in the cosmic setup. This chapter will focus on presenting available information on the attitudes of specific ethnic groups in Nigeria and Africa toward fertility, family size, and abortion. The chapter will also examine some of the sayings, proverbs, and societal practices to aid our understanding of the general cultural beliefs about what constitutes appropriate family size and the actual practices extant in the country.

Demographically, Nigeria is one of the rapidly growing nations of the world. Its population in 1970 was 55.1 million, in 1995, 117.1 million, and in the year 2015 it is estimated that the population will be 190.0 million. However, Nigeria has also been witnessing a very gradual decline in its total fertility rate. The fertility rate in 1960 was 6.5; in 1990, 6.0; and in 1998, 5.1. The average rate of reduction in fertility rate was 0.3 percent between 1960 and 1998.[1] However, compared with other countries, the fertility rate for Nigeria, though declining, is still high. There are also regional differences in fertility rates within the country. The fertility rate in the North is said to be higher than those for the south. What sociocultural factors appear to be supportive of this high fertility in Nigeria and indeed in most parts of sub-Saharan Africa?

In many societies in sub-Saharan African countries, women generally attribute to God the number of children they have. As John Mbiti has written, marriage and having children is viewed as a religious duty. To be unmarried and childless is regarded "as stopping the flow of life . . . and hence the diminishing of mankind upon earth."[2] In fact, one of the most sensitive questions to ask in any survey is, "How many children do you have?" Among the rural-dwelling Yoruba such questions cannot be asked directly because of the common saying *"A ki ka omo fun olomo"* ("You must not count someone else's children"). Demographers working in the field are familiar with the occurrence of nonnumeric responses to the question, "How many children do you wish to have?" God is perceived as the only one who can answer such a fundamental question. Among the Edos of Nigeria, for example, God is referred to as "bringer of children"[3] and the Yoruba regard children as God's gift or blessing from heaven that cannot be refused. Jacob Olupona writes that in 1992, "Nigeria decided to produce a population blueprint to guide policy on birth control and fertility." Within a week, there was such a popular uproar led by religious leaders from the indigenous religions and also Christians and Muslims, that the state had to back off. The policy was seen as an infringement on the people's private religious prerogatives.[4] The Rwandans place such a high premium on the task and privilege of transmitting life that they believe that the number of offspring should not be limited but should be accepted as God-given. The possible fecundity of a would-be bride is an important consideration in approving and forging marriage ties among the Yoruba of Nigeria. Infertility is regarded as justifiable excuse for a husband to seek additional wives.[5] The idea that the infertile partner may be the male usually receives little or no attention. This high desire to prove fertility is also linked with the desire to demonstrate it in a large number of children. The Yorubas expect the new bride to become a mother within the first year of marriage. A typical prayer at wedding ceremonies is, "by this time next year, we will all gather together again to welcome your child."

Olupona observes that he was struck when he read that Princess Diana, when she was pregnant with Prince William, said that she felt that all of Britain was carrying the child with her. Says Olupona: "In African communities this is not just the privilege of royals; the pregnancy of any village woman has special significance for the community."[6] If the whole village feels it is pregnant with your prospective child, your reproductive freedom is limited.

This stress on fecundity is woven into much of African culture. In the popular novel *Things Fall Apart*, by Chinua Achebe, the hero's Uncle Mbata has this advice for him: "We do not ask for wealth because he that has health and children will have wealth. We do not pray to have more money but to have more kinsmen."[7]

A number of factors fuel the ideal of a large family size. Among these factors is what can be called an insurance strategy.[8] This is the practice of having more than the desired number of children because of the fear of infant and child mortality, to ensure survivorship of sons to continue the lineage. In times past the infant mortality rates for most parts of Africa were quite high.[9] Among the Yoruba, the infant mortality rate was so high that the concept of "Abiku" (children who are born, only to die shortly thereafter) was quite widely accepted. Various rituals were performed on those children at death to mark them or to discourage them from returning to the same family. Similarly, many rituals and practices, including scarring of the face and body of the baby, are performed to prevent a currently living baby from supposedly associating with his/her unseen friends in the spirit realm who may take him/her away. Therefore, because a woman was never really sure which of her living children would survive, it made good sense to have as many as she could possibly have. However, because of the general improvement in sanitation and the active immunization drive in the country, infant mortality seems to be on the decline. A particularly useful index is the under-five mortality rate. This is the probability of dying between birth and exactly five years of age, expressed per 1,000 live births. For Nigeria in 1960, the under-five mortality rate was 207, and in 1998, 187. Though gradually decreasing, the rate of decrease is still far from satisfactory, particularly when it is observed that in 1994, the under-five rate for Kenya was already 74.

A second factor most probably associated with large family size is the economic contribution of child labor to the household economy. The larger a man's household, the larger his potential pool of workers. The larger the number of children, the larger the acreage that could be farmed. With modernization, the introduction of Western education, wage employment, and the rural-urban migration, young children who cannot yet hold full formal employment or who have no opportunity to migrate to the urban centers still assist their parents on the farm. However, an increasing proportion of children now assist with enlarging the pool of the family's income by engaging in such activities as street hawking, serving as domestic servants to elite families in the urban centers, and other economic activities. Regrettably, children (under 15 years of age) engage in these activities which are often deleterious to their physical and emotional health, and which deprive them of the opportunity to enroll or remain in schools. Thus, not having gained any additional educational or vocational skills, they have little chance for futures better than those of their parents. Hence, the cycle of poverty continues into the next generation, with an enduring and predictable impact on population increases.

A third factor most probably responsible for the large number of children is the expectation of assistance from adult children during old age. There is no formal public assistance for those elders who worked in the informal sector of the economy. Therefore, in old age, with its diminished economic activity, there is usually a total reliance on support from adult children. Under this situation, ideally, the greater the number of adult children a person has, the greater the degree of assistance he/she can expect in old age.[10]

A related factor in understanding the persistence of high fertility rates is the role of women in reproductive decision making. Among the Yoruba generally, with very few exceptions, the role of the woman in reproductive decision making is constricted by societal expectations and cultural norms. Before marriage, she is under the authority of her parents in matters of her sexuality, as well as other matters. At marriage, these rights are transferred to her husband, whom she publicly declares during the ceremony to be "her friend, her older brother, and her father." In Nigeria it used to be that an unmarried girl had to bring her parents to get family planning services and a married woman had to show she had the husband's consent. A woman who refuses to bear more children, when able to, is likely to incur the displeasure of her husband and her in-laws. The latter might give all encouragement to the husband of the "stubborn" woman to acquire additional younger wives who will gladly oblige him. Given this high price placed on children, it is encouraging to report that there are positive attitudes also toward family planning in Nigeria.

Among the Yoruba, postpartum abstinence and the operation of sex taboos associated with breastfeeding are some of the cultural devices that make it possible for children to be spaced. It is reported that the average space is about 2 to 2½ years.[11] This practice works best when the family is an economic unit and the family structure polygamous so that the husband's sexual desires can be met by other wives. The demands of breastfeeding also assumes that the child is kept within the reach of the mother almost all of the time. With the participation of the women in the formal labor force and the introduction of baby formula and creches at the urban centers, this cultural device of birth spacing is becoming unworkable for the urban, educated women living in monogamous family settings. There is therefore a recourse to the newer methods. Studies conducted in Southwestern Nigeria report that a substantial proportion of women approve family planning in principle. Studies further reveal that acquisition of some formal education and skills are vital in gaining family planning information either directly from the mass media or through the public health institutions. The younger and urban based-women have higher approval rates of family planning. Among the reasons given for approving family planning are the mother's health, ability to care for the child, and ability to provide for the child later. There is still, however, the broad opinion that methods of birth control are risky. It is to be noted that there are indigenous methods of birth control that have not been adequately studied.[12]

Regarding the attitude toward family planning, mention must also be made of what has been known as the "male factor" in family planning in sub-Saharan Africa. It has been found in Ghana, Nigeria, and Sudan, for example, that the male partner plays an important role in decision making regarding contraception use, timing, and the number of a couple's children. The tradition of polygamy is also a complicating factor in Africa. Traditionally, polygamy symbolized prestige and affluence, and was an indication of wealth.[13] Polygamy is also associated with men's reproductive preferences. Men may either have more than one wife because they want more children or want more children because they have more wives. For instance, a government proclamation in Nigeria during the reign of President Babangida that recommended four children per woman was generally interpreted to mean that a man who had four wives could then have sixteen children! The fertility preferences of wives in polygamous unions are often not very clear. Wives in such unions may want more children in order to compete favorably with cowives in terms of childbearing and status in the household. On the other hand, this desire may be curtailed by the fact that women in polygamous unions tend to shoulder greater responsibilities in rearing their children than those in monogamous marriages. In general, what can be concluded is that most people (women in particular) hold two sets of opposing ideas when it comes to contraceptives and family planning: belief that children are a blessing from God and should be accepted and also the belief that family planning is desirable to ensure the health of the mother and the proper upbringing of the children. The pronatalist forces are such that it limits success in the family planning area. For example, contraceptive prevalence for Nigeria for 1990–99 was only 6 percent as compared with a 59 percent for Morocco and 82 percent for the United Kingdom. This may not take account of indigenous methods, the prevalence of which is not known with any precision.

Abortion

Concerning abortion, the picture is clearer. There is government legislation against abortion in Nigeria, and the general view is that only unmarried people have abortions. The Yoruba disapprove of pregnancy in young girls but they also disapprove of "grandmother pregnancy." To avoid the likelihood of the latter, most Yoruba women abstain from sexual intercourse once their children are married and they become grandmothers. Women consider the occasion of grandmother pregnancy serious enough to call for abortion. Aside from this, abortion is generally perceived as dangerous, immoral, and shameful, but there is strong evidence that it is still resorted to. Despite the seeming public condemnation of abortion in Africa, available evidence suggests that the practice is prevalent. In Nigeria in particular, the most recent information on the issue reveals that at least 610,000 pregnancy terminations occur in Nigeria yearly and 60 percent of the abortions are performed by "nonphysician providers." Included in these nonphysician providers could be fake doctors or herbal doctors, most of whom have knowledge of traditional abortifacients.

The criminalization of abortion has led to an increase in the health risks associated with having illegal abortions and the economic costs of having a proper abortion. Adolescent pregnancy is perceived as a shame not only for the girl but also for the family. It disrupts the girl's education and stigmatizes her. The only one possible option is abortion, a choice society has made unsafe by driving it underground. Estimates on the relationship of maternal deaths to abortion vary from 20 to 30 percent, and, obviously, data is not easy to confirm.

Gaps between the normative prescriptions concerning family reproductive matters and the actual experiences in Nigeria today are revealed in popular sayings and current practices on the social scene. Among the commonest Yoruba idiomatic expressions concerning reasonable family size is: *"Omo beere oosi beere"* ("Many children, many afflictions"). The Yoruba appear to believe that having too many children leads to poverty in the family. Another popular saying is *"Bi a bi okan oga, o ya ju egberun obun omo lo"* ("Better to have just one successful child than to have a thousand useless ones").

The Kikuyu people of Kenya have a saying that many births mean many burials.[14] There is also a general belief among the Yoruba that the larger the family size, the greater the possibility of having abnormal children. It is therefore expected that among children of kings and important personalities who have large families, there will be one or two with deformity or aberrant behavior. Thus, within the same cultural group where children are highly valued, we find in existence elements cautioning against excessive large family size or at least acknowledging the potential problems of having a large family.

Another indicator on the social scene suggests that the cultural stance of zero tolerance for abortion is leading to the practice of abandonment, especially by young mothers, a practice very common in Christian medieval Europe. Traditionally, if any child was abandoned, it was a child with a gross deformity believed to be brought upon the family by malevolent spiritual forces. A few of such children were abandoned. But nowadays, the neonates abandoned are healthy ones. The society has no long-term plans for these abandoned neonates.

Secondly, because of the changes in the socioeconomic conditions and the effects of globalization, both the direct and indirect costs of raising children have increased tremendously. The instrumental values of children to parents appears to be diminishing over time. The economic benefits they provide as extra labor hands, old age support, and risk insurance have declined over time. Current gerontological studies in Nigeria suggest that the expectation of old-age support from adult children may no longer be realistic, as there is already an increase in the visibility of destitute elderly beggars in the major urban centers. Furthermore, transnational migration by an increasing number of youths may mean decreased availability of younger people to care for the aged.

A third factor, which needs to be part of the campaign for a just, humane, and reasonable reproductive health stance, is the AIDS scourge in much of Africa. It has been said that more people have died from AIDS in Africa than have died from the various wars fought on the continent. Furthermore, for developing countries, unsafe sex comes second only to malnutrition among the risk factors associated with percentage of disability-adjusted life years.

Thus, the previously prevailing socioeconomic conditions that provide justification for the pronatalist orientation to reproductive health are no longer salient although they have not quite disappeared either. New health risk factors—for example, AIDS—with potentially devastating and confounding effects on population dynamics have also emerged on the scene. Within this rather fluid context, therefore, an individual's practice with respect to family planning and abortion will depend upon their location in the socioeconomic scale and more especially on their appraisal of the incentives for a reduced family size. Among the poor, rural dwellers where there is always the need to marshal all resources including those of children to meet the basic economic needs of the family, small family size may still be undesired. But among the educated, westernized, urban population, family planning has wider acceptance because the existential living conditions in the urban centers may make large family size a burden rather than a help. Thus, although cultural norms in general extol the desirability of large family size, compliance with that and other norms concerning reproductive decisions depends on the extent to which the norms facilitate the individual's pursuit of his/her existential needs. Hence, as norms shape practice, existential conditions seem also to be shaping the norms in reproductive matters. It is a fluid situation.

NOTES

1. For references to African fertility rates, see *The State of the World's Children,* an annual publication of UNICEF, The United Nations, New York.

2. John Mbiti, *Introduction to African Religion* (New York: Heinemann, 1991), p. 98.

3. Ibid.

4. Jacob Olupona, "African Religions and Global Issues," in *Visions of a New Earth: Religious Perspectives on Population, Consumption, and Ecology* (Albany: State University of New York Press, 2000), pp. 181–82.

5. For discussion of polygamy in African cultures, see N. A. Fadipe, *The Sociology of the Yoruba* (Ibadan: Ibadan University Press, 1970).

6. Olupona, *Visions of a New Earth,* p. 194.

7. Chinua Achebe, *Things Fall Apart* (London: Heinemann, 1958), p. 146.

8. C. B. Lloyd, "The Effects of Improved Child Survival on Family Planning, Practice, and Fertility," *Studies in Family Planning* 19, 1988, pp. 141–61.

9. J. F. May, M. Mukamanzi, and M. Vekemans, "Family Planning in Rwanda," *Studies in Family Planning,* 21, 1990, pp. 20–31.

10. Funmi Togonu-Bickersteth, "Gender Differences in Expressed Satisfaction with Care from Adult Children Among Older Rural Yoruba," *Southern African Journal of Gerontology,* 6, 1997, pp. 3–6; F. Togonu-Bickersteth, E. O. Akinnawo, O. S. Akinyele, and E. Ayeni, "Public Alms Solicitation Among the Yoruba Elderly in Nigeria," *Southern African Journal of Gerontology,* 6, 1997, pp. 26–31.

11. E. T. Dow, "Breastfeeding and Abstinence Among the Yoruba," *Studies in Family Planning,* 21, 1981, pp. 272–77.

12. See Olupona, *Visions of a New Earth,* p. 195

13. Ibid.

14. G. Barra, *Kikuyu Proverbs* (Nairobi, Kenya: Kenya Literature Bureau, 1939), p. 261.

8

Reproductive Rites and Wrongs

Lessons from American Indian Religious Traditions, Historical Experience, and Contemporary Life

MARY C. CHURCHILL

Spiritual consciousness is the highest form of politics.

In 1998 eleven Dakota girls "lived alone" for the first time in over one hundred years. Under the guidance of their female elders, these child-beloveds participated in a ceremony that had been prohibited by the U.S. government for five generations, the *Ishna Ti Awica Dowan*, or "singing for those who live alone."[1] In the 1880s this coming-of-age ceremony, along with all other traditional religious practices, became a crime under the "Indian Offenses" policy, which established a tribunal to eliminate the "savage rites and heathenish customs" of American Indians.[2] It would not be until the passage of the American Indian Religious Freedom Act in 1978 that the Dakota could again hold the girls' puberty ceremony publicly and legally.[3] With the return of the *Ishna Ti*, Dakota girls once again became women in the traditional way. Stressing humility, strength, and self-respect, the elders taught the initiates the roles and responsibilities of womanhood and its meaning in Dakota culture. Whether they knew it or not, these women and girls fulfilled a hope articulated a decade earlier by Lakota scholar Beatrice Medicine. Recognizing the relationship between the loss of the *Ishna Ti* and the erosion of family responsibility, Medicine had called for the return of the girls' puberty ceremony, arguing, "We must understand and recapture this [rite] as a tremendously important means of revitalizing the best of our values."[4]

Reproductive rites, such as puberty ceremonies, and reproductive wrongs, such as the banning of religious practices, are at the heart of any discussion of reproductive health issues in Indian country. Although American Indian people have developed rich ritual, mythic, and social traditions concerning reproduction, the history of genocide—a genocide that targeted Native women and children—has made issues like overpopulation and contraception subjects fraught with conflict. Certainly, Native philosophies and religious practices have much to contribute to the question of population growth. However, the complexity of these issues for indigenous people necessitates that we also examine Native historical and contemporary experience. Only with this grounding in the realities of American Indian life is it possible for us to consider seriously Native religious traditions bearing on these issues. Achieving this understanding is more than a prelude to considering solutions to global overpopulation, however, for the history and contemporary experience of Native people have the potential to reframe the population question entirely.

In North America there exist hundreds of indigenous nations that predate the establishment of the United States and Canada. Each of these nations has its own unique religious traditions based largely on the particular region it calls home. Due to this variety in American Indian traditions, there is no one "Native American religion" per se. Even the word *religion* in this context is a misnomer because these traditions are usually so fully integrated into every aspect of life as to be synonymous with culture. Despite the variation in these traditions, there are significant similarities among them, including the importance of ritualism and healing, the primacy of the oral tradition, the privileging of the common good, and the belief in the sacrality of Mother Earth and the interrelatedness of all life.

These nations came under attack, however, beginning in the fifteenth century, first with the European colonization, then with the anti-Indian policies of the U.S. government. Genocide, combined with theft of land and systematic cultural destruction, led to significant loss of traditional religious knowledge and practices. Despite the devastation, many indigenous North American traditions have managed to survive, although changed to greater or lesser degrees. Moreover, new forms of Native religious traditions have emerged, such as the Native American Church and indigenous Christian churches. Today, American Indian people engage in Native religious traditions in reservation, rural, and urban contexts. The importance of land to these traditions has meant that reservations, sacred sites on public land, and ceremonial sites on private land are the main centers of Native American religious practice today.

The oral traditions of many Native nations attest to concerns with population size dating back to the time of creation. The Cherokee sacred story of the origin of disease, for instance, explains that animals introduced afflictions into the world because humans were overpopulating the earth and treating them carelessly.[5] And in the Navajo account of creation, Coyote warns the people, "If we all live, and continue to increase as we have done, the earth will soon be too small to hold us, and there will be no room for the cornfields."[6] Along with mythic sources, Native traditional knowledge and practices of birth control also indicate concern with population size. These sources suggest that prior to European contact Native people generally strived to live in harmony with their environment, balancing their population size with the resources available in their regions.

Native concern about population size changed dramatically, however, as a result of European colonization, American domination, and Christian missionization. The emphasis shifted from living in proper relationship with Mother Earth and her inhabitants to trying to survive in the face of seemingly inevitable extinction. Native American population expert Russell Thornton estimates that at the nadir of American Indian population decline in the United States only about 7 percent of the aboriginal population remained (150,000 people at most).[7] As historian David E. Stannard argues, "The destruction of the Indians of the Americas was, far and away, the most massive act of genocide in the history of the world."[8] This slaughter was carried out not only through contagion and warfare but also through what could be called "reproductive genocide," the attempted eradication of people and practices essential to or associated with Native reproduction.[9] In other words, instead of sparing women and children, Europeans and Americans targeted them for sexual violence and death.[10] In the conquest of California, for instance, sexual assault served to ensure the subordination not just of indigenous women but of entire communities.[11] Neither women nor children could escape the Spanish soldiers who sought to rape them, and indigenous men who interfered were killed.[12] One of the consequences of this sexual reign of terror, syphilis, was as pernicious as the predation itself. It became the most prevalent disease throughout the mission Indian population, leading to stillbirths and maternal death in childbirth and leaving its victims vulnerable to other epidemics.[13]

Another significant example of reproductive genocide is the massacre at Sand Creek, Colorado, in 1864, a military raid on a Cheyenne and Arapaho camp that was already under government control. Guided by the philosophy of, in his words, "Nits make lice," Colonel John Chivington directed his troops to annihilate an unarmed village he knew consisted mostly of women and children.[14] As if the killing of women were not enough, the soldiers mutilated their victims' genitalia, exhibiting them on sticks, hats, and saddle-bows; and they "ripped open women," even cutting out at least one woman's unborn child.[15] Though extreme, these two cases merely exemplify the pattern of violence dubbed by Cherokee scholar and activist Andrea Smith the "sexual colonization" of Native women.[16]

Though more subtle, the loss of reproductive health knowledge and practices was no less devastating. First and foremost, the dislocation of American Indians from traditional homelands caused irreparable damage. The keepers of traditional knowledge, the elders, and the future generations, the youth and children, died in significant numbers during the forced marches conducted by the federal government. Communities also lost access to ceremonial sites and locations where medicinal plants grew. Perhaps most important, however, was the change sustained in the relationship between the people and the sacred powers of their homelands. As Laguna scholar Paula Gunn Allen argues, many female sacred beings were replaced by male-gendered creators, such as the "Great Spirit"[17] and the Christian God, the Father. Simultaneous to the loss of these female powers was the growing repression experienced by women. The colonies and eventually Indian nations themselves demoted and disenfranchised women in a variety of ways. The imposition of Western forms of religion, education, and government institutionalized patriarchal authority in Indian America.

While many may believe that reproductive genocide ended with the Indian Wars in the 1880s, the assault on Native reproduction has actually continued into the twentieth and twenty-first centuries. Until the late twentieth century, for example, Native American children were being adopted into non-Indian homes or placed in foster care at high rates, a trend that was partially reversed only with the passage of the Indian Child Welfare Act in 1978.[18] It was also discovered in the 1970s that the branch of the U.S. government responsible for health service to Native Americans, the Indian Health Service (IHS), was performing sterilizations on Native women without informed consent.[19] Dr. Connie Uri, the Choctaw/Cherokee doctor who uncovered the practice, estimates that more than a quarter of all Native women had been forcibly sterilized in this way.[20] In 1989, the IHS denied charges that doctors were again conducting such sterilizations.[21] The IHS use today of the contraceptives Depo-Provera and Norplant in American Indian communities should also be seen as ongoing genocide, according to Charon Asetoyer of the Native American Women's Health Education Resource Center.[22] She points out that these contraceptives place control in the hands of doctors, not women; that they are prescribed without uniform protocols for administration; and that they pose special dangers to Indian women because of the medical conditions they commonly face.[23]

In addition to the theft of Native children and the control of indigenous

women's reproduction, environmental racism affects American Indian reproductive health as well. For instance, large corporations have dumped industrial
waste into the St. Lawrence Seaway for four decades, contaminating the food
chain and, ultimately, the breast milk of Mohawk women. One of the corporations, General Motors (GM), whose factory is only 100 yards from the homes
of some Mohawks, has been fined for contaminating the local groundwater.
Nevertheless, chemicals continue to leach into the river, as GM only "capped"
the landfill without installing a liner under the waste.[24] Understanding mothers' bodies as the "first environment," Mohawk midwife and activist Katsi Cook
sadly recognizes, "[O]ur bodies are in fact, a part of the landfill."[25]

Through centuries of domination, then, Native people have witnessed the
decimation of their populations and the loss of land and livelihood. At the
same time, they have been spectators to their oppressors' growing numbers,
landbase, wealth, and power. This inverse relationship has made Native people
acutely aware of the role of power in structuring social, economic, and political
relations. As a result, Native people are understandably resistant to any form
of population regulation, especially when unequal power relations inform such
policies. The experience of Native people therefore suggests that we must question, resist, and undermine these power structures in order to arrive at just
and equitable solutions.

Underlying the power relations that structure discourse and policy on population has been and continues to be the Malthusian paradigm. While many
may claim that Malthusian thinking has lost its influence, population scholar
Asoka Bandarage argues otherwise:

> Given the deep entrenchment of Malthusian thinking in academic
> and policy planning circles and the extensive publicity given to fears
> of "overpopulation" in every imaginable medium of communication,
> most educated people in the world tend to be predisposed toward a
> Malthusian view of the world. Indeed, it can be argued that Malthu-
> sianism has shaped modern consciousness, determining the moral
> spirit of our age.[26]

Population analyst Betsy Hartmann concurs: "So pervasive are [Malthusian]
assumptions that many of us have internalized them without even realizing
it."[27] The Malthusian ethic regards overpopulation as the cause of hunger,
poverty, environmental destruction, and resource depletion, among many
other social, political, and economic ills. In its narrow focus on overpopulation,
this approach fails to interrogate the central role of racism, classism, sexism,
colonization, imperialism, and transnational corporate capitalism in creating
the social, political, economic, and environmental ills it lays at the doorstep of

overpopulation.[28] In so doing, the Malthusian paradigm attempts to treat the symptom of population increase rather than the disease of domination.[29] Therefore, to target overpopulation without seriously challenging dominant society and First World structures and institutions of power, including such practices as overconsumption, environmental exploitation, and militarism, suggests the same kind of genocidal philosophies and practices faced by American Indians for centuries. The American Indian experience therefore demonstrates that the question of population has to be reframed entirely. Native religious traditions suggest that instead of narrowly focusing on human needs, we need to address the larger question of how humanity as a whole can facilitate planetary health, including the well-being of all life forms. This framework calls upon all human beings and all nations to take responsibility for their role in Mother Earth's decline and for her return to health. The impulse for change must therefore come from initiative within instead of coercion without.

What, then, might be the responsibility of American Indians in this case, and what might be the Native contribution to these discussions?[30] Determining the responsibility of American Indians is a rather complex matter. Allen makes the point that "American Indians take the fact of probable extinction for granted in every thought, in every conversation."[31] It is likely, therefore, that many, if not most, Native people would agree that indigenous people have made enough of a sacrifice. As Lakota holy man Lame Deer put it in the 1970s,

> the population explosion doesn't worry us much. All these long
> years, when the only good Indian was a dead Indian, the bodies at
> Wounded Knee, the Sand Creek Massacre, the Washita, all this kill-
> ing of women and children, the measles and small pox wiping out
> whole tribes—the way I see it, the Indians have already done all the
> population control one could ask of them a hundred times over. Our
> problem is survival. Overpopulation—that's your worry.[32]

In light of this philosophy, we would therefore expect to see unrestricted growth in the American Indian population. Certainly, increased fertility rates have contributed significantly to Indian demographic recovery, which started at the turn of the twentieth century but did not begin in earnest until the end of World War II. But since the baby boom, Native fertility rates, like those of other Americans, have dropped consistently, leaving these rates only slightly higher than those of whites and blacks.[33] Although this drop was due in part to the sizeable number of people who identified as Indian for the first time, Thornton looks to the increasing number of intermarriages, the growing urbanization of the American Indian population, and other factors to argue the likelihood of modest population growth:

[W]e can expect the American Indian population to continue to grow somewhat, as the total United States population will grow somewhat, but the percentage of the total United States population represented by the American Indian population will very likely become more or less constant as the growth rates of both populations converge. American Indians will then represent a small, stable subpopulation of the United States.[34]

He also recognizes that these factors may well lead to population decline instead.[35] In either case, American Indians will likely continue to remain a relatively small population. In light of the great demographic losses suffered by American Indians and their limited anticipated population growth, advocating for a policy of Native population regulation is not only unethical and neocolonial but also ill-founded. Native Americans' share in the responsibility of facilitating planetary health therefore lies in means other than population regulation.

Indeed, since the beginning of time, indigenous people across the continent have understood their responsibility to be in creating, maintaining, and restoring harmony. This imperative includes not only living in right relationship with oneself and with others but also living in balance with the (super)natural world.[36] In this indigenous "harmony ethic" we find values essential to maintaining and reinvigorating traditional Native reproductive philosophies and practices, as well as perspectives relevant for non-Indians discerning how they might contribute to efforts to heal the planet.

American Indian nations today are in dire need of revitalizing reproductive health traditions. With the loss of significant traditional knowledge and many religious practices concerning reproduction, Native American communities, like the American population as a whole, find themselves in the midst of what might be called "reproductive chaos"—in the case of American Indians, conditions out of sync with traditional tribal behaviors and values concerning reproduction and out of balance with the (super)natural world. The issue of teenage pregnancy serves as a telling example. Teenage motherhood, in and of itself, is not the central problem; historically, once a girl completed her puberty ceremony, the community considered her ready for marriage and childbirth. Rather, the circumstances that lead to teen pregnancy cause great concern. One national study, "The State of Native American Youth," found that 18.9 percent of Native American young women across the country were pregnant by the twelfth grade and that 12.2 percent of Native American men had impregnated someone before they themselves had completed high school.[37] Specialists in the area of Native teen parenting cite several reasons for such

high rates: lack of good role models, family disintegration, pressure from partners, limited access to or failure to use contraceptives, low self-esteem, lack of
sexual self-respect, and the desire to be loved, among others.[38] Native girls also
experience sexual abuse at high rates, which can ultimately lead to unintended
pregnancy. One study that included 320 American Indian young women
showed that of the Native teens who had become pregnant, 50 percent had
been coerced into sex, over 30 percent had experienced attempted rape, and
over 40 percent had been raped.[39] High rates of intimate partner violence and
substance abuse likely contribute to these rates as well.

Other indicators of reproductive disorder are low birth weights and substantial infant mortality rates. Approximately 6–7 percent of American Indian
babies are born with low birth weights.[40] American Indians also have the second highest infant mortality rate in the country (13 deaths per 1,000 live
births).[41] In recent years, infant mortality rates on reservations in South Dakota
have reached as high as 23.8 deaths per 1,000 live births.[42] These outcomes
arise from a variety of sources, including inadequate prenatal care, high rates
of maternal smoking, diabetes, fetal alcohol syndrome, and sudden infant
death syndrome.[43] I call attention to these indicators not to blame Indian
women, men, and youth—these conditions are clearly the legacy of colonial
rule and American oppression—rather, they illustrate the great need to regain
traditional reproductive health teachings and practices and reincorporate them
into daily life.

Like American Indians, other communities face some of the same challenges. Before we can consider how an indigenous harmony ethic might be
useful for non-Indians, however, I must issue a word of caution. It is often
thought that American Indian traditions hold the answers to many of today's
pressing questions on the environment, global peace, spiritual fulfillment, and
the like. Even Lakota scholar Vine Deloria Jr. has commented,

> It may be that American Indians contain the last best hope for spiri-
> tual renewal in a world dominated by material considerations. The
> multitude of non-Indians arriving at reservation doors seeking an-
> swers would seem to indicate an intuition in many hearts that Indi-
> ans do give us the last hope of resurrection.[44]

Religion scholar Joseph Epes Brown has also suggested that American Indian
traditions offer "models" for resolving contemporary society's dilemmas.[45]
While Native traditions do contain valuable knowledge and practices for individual, communal, and planetary health, this savior-seeking is largely mis-
guided, not to mention opportunistic. In reality, the energies of many American Indian nations are and must necessarily be directed at resolving

environmental, social, and economic problems in their own communities. Moreover, it is a sad irony that as non-Indians seek Native spiritual guidance for inner peace and world redemption, dominant society simultaneously undermines the viability of indigenous religions.

In the case of articulating and defending the right to family planning, contraception, and abortion, however, I believe it is not only appropriate but necessary to include American Indian perspectives. Here, in this project of the Religious Consultation on Population, Reproductive Health, and Ethics, Native American values have not been singled out as the only source of wisdom; rather, they contribute to a dialogue that must necessarily integrate indigenous perspectives in order to succeed. In actuality, many publications featuring "world religions" fail to recognize what some call the "Fourth World"—the seemingly invisible indigenous communities and nations that defy the boundaries of the First and Third worlds yet supply these worlds with much of their wealth. Lacking an organized worldwide structure, indigenous traditions cannot be easily categorized as a "world religion," despite the similarity in ways of life and experiences of religious oppression shared by indigenous nations. The inclusion of American Indian religious traditions in this volume therefore signals a recognition of the importance of Native perspectives to dialogues on global issues and the validity of indigenous practices and philosophies in the study of religion. Indeed, as victims of centuries of population control, American Indians are among the most important participants in discussions on the population question.

With this background, therefore, let us turn our attention to the values inherent in an indigenous harmony ethic that stand to inform our thinking on reproduction and population growth. In order for us to understand this emphasis on harmony, we must appreciate the relationship between rights and responsibilities in Indian country. American Indians today employ the language of rights to fight for many aspects of traditional life, including the right to freedom of religion, the right to hunt and fish in traditional ways, and the right to self-determination. Native women also use rights discourse to advocate for indigenous women's reproductive freedom. The Native Women for Reproductive Rights Coalition, for instance, has created an "Agenda for Reproductive Rights" that clearly articulates the rights of Native women to family planning, contraception, and abortion.[46] It, too, reflects traditional Native religious values. Although rights discourse in the West implies individual entitlement under the liberal "rights" paradigm, in traditional Indian thought rights cannot be extricated from Native American religious traditions, or rites. Rights exist only within the context of sacred responsibilities that have been entrusted to Native people since time immemorial. Under this "rites" paradigm, to insist on individual or group rights that conflict with these responsibilities is to court chaos, for at the core of these sacred obligations lies the requirement for creating, maintaining, and restoring harmony. By the same token, to fight for rights as a means to honor or fulfill these responsibilities is to promote and perpetuate harmony. As we shall see, the fight for traditional reproductive rights has just this potential.

In everyday terms, the pursuit of harmony translates into living in proper relationship with oneself and others and living in balance with the (super)natural world.[47] In considering these relationships, we find not only important means for addressing the reproductive issues that face American Indians but also useful resources for examining the population growth issues that challenge humanity as a whole. We discover the basis of Native women's reproductive authority as well.

Although the process of maintaining or restoring right relationship with oneself begins early in life, religious traditions that honor a youth's coming-of-age and virginity are an essential means of fostering self-respect. As Carole Anne Heart Looking Horse has indicated about the Lakota girls' puberty rite, "The Womanhood Ceremony is a sacred ceremony that lets you know that you are making a transformation from child to woman, you're able to bear children, you have to have respect for yourself, you have to be modest."[48] In these ceremonies the girls often learn about many aspects of adult life. For instance, they learn about sexuality, married life, and childcare so that they can make responsible choices and fulfill their responsibilities honorably. According to Delfina Cuero, a Kumeyaay woman born in 1900,

> In the real old days, grandmothers taught these things about life at the time of a girl's initiation ceremony, when she was about to become a woman. Nobody just talked about these things ever. It was all in the songs and myths that belonged to the ceremony. All that a girl needed to know to be a good wife, and how to have babies and to take care of them was learned at the ceremony, at the time when a girl became a woman.[49]

Today, the elder women do not necessarily present motherhood as the next stage in a girl's life, however. They encourage the initiates to stay in school, to go to college, to prepare themselves to contribute to their nations. They stress the value of hard work, and many ceremonies require the initiates to perform traditional tasks, some of which test the girls' endurance. In some traditions, the elders introduce them to alcohol and tobacco at this time to educate them about their appropriate use and to facilitate moderation and responsible decision making. All of these steps are thought to "mold" the girls—anything that they experience during the ceremony establishes a pattern for the rest of their lives. The aspect of the ceremony that shapes them most profoundly, however, is their growing understanding of the power of women and of their own sacred nature. In the Apache and *Diné* (Navajo) ceremonies, for example, girls actually become during the ceremony the most powerful female being in the tradition, White-Painted Woman (Apache) or Changing Woman (*Diné*). From then on, the initiates must lead their lives in her footsteps.[50]

In order to protect this sacred power until the appropriate time, some nations stress the value of virginity. Through stories, for instance, elders warn girls about the dangers of men. Delfina Cuero was told the story of coyote's attempt to capture two beautiful girls who were crows. "This story explains how we have to watch men—there are some good and some bad men," she comments. "We knew that these stories were told to teach us how to behave and what to expect."[51] Native women also kept a watchful eye over girls and young women. Beverly Hungry Wolf, noting the value of female virtue in Blackfoot culture, reports that Blackfoot mothers and aunts strictly watched girls who were at the age of marriage.[52] In Lakota culture, mothers had special means to protect their daughters against uninvited "guests." According to Lame Deer, "[I]f you were a tipi-creeper you'd find out that mothers had a habit of tying a hair rope around their daughters' waists, passing it through their legs. This was a "No Trespassing" sign. If a boy was found fooling around with that rope, the women would burn his tipi down or kill his horse."[53] Ritual also promoted the value of virginity. Lakota warrior societies, for instance, sought out virgins to sing the society's ritual songs.[54] A virgin woman also performs the role of doorkeeper during the sweatlodge rite of Lakota Sun Dance.[55] Perhaps most important, however, only virgin women were allowed to symbolically chop down the sacred Sun Dance tree. Like the puberty ceremony initiates, they too experience sacred female power at this time, for they embody the White Buffalo Calf Woman.[56]

Central to identity development, therefore, are puberty ceremonies and other traditions that establish and preserve not just a girl's value but her divinity. There can be, perhaps, a no more profound means to self-respect than in embodying the sacred power of White-Painted Woman or White Buffalo Calf Woman. Restoring reproductive balance therefore entails upholding these traditions, many of which continue in part or whole today, and adapting them, if necessary, to contemporary life. Like the Lakota who restored the *Ishna Ti Awica*, communities must also reinvigorate relevant traditions that have been lost, including the traditions that transform boys into responsible men.

In addition to creating right relationship with oneself, establishing appropriate relationships with others also facilitates harmony. Of primary importance here is the equal value of women and men, both in the family and in society as a whole. In regard to her own people, for instance, Debra Lynn White Plume points out, "Deeply enmeshed in prereservation Lakota philosophy was the reality of adult men and women existing as equal human beings. . . . Men and women each held definite roles in society that were considered of equal importance to the Nation."[57] In contrast to the white feminist approach of stressing the sameness of women and men, Native women honor the distinctions between the male and female genders and stress their complementary balance.[58] In some traditions, women were considered even more powerful than men. A Papago woman explained to anthropologist Ruth Underhill, " 'Don't you see that without us there would be no men? Why should we envy men? We *made* men.' "[59] As a result of this balance, domestic violence rarely occurred in Indian families historically. Instead, women and men participated in nearly all spheres of society, including the family. In some cultures, such as the matrilineal Cherokee and the Iroquois, the home belonged to the women, and their children, to the mother's clan. The most important male in a child's life in this case was not the father but the clan uncle, the mother's brother, who shared responsibility for his sisters' children. This arrangement facilitated the equality of women and men in domestic matters and enabled failed marriages to dissolve without significant harm to the children. In this case, men did not always live with their wives and sometimes resided in structures where men commonly gathered.

The separation of genders, in fact, was historically a common feature in most if not all American Indian societies. Men and women had their own spheres of responsibility, which often entailed physical separation as well. In many societies, ceremonial requirements, hunting, waging war, and healing from bloodshed, required men to live in seclusion for periods of time. Similarly, women often lived alone for up to seven days during menstruation. Ruby Modesto, a Desert Cahuilla medicine woman, describes menstrual seclusion among her people:

> [W]omen didn't feel that they were being imposed upon when they
> retired to the menstrual hut. They got to be by themselves for three
> or four days. It was a ceremonial occasion which enabled a woman
> to get in touch with her own special power. It was a time to Dream
> and have visions. Each month the women went to their own vision
> pit. The men had vision pits too, places to Dream and pray, way up
> in the mountains. This was how the people learned. Dreams were
> the source of all wisdom.[60]

When women and men did live together, gender segregation was maintained by dividing structures in half, one side for men, the other for women. One Dakota woman reported, for instance, "Mother and father never slept together, men and women slept on different sides of lodges. Men and women slept separately. Maybe we have to do that again."[61]

Recognition of the power and danger of sexuality likely underlies some of these traditions. As one Dakota woman recalls, "The Elders used to tell us that sexuality is not a play-thing."[62] The Lakota sacred story of the White Buffalo Calf Woman, for instance, suggests the need to control the impulse for self-gratification. In this story, one of the men who first met the White Buffalo Calf Woman recognized that she was holy and kept his distance. Another man approached her, however, intending to fulfill his desire for her. While she spared this first man, she enveloped the second in a cloud, leaving only a pile of bones when the vapor had dissipated.[63] Lame Deer explains, "Desire killed that man, as desire has killed many before and after him. If the earth should ever be destroyed, it will be by desire, by the lust of pleasure and self-gratification, by greed for the green frog skin, by people who are mindful only of their own self, forgetting about the wants of others."[64] It is enlightening that Lame Deer makes clear the potential of self-gratification to cause planetary destruction.

Among the Diné, men and women are to avoid sexual indulgence. Anthropologist Gladys A. Reichard explains, "[S]exual needs must be allowed expression but should be controlled."[65] According to the Navajo creation story, floods resulted from a preoccupation with sexual indulgence.[66] It is believed that one can become a victim of or suffer from "Frenzy Witchcraft," a condition in which one has excessive sexual desire. Although rare today, ceremonials exist for the treatment of this condition among women and men.[67]

For the Ojibwe, the results of excessive sexual indulgence were considered disgraceful; as one woman put it, it was "a disgrace to have children like steps and stairs." According to Ojibwe women,

> "Parents preached to the men and to their daughters to stay away
> from each other." "If a man had sense, he didn't bother his wife
> while a child was young." "Some had many children, but none had
> them like steps and stairs; the men and women kept away from
> each other." "I didn't live with my man as husband until the baby
> was able to walk. I slept alone."[68]

Other nations recognized the benefits of controlling one's sexual "energy." Among the Cheyenne, for instance, some men vowed to remain celibate for extended periods in order to devote that energy to one child. E. Adamson Hoebel explains:

> Sexual energy is a limited quotient which must be spent sparingly. Therefore the man of strong character and good family vows at the birth of his first child (especially if it is a boy) not to have another child for either seven or fourteen years. All of the father's growth powers are then concentrated on the development of this one child rather than being dissipated among several. It is necessary to understand that more than the semen of conception goes into growing a child; there is a continuing transfer of the father's "energy" from parent to offspring. . . . During the long period of seven or fourteen years the father must practice absolute celibacy, unless he has more than one wife. The mother of the dedicated child is without question celibate throughout the period. . . . Should a parent break the vow of dedication, it is believed it will kill the child.[69]

Native peoples have recognized, therefore, the power of sexuality to cause great harm and to bestow great blessing. As with any polyvalent force, however, sexuality must be brought under control. While there are a variety of ways to do so, none is perhaps as important as separating women and men as a means of establishing a proper relationship between them in families and in society as a whole.

Consistent with this gender segregation, men did not interfere with women's matters, especially concerning sexuality. Historically, women made their own decisions about family planning, contraception, and abortion, all of which have been practiced in American Indian societies to greater or lesser degrees. Native women today continue to abide by this philosophy. A 1991 Women of Color Reproductive Health Poll, for instance, found that 80 percent of Native American women believe every woman should decide for herself whether or not to have an abortion.[70] As one Lakota woman put it, " 'Anything that has to do with our bodies . . . is really our business as women, and as Lakota women, it is part of our culture to make our own decisions about [abortion]. . . . [I]t is our privilege as Lakota women to make decisions about our bodies.' "[71] More than a privilege, it is women's sacred right and responsibility to live in reproductive balance. Some indigenous women locate this authority in each woman's relationship with the divine. According to the Native Women for Reproductive Rights Coalition, for example, "Traditionally reproductive health issues were decisions made by the individual, and were not thrust into the political arena for any kind of scrutinization. The core of decision-making for Indigenous women is between her and the Great Spirit."[72] But this authority has even more profound roots.

In the case of the *Diné* girls' puberty ceremony, if not all female coming-of-age rites, the initiate is entrusted with the power to control her own fertility by virtue of her *becoming* the deity, not just communicating with her. In the *Kinaaldá* ceremony, the girl is transformed into the most powerful and sacred of divinities, Changing Woman. According to Reichard,

> Changing Woman is Woman with a sphinxlike quality. No matter
> how much we know about her the total is a great question mark.
> She is the mystery of reproduction, of life springing from nothing,
> of the last hope of the world, a riddle perpetually solved and peren-
> nially springing up anew, literally expressed in Navaho: ". . . here the
> one who is named Changing Woman, . . . here her name is pretty
> close to the [real] names of every one of the girls."[73]

Becoming the very "mystery of reproduction," the initiate gains the ability to have children through the ceremony. But with Changing Woman's power also comes her burden of responsibility.[74] At Changing Woman's own *Kinaaldá*, which became the pattern for all future Navajo girls' puberty ceremonies, it was said that she would "now be made holy [so that] in the future, life can be regulated by her. . . ."[75] Because Changing Woman and Mother Earth are one and the same, it is understood that, like seasons, women undergo periods of dormancy as well as fecundity. Through this rite, therefore, the initiate gains the sacred right and responsibility of regulating her reproduction, just as the Earth regulates her own. Men who live in proper relationship to women rec-ognize this authority. They understand that the power to give, withhold, and take away life—especially evident during menstruation and childbirth—can weaken their own spiritual power and that of their sacred objects if they come too close. Beyond the social structure of gender segregation, then, divine in-junction prohibits interference with the sacred duties of each gender and each individual.

It is not surprising, therefore, that Native women regard a woman's re-productive freedom as "taking care of herself" or as maintaining "control" over her body. According to the Native Women for Reproductive Rights Coalition,

> Within traditional societies and languages, there is no word that
> equals abortion. The word itself is very harsh and impersonal. When
> speaking to traditional elders knowledgeable about reproductive
> health matters, repeatedly they would refer to a woman knowing

which herbs and methods to use "to make her period come." This
was seen as a woman taking care of herself and doing what was
necessary.[76]

As the embodiment of the female sacred power, she must exercise reproductive
care and do what is necessary to maintain right relationship with the (super)natural world. Even the sacredness of children cannot deter her from this
obligation. The Lakota, for example, regard children as *wakanyeja*, literally,
"sacred beings."[77] Although Lakota women acknowledge that children are sacred, this belief does not serve as a justification for surrendering her reproductive autonomy. As one Native woman expressed it, " 'Our children are very,
very sacred and they are treated in a sacred manner. But that does not mean,
at the same time, we can continue to give up control of our bodies to government and organized religions."[78] So strong is this tradition that American laws
and religious institutions cannot force her to acquiesce. So powerful is the
belief in her reproductive authority that another tenet of her tradition—the
sacrality of children—cannot compel her to sacrifice what is divinely hers.
Maintaining and reestablishing balance between Native women and men
therefore has great potential for restoring order in the face of reproductive
chaos.

It would seem to make sense, now, to turn to the relationship between
humans and the (super)natural world. The outline of the argument earlier
["living in proper relationship with oneself and others and living in balance
with the (super)natural world"] as well as the Western belief in the "closeness"
of Native people to "nature" would seem to call for this elucidation. Certainly,
much has been made of the extensive means indigenous people employ to live
in balance with the (super)natural world. Those interested in the environment,
for instance, often turn to Native philosophies of the land. In many ways it is
appropriate for them and others to do so, for land is at the heart of indigenous
traditions. In this case, however, it would be a misstep, as the conclusion of
this chapter is about to show.

In my discussion of the relationship with oneself and with others, I have
been addressing this very subject of living in balance with the (super)natural
world. To miss this point is to overlook perhaps the most important lesson—
we *are* the sacred Earth. The girls' puberty ceremony tells us that humanity
can share the indwelling spirit of the Earth. No discussion of the importance
of not overhunting or overfarming can convey this message as powerfully. By
living in proper relationship with others—maintaining the sacred ties that keep
the genders separate and the keep the people whole—humanity belongs to the
beloved (super)natural world. Discussions of the details of reciprocity and sac-

rifice only hint at this understanding. But while these ideas are profoundly beautiful and important, the Earth suffers. We suffer. The Sun Dance of the Lakotas, the Green Corn of the Cherokees, the World Renewal of the Yurok each recognizes that the Earth and her people cycle through the seasons of chaos and harmony; these ceremonies exist to balance these powerful forces. But Native leaders and healers across the continent and Native prophecies throughout the centuries warn about living in chaos for too long. In the words of Mohawk midwife Katsi Cook,

> We're waging our struggle in this time when all the signs that were prophesied about the earth—that very young women, very old women will begin conceiving and having babies and the trees will begin to die—all of these things are being told in our community still and we see it happening.[79]

These prophecies should not be mistaken for visions of doom, however. They do not predict the inevitable, but identify the possible. It is possible, still, to renew the world. Importantly, the *Kinaaldá* does precisely this. As a form of the Navajo Blessingway, the girls' puberty rite creates the world anew with each ceremony. Through the power of thought and speech, Navajo singers remake the world in all its beauty and power. In so doing, both a woman is born and the Earth, reborn. Simultaneously. Finally, it is possible for us to understand that assuming reproductive power in a balanced and sacred way goes hand-in-hand with renewing and enlivening the world. From this perspective, reproductive health and planetary health are one and the same.

Sadly, reproductive wrongs threaten the viability of these ceremonies. For instance, lack of access to public lands—an issue of freedom of religion—has prevented the Mescalero Apache from gathering the sacred plants and other materials necessary for the girls' puberty ceremony.[80] Nevertheless, the Mescalero and other Native nations persevere for the right to religious freedom and, consequently, the right to reproductive freedom. All inhabitants are called to this same struggle. Regardless of our particular traditions, each of us is the Earth. Her future and the future of the next seven generations depends on answering her call to harmony.

NOTES

For this chapter's title, I owe credit to Betsy Hartmann, whose book title *Reproductive Rights and Wrongs: The Global Politics of Population Control* (Boston: South End Press, 1995) was the inspiration for my own. I would also like to thank Michelene

Pesantubbee, Susan Harding, and Marcia Westkott for their support and advice on this project. My gratitude goes to the University of Colorado at Boulder as well for its financial support of my work on Native American women and religious traditions.

The epigraph is from the following: Haudenosaunee Delegation to the United Nations Non-Governmental Organization Conference on Discrimination Against the Indigenous Populations of the Americas, *A Basic Call to Consciousness*, ed. Akwesasne Notes, rev. ed. (Summertown, Tenn.: Book Publishing, 1981), 71.

1. Tessa Lehto, "Ishna Ti Awica Dowan Ceremony Revived," *Indian Country Today*, 3 Aug. 1998, sec. B, p. 5. *Ethnic Newswatch*. CD-Rom. Softline Information, 1999.

2. Francis Paul Prucha, "Courts of Indian Offenses," in *Documents of United States Indian Policy*, 2d ed. expanded (Lincoln: University of Nebraska Press, 1990), 160–62.

3. Francis Paul Prucha, "American Indian Religious Freedom," in *Documents of United States Indian Policy*, 2d ed. expanded (Lincoln: University of Nebraska Press, 1990), 288–89. Despite the passage of this act, Native religious freedom remains circumscribed. As a general policy statement, the act had no provision for enforcement and has had limited impact on litigation involving religious freedom.

4. Beatrice Medicine, "Indian Women and the Renaissance of Traditional Religion," in *Sioux Indian Religion: Tradition and Innovation*, ed. Raymond J. DeMallie and Douglas R. Parks (Norman: University of Oklahoma Press, 1987), 169.

5. James Mooney, "Myths of the Cherokee," in *Nineteenth Annual Report of the Bureau of American Ethnology*, 1897–98, Part 1 (Washington, D.C.: GPO, 1900; reprint, "Myths of the Cherokee," in *Myths of the Cherokee and Sacred Formulas of the Cherokees*, Nashville: Charles and Randy Elder, 1982), 250 (page references are to reprint edition).

6. Washington Matthews, *Navajo Legends* (Boston: Houghton, Mifflin, 1897; reprint, Salt Lake City: University of Utah Press, 1994), 77 (page references are to reprint edition).

7. Russell Thornton, *American Indian Holocaust and Survival: A Population History Since 1492*, Civilization of the American Indian Series (Norman: University of Oklahoma Press, 1987), 42.

8. David E. Stannard, *American Holocaust: Columbus and the Conquest of the New World* (New York: Oxford University Press, 1992), x.

9. Ward Churchill proposes a useful way of thinking about genocide in *A Little Matter of Genocide: Holocaust and Denial in the Americas, 1492 to the Present* (San Francisco: City Lights, 1997). While genocide is often synonymous with killing, Churchill argues that genocide, broadly speaking, is "a denial of the right of existence of entire human groups," which may or may not involve killing (431). He identifies three forms of genocide: physical, cultural, and biological. Physical genocide entails the killing of members of the targeted people. Cultural genocide includes the destruction of a people's means of survival; prohibition of language use and religious, social, and political practices; and forced dispersal of the population. Biological genocide involves the direct or indirect prevention of births among a people (432–33). Reproductive

genocide, as I have formulated it, most closely resembles Churchill's biological genocide, but, as examples will show, it includes physical and cultural forms of genocide as well.

10. Stannard, *American Holocaust*, 118–19.

11. Antonia I. Castañeda, "Sexual Violence in the Politics and Policies of Conquest: Amerindian Women and the Spanish Conquest of Alta California," in *Building with Our Hands: New Directions in Chicana Studies*, ed. Adela de la Torre and Beatríz M. Pesquera (Berkeley: University of California Press, 1993), 29.

12. Edward D. Castillo, "Gender Status Decline, Resistance, and Accommodation Among Female Neophytes in the Missions of California: A San Gabriel Case Study," *American Indian Culture and Research Journal* 18, no. 1 (1994): 70–71; Castaneda, "Sexual Violence," 15–17.

13. Albert L. Hurtado, "Sexuality in California's Franciscan Missions: Cultural Perceptions and Sad Realities," *California History* 71, no. 3 (fall 1992): 384.

14. Stannard, *American Holocaust*, 129–34.

15. Ibid., 132–33.

16. Andy [Andrea] Smith, "Christian Conquest and the Sexual Colonization of Native Women," in *Violence Against Women and Children: A Christian Theological Sourcebook*, ed. Carol J. Adams and Marie M. Fortune (New York: Continuum, 1995), 377–403.

17. Paula Gunn Allen, *The Sacred Hoop: Recovering the Feminine in American Indian Traditions* (Boston: Beacon Press, 1986), 41.

18. Francis Paul Prucha, "Indian Child Welfare Act," in *Documents of United States Indian Policy*, 2d ed. expanded (Lincoln: University of Nebraska Press, 1990), 293–95.

19. Brint Dillingham, "Indian Women and IHS Sterilization Practices," *American Indian Journal* 3, no. 1 (Jan. 1977): 27–28; Brint Dillingham, "Sterilization of Native Americans," *American Indian Journal* 3, no. 7 (July 1977): 16–19; Charles R. England, "A Look at the Indian Health Service Policy of Sterilization, 1972–76," *Red Ink* 3 (spring 1994): 17–21.

20. Women of All Red Nations, *W.A.R.N.* (Porcupine, S.D.: We Will Remember Group, 1978), 14.

21. "Oklahoma: Sterilization of Native Women Charged to I.H.S.," *Akwesasne Notes*, 31 Jan. 1989, p. 11. *Ethnic Newswatch*. CD-Rom. Softline Information, 1999.

22. Charon Asetoyer, "Population Controls: What's in Store for Indigenous Peoples," *Indigenous Woman* 2, no. 4 (1997): 10–12.

23. Lin Krust and Charon Asetoyer, *A Study of the Use of Depo-Provera and Norplant by the Indian Health Services*, Rev. ed. (Lake Andes, S.D.: Native American Women's Health Education Resource Center, 1993), 3, 7, 9, 14–21.

24. Winona LaDuke, "Akwesasne: Mohawk Mothers' Milk and PCBs," in *All Our Relations: Native Struggles for Land and Life* (Cambridge, Mass.: South End Press, 1999), 18–19.

25. Katsi Cook, "Breastmilk, PCB's, and Motherhood: An Interview with Katsi Cook, Mohawk," *Indigenous Woman* 1, no. 2 (1991): 2.

26. Asoka Bandarage, *Women, Population, and Global Crisis: A Political-Economic Analysis* (London: Zed Books, 1997), 30.

27. Hartmann, *Reproductive Rights and Wrongs*, 14. I, myself, have even seen an automobile bumper sticker with the slogan, "Malthus was right."

28. The approaches of Black Feminist Thought, Critical Race Feminism, and Global Critical Race Feminism require that we treat the oppressions of race, gender, class, sexuality, and nation simultaneously, understanding the ways in which they reinforce and mediate not only each other but also the structures of domination within individual nations and in the transnational context. See Patricia Hill Collins, *Black Feminist Thought: Knowledge, Consciousness, and the Politics of Empowerment*, 2d ed. (New York: Routledge, 2000); Adrien Katherine Wing, ed., *Critical Race Feminism: A Reader* (New York: New York University Press, 1997); and Adrien Katherine Wing, ed., *Global Critical Race Feminism: An International Reader* (New York: New York University Press, 2000).

29. Hartmann, *Reproductive Rights and Wrongs*, xx.

30. As a mixed-blood Cherokee academic, I hope to shed light on Native experiences, perspectives, and religious traditions; I am not, however, empowered to speak for American Indians. While I rely extensively on sources by Native people, the conclusions that I reach are based on my own interpretation and analysis.

31. Allen, *Sacred Hoop*, 156.

32. John (Fire) Lame Deer and Richard Erdoes, *Lame Deer: Seeker of Visions* (Pocket Books, 1976), 143.

33. Nancy Shoemaker, *American Indian Population Recovery in the Twentieth Century* (Albuquerque: University of New Mexico Press, 1999), 12.

34. Thornton, *American Indian Holocaust and Survival*, 236. Gary D. Sandefur and Carolyn A. Liebler report increases over time in the percentages of young American Indian women who have never married or who have become divorced. While the authors do not speculate on the ramifications of these trends, one wonders if these circumstances may lead to limited population growth. Gary D. Sandefur and Carolyn A. Liebler, "The Demography of American Indian Families," *Population Research and Policy Review* 16 (1997): 95.

35. Thornton, *American Indian Holocaust and Survival*, 239.

36. While *supernatural* suggests a state of being above or beyond the natural world, I employ *(super)natural* to suggest the simultaneous immanence of the sacred in the natural world and in nonmaterial reality.

37. Michael Casey, "Having a Baby: Teen Parents Struggle Against Dysfunctional Families and Economic Barriers," *The Circle*, May 1992, p. 5. *Ethnic Newswatch*. CD-Rom. Softline Information, 1999.

38. Ibid.

39. Janet W. Kenney, et al. "Ethnic Differences in Childhood and Adolescent Sexual Abuse and Teenage Pregnancy," *Journal of Adolescent Health* 21, no. 1 (1997): 7.

40. Lillian Tom-Orme, "Native American Women's Health Concerns: Toward Restoration of Harmony," in *Health Issues for Women of Color: A Cultural Diversity Perspective*, ed. Diane L. Adams (Thousand Oaks, Calif: Sage, 1995), 37.

41. "Preventive Health Care Services; Birth Outcomes: Infant Mortality," *Women of Color Health Data Book*, National Women's Health Information Center, 25 May 2000 <http://www.4women.gov/owh/pub/woc/toc.htm>.

42. Native American Women's Health Education Resource Center, *Dakota Roundtable II: A Report on the Status of Native American Women in the Aberdeen Area* (Lake Andes, S.D.: Native American Women's Health Education Resource Center, 1994), Pt. 6, Accession no. 01016519. *Contemporary Women's Issues*. Online. First-Search. 7 May 1998.

43. "Preventive Health Care Services; Prenatal Care," *Women of Color Health Data Book*, National Women's Health Information Center, 25 May 2000 <http://www.4women.gov/owh/pub/woc/toc.htm>; Tom-Orme, "Native American Women's Health Concerns," 37–38; David Rooks, "Surgeon General Reports Higher Tobacco Usage Among Indians," *Indian Country Today*, 18 May 1998, sec. A, p. 1. *Ethnic Newswatch*. CD-Rom. Softline Information, 1999; Jennifer Peterka, "Sugar Levels May Affect Fetal Health," *Indian Country Today*, 7 December 1998, sec. A, p. 7. *Ethnic Newswatch*. CD-Rom. Softline Information, 1999.

44. Vine Deloria Jr., "Out of Chaos," in *I Become Part of It: Sacred Dimensions in Native American Life*, ed. D. M. Dooling and Paul Jordan-Smith (New York: Parabola Books, 1989), 268.

45. Joseph Epes Brown, "Becoming Part of It," in *I Become Part of It: Sacred Dimensions in Native American Life*, ed. D. M. Dooling and Paul Jordan-Smith (New York: Parabola Books, 1989), 10.

46. "Native Women's Reproductive Rights Agenda," *Indigenous Women's Reproductive Rights and Pro-Choice Page*, Home page, Native Women for Reproductive Rights Coalition, 10 Oct. 1999 <www.nativeshop.org/pro-choice.html>; Native Women for Reproductive Rights Coalition, "For Native Women Reproductive Rights Mean . . . ," in *Women's Health: Reading on Social, Economic, and Political Issues*, 3d ed., ed. Nancy Worcester and Mariamne H. Whatley (Dubuque, Iowa: Kendall/Hunt, 2000), 386. See also Donna Haukaas, "Empowerment Through Dialogue: Native American Women Hold Historic Meeting," in Worcester and Whatley, *Women's Health*, 384–85.

47. The idea of an ethic based on harmonious relations has been proposed by Cherokee scholar Robert K. Thomas in his unpublished manuscript "Cherokee Values and World View" (Cross-Cultural Laboratory, University of North Carolina, 1958). The ethic Thomas describes has become known in the literature as the Cherokee "Harmony Ethic" (see John D. Loftin, "The 'Harmony Ethic' of the Conservative Eastern Cherokees: A Religious Interpretation," *Journal of Cherokee Studies* 8, no. 1 (spring 1983): 40–45. An indigenous harmony ethic, however, is not based on the values of any particular Native nation, but reflects a philosophy and practice that can be found in many indigenous traditions.

48. Carole Anne Heart Looking Horse, "Our Cathedral Is the Black Hills," in *Messengers of the Wind: Native American Women Tell Their Life Stories*, ed. Jane Katz (New York: Ballantine, 1995), 294.

49. Delfina Cuero, *Delfina Cuero: Her Autobiography: An Account of Her Last*

Years and Her Ethnobotanic Contributions, ed. Florence Connolly Shipek (Menlo Park, Calif.: Ballena Press, 1991), 42–43.

50. Inés Talamantez, "Images of the Feminine in Apache Religious Tradition," in *After Patriarchy: Feminist Transformations of the World Religions*," ed. Paula M. Cooey, William R. Eakin, and Jay B. McDaniel (Maryknoll, N.Y.: Orbis Books, 1991), 143; Bruce Lincoln, *Emerging from the Chrysalis: Studies in Rituals of Women's Initiation* (Cambridge, Mass.: Harvard University Press, 1981), 25. For a detailed description of the Navajo girls' puberty ceremony, see Charlotte Johnson Frisbie, *Kinaaldá: A Study of the Navaho Girl's Puberty Ceremony* (Middletown, Conn.: Wesleyan University Press, 1967; reprint, Salt Lake City: University of Utah Press, 1993).

51. Cuero, *Delfina Cuero*, 41–42.

52. Beverly Hungry Wolf, *Daughters of the Buffalo Women: Maintaining the Tribal Faith* (n.p.: Canadian Caboose Press, 1996), 43.

53. Lame Deer and Erdoes, *Lame Deer*, 129.

54. Marla N. Powers, *Oglala Women: Myth, Ritual, and Reality* (Chicago: University of Chicago Press, 1986), 73.

55. Debra Lynn White Plume, "The Work of Sina Wakan Win Okolakiciye—Sacred Shawl Women's Society," in *Cante Ohitika Win (Brave-Hearted Women): Images of Lakota Women from the Pine Ridge Reservation, South Dakota*, ed. Carolyn Reyer (Vermillion: University of South Dakota Press, 1991), 69.

56. Beatrice Medicine, "Indian Women: Tribal Identity as Status Quo," in *Woman's Nature: Rationalizations of Inequality*, ed. Marian Lowe and Ruth Hubbard (New York: Pergamon Press, 1983), 68.

57. White Plume, "The Work of Sina Wakan Win Okolakiciye," 69.

58. Ingrid Washinawatok, "Our Responsibility," in *Indigenous Women Address the World: Our Future—Our Responsibility*, ed. North American Indigenous Women's Working Group (Rapid City, S.D.: Indigenous Women's Network, 1999), 20.

59. Ruth M. Underhill, *Papago Woman* (Prospect Heights, Ill.: Waveland Press, 1979), 92.

60. Ruby Modesto and Guy Mount, *Not for Innocent Ears: Spiritual Traditions of a Desert Cahuilla Medicine Woman* (Arcata, Calif.: Sweetlight Books, 1980), 42.

61. Native American Women's Health Education Resource Center, *Dakota Roundtable II: A Report on the Status of Native American Women in the Aberdeen Area* (Lake Andes, S.D.: Native American Women's Health Education Resource Center, 1994), Pt. 4, Accession no. 01016506. *Contemporary Women's Issues*. Online. First-Search. 7 May 1998.

62. Ibid.

63. Lame Deer and Erdoes, *Lame Deer*, 240–41.

64. Ibid., 241.

65. Gladys A. Reichard, *Navaho Religion: A Study of Symbolism* (New York: Bollingen Foundation, 1950; reprint, Princeton: Princeton University Press, 1974), 31 (page references are to reprint edition).

66. Ibid.

67. Bernard Haile, *Love-Magic and Butterfly People: The Slim Curley Version of the*

Ajilee and Mothway Myths. American Tribal Religions Series (Flagstaff, Ariz.: Museum of Northern Arizona Press, 1978), 157; Clyde Kluckhohn, *Navajo Witchcraft* (Boston: Beacon Press, 1967), 36–42.

68. M. Inez Hilger, "Chippewa Child Life and Its Cultural Background," in *Bureau of American Ethnology Bulletin 146* (Washington, D.C.: GPO, 1951), 3–4.

69. E. Adamson Hoebel, *The Cheyennes: Indians of the Great Plains,* 2d ed. Case Studies in Cultural Anthropology (Fort Worth, Tex.: Harcourt Brace Jovanovich, 1988), 84.

70. "First Women of Color Poll on Reproductive Health," *Sun Reporter,* 18 September 1991, p. 3. *Ethnic Newswatch.* CD-Rom. Softline Information, 1999.

71. Bonnie London, "Group Fights for Women's Rights," *Indian Country Today,* 28 January 1993, sec. A, p. 7. *Ethnic Newswatch.* CD-Rom. Softline Information, 1999.

72. *Indigenous Women's Reproductive Rights and Pro-Choice Page,* Home page, Native Women for Reproductive Rights Coalition, 10 Oct. 1999 <www.nativeshop.org/pro-choice.html>.

73. Reichard, *Navaho Religion,* 407 (brackets in original).

74. Lincoln, *Emerging from the Chrysalis,* 28.

75. Leland C. Wyman, *Blessingway,* recorded and translated by Bernard Haile (Tucson: University of Arizona Press, 1970), 197 (brackets in original).

76. *Indigenous Women's Reproductive Rights and Pro-Choice Page,* <www.nativeshop.org/pro-choice.html>.

77. Looking Horse, "Our Cathedral Is the Black Hills," 286.

78. London, "Group Fights for Women's Rights."

79. Katsi Cook, et al., "Seeking the Balance: A Native Women's Dialogue," *Akwe:kon Journal* 2 (summer 1993): 18.

80. David L. Carmichael, "Places of Power: Mescalero Apache Sacred Sites and Sensitive Areas," in *Sacred Sites, Sacred Places,* ed. David L. Carmichael, et al. London: Routledge, 1994), 94–96.

9

Heavenly Way and Humanly Doings

A Consideration of Chinese Man's Body Management During the Late Imperial Period

PING-CHEN HSIUNG

The Duty of a Man

There is a marked tendency in both contemporary scholastic and popular culture to present males as the irresponsible and irrepressible sexual actor. Such commonly held modern notions assume that men are always and by nature negligent of the possibilities of conception in heterosexual sex. In this imagery men, riven by endless carnal desires, are the naturally wild party always ready to indulge and hardly capable of constraint. Modern statistics documenting the difficulties in receiving male cooperation in the promotion of family planning and contraceptive methods seem to reinforce the general impression that men are far less interested in limiting the number of children or restraining their sexual conduct. Thus, many research projects operate on these preconceptions and their studies are tilted to yield supportive data. Women are taken to be the only parties interested in controlling reproduction. This chapter intends to show contrasting convictions and practices of male reproductive behavior in imperial China that will fend off over-generalization based on the modern thesis about men's sexual irresponsibility.

From the very beginning, it was clear that multipurpose functions assigned to male sexual conduct in the traditional Chinese context (for self-cultivation, physical immortality, and good breeding) made for a much more complex picture of the male sexual ethos. Such comparisons are useful since they break the stranglehold of false blueprints that get absolutized into caricature. First of all, in terms of agency, men in imperial China were given the greatest duty in observing and controlling their carnal activities because in concept and in practice they were perceived as the active party playing a leading and decisive role in sex-related matters. Thus, answering all the questions of how (the frequency and techniques), which (to whom), when (the timing), whether (temporary or permanent abstinence), and what (the specific goal of each and every act) remained a male-centered obligation. From this perspective, the appearance of Taoist manuals that call for the cultivation of sexual practices based on gender equity are noteworthy. They relate sexuality to both physical and spiritual cultivation. Often these manuals were misunderstood as exotic literature advocating free indulgence in romantic passions and purely lustful sexual consumption.

Actually, the inner logic of the traditional advice on male sexuality asked men to try to be temperate, selective, and watchful in their coital engagements. (They are to choose the right match, the right time, the right occasion, and adopt the best mental attitude as well as superb physical skills. All of this points to anything but promiscuous and thoughtless behavior.) This advice was braced by promises of beneficent results: good health, good spirit, and successful production of bright and filial (loyal and respectful) sons. Individual men, because of their particular philosophical, religious, and social beliefs, might have favored one of these promised values over the others. For example, one man may elect to pursue personal happiness in the Taoist style or religious salvation in the Buddhist sense, thus giving up on the Confucian social obligation to reproduce, which put less stress on issues of personal salvation. None of this plays out in a uniform pattern, because in Chinese society in the past as today, there were as there are competing philosophical, religious, economic, and social-ethical forces at work that allow for a fierce interaction and interplay of competitive and conflicting views. Sexual mores are never simple.

What was much debated was whether the duty of a man was first toward his own spiritual salvation and physical preservation or toward his ancestral clan and family procreation. Thus it is that we see a rich variety in all the various methods and recipes teaching the secrets and offering magical aids toward advancing one aim or the other or all of them. What is clear is that imperial Chinese men were not let off the hook regarding sexual and reproductive behavior. All the burdens were not to be put on the women as though reproduction were their business since they were the ones who got pregnant. There is always a tendency to put the burden of contraceptive usage on women since it is easier to manipulate or control the female reproductive organ or function. There were practices and medical-pharmaceutical devices that focused on the male mechanisms in reproductive processes, since male responsibility is both possible and reasonable.

The Emphasis on Increasing Offspring

Given the conditions in premodern times, traditional Chinese interest in procreation should not be a surprise. Ancestor worship and the Confucian value of family only work to enhance instinctive concerns for biosocial succession. China's technical knowledge, together with its social ethics and cultural institutions, had long been there to facilitate this need to produce. The existence of a branch of Chinese medicine called the specialty on "spreading (or increasing) one's offspring (*kuang-ss'u*)" represented one such instance. In this form of medicine, medical and behavioral advice and practical recipes to create or enhance the chances of conception and successful gestation were meticulously laid out for interested men and women. The female section of this discipline converged with other discussions on the female body to constitute traditional Chinese "gynecology (*fu-k'o*)" as we know it. The male part of this *kuang-ss'u* tradition, interestingly enough, also came into a separate practice, at times called the "medicine for men (*nan-k'o*)," or "andronology" if we will. As the only known medical specialty attentive to the bodily conditions and reproductive problems of the male population, this traditional Chinese medicine for men provides a vital glimpse into the physical culture of men and male reproductive habits, as well as the medical knowledge and technical assistance in the related area. The picture obtained from such materials suggest that the need to produce children and the interest in increasing offspring, though of predominant concern, represented nonetheless a conditional value coached and modified by numerous other factors. The conventional reference to the Chinese preference for "many sons (or children) and numerous grandsons (grandchildren) (*tuo-tzu tuo-sun*)" is but a simplified rhetoric awaiting further elucidation.

At a time when infant and child mortality was high, when artificial insemination was yet unknown, and when social interest in family reproduction was strong, the emergence of a literature and a practice to facilitate people's need in successful breeding needs especially close consideration. Alongside this pronatalist concern, there was also a counter literature that studied how to lessen the chances of impregnation.[1] What was intriguing in this textual and vocational tradition was that, due to a complicated combination of religious eclecticism, philosophical evolution, and medical-technological developments, there developed a stress on having less but more intense sex, sex that was more intensely planned and more thoughtfully acted out. A philosophy developed that taught that refraining from carnal activities promoted the elevation and tranquility of the human spirit. Physically, thriftiness in coital intercourse and more sparing seminal emission promised a strong faculty and improved "male essence." This meant, in a way, saving up for the rightful moment. Ancient Taoist recommendation for "less (frequent) engagement" so as to preserve the spirit and energy, as well as the precious fluid, for the vital occasion was a leitmotif reworked and played out in many late imperial "life-nurturing" texts. The Neo-Confucian emphasis on "reducing the human desires for the pres- ervation of heavenly principles" helped to provide additional intellectual backup, cautioning people to carefully moderate their propensity for material gains and physical indulgence. The inherent Buddhist misgivings toward food and sex taught people that carnal needs and greediness toward beauty were among the gravest of worldly traps and human sins. People were encouraged to labor toward a state where sex represented the ultimate emptiness promised in the final enlightenment. With these various cultural accents in place, it is easy to see the makeup of the sex culture in the later centuries of the Chinese Empire. It stressed the art of lessened but focused sex.

Any man interested in self-cultivation, longevity, or fine breeding was ad- vised to take his chamber activities seriously and cautiously. And for their practical consumption, Taoist authors freely quoted Neo-Confucian teachings that urged all to try "keeping a clean heart and refraining from many desires." They developed pharmaceutical recipes and offered technical tricks based on the idea that the art of the bedchamber required saving up rather than letting go of masculine fluids. This was the treasured secret. Buddhist advocacy in puritanical celibacy can, thus, be melded with the Taoist preference for coitus interruptus to make a case for scarce but potent and more satisfying sex. All of this was an aid to the Confucian value of ethical and aesthetic self-cultivation and also fulfilled one's social duty to successfully breed. For the fulfillment of any or all of the above, the very rare yet well-executed "high sex" seemed a perfect answer. Mid-sixteenth-century manuals such as *The Secret Disclosure in Planting the Seeds* and *The Compendium on Life Management*, both authored by the Taoist convert Hung Chi, claimed to supply the arts and acts of high sex.[2] As China's literacy increased for both men and women (more in wealthy urban centers but also in rural ordinances), there was a booming publishing industry serviced by the prospering domestic commerce and enlivening popular culture. This literature presented a complicated and contrived yet dynamic envisioning of sexuality.

When we look at the nuanced details of this *Kuang-tzu* literature, moreover, it becomes clear that although ostensibly concerned with man's duty to widen the branches and spread out their seeds, these medical-philosophical texts were not solely devoted to the "art of the bedchamber." Nor was successful reproduction their sole purpose. In fact, along their line of argument, the literature addresses a host of considerations and assorted conditions. Every act and the art of sex itself were studied in great specificity. For example, they took into account one's ethical state, the level of one's personal cultivation, and one's inherited social record (whether positive or negative). They also looked to the particular spiritual-ecological-physical environment where the copulation was to take place. All of these were seen as key influences on truly successful sex.

What was involved here was the likelihood of success for enjoyable coital intercourse or successful conception leading to healthy, bright, high-achieving, and long-living offspring. All these felicitous results could depend on having not "more" but "less" sex.

The Taoist Reverence for Nature and the Humanly Effort to Enhance It

There is, moreover, a distinct appreciation for Nature manifested in ancient Chinese cosmology. Taoist philosophy and Taoist popular religion later on inherited and built on the essence of this spirit, and other schools of thought such as Confucianism or even Legalism showed their interest also in certain values in this common heritage. Out of this deep respect for the forces of nature, concepts such as life, heaven, and genuineness were fundamentals that function as core manifestations in this cultural discourse. Within this system a frank recognition of human bodily needs (such as food and sex) became important corollaries to the main belief in naturalness. To enable a natural continuation and a healthy abundance of life, principles and activities related to sex and procreation can, therefore, appear to be of graver concern than philosophical explanations pertaining to the origins of creation. Humans need to investigate carefully and learn gradually, in idea and practice, sensible ways to manage their bodies as first lessons toward a way of good living. Sex was not separated from a holistic sense of human well-being.

An intriguing characteristic of this long-held belief in the works of nature, however, is a parallel notion that human beings somehow, as important participants in the universe, can and should in fact "nurture" and "enhance" Heaven's doing by their own proper actions. Whether termed "life nurturing (*yang-sheng*)," "life elongating (*chang-sheng*)," "life caring (*she-sheng*)," or some other similar name, this millennia-old tradition pointed at a conviction that the life-bearing and life-creating force was at the heart of the order of nature, and as dutiful members of that cosmos humans should make it their duty to be as friendly to and protective of their own bodies and all other procreational elements as best they could. They should certainly feed themselves well, sleep well, and try their best to breed successfully. If necessary, these should and could be helped along by external measures: breathing, exercise, special diet, even medicine. It is also obvious that, under this scheme, sex and procreation are looked upon in a positive light. Both are the most natural among the natural forces. The pleasure in sex was also to be affirmed, since from very early on, it was observed that happiness in coital activities was essential to the health of the parties involved, as well as to the good success of intended reproduction.

Ancient Chinese textual and pictorial evidence, showing early beliefs and practices concerning sex, reproduction as well as religion and health, pointed to a world whereby human control and self-management in such affairs were possible and commendable. And far from a passive or careless party in sexual and reproductive activities, the male was to take active interest and bear key responsibility for the successful handling of the engagement. The manuals, providing specific recipes as well as other technological devices to help people reproduce satisfactorily and wisely, embodied the fundamental kernels of this tradition. This human intervention in and technical manipulation of people's sex life or reproductive experience not only were acceptable and legitimate but also were seen as positive, necessary, and exciting. Sex was not seen puritanically as opposed to, or a departure or deviation from, the paths of nature, but as the enhancing, facilitating, and indispensable human activity that would sharpen, deepen, and in the end drive home and make clear the true meaning of a "heavenly" intention.

This intense interest in life inherent to Taoism, whether in its preservation or in its elongation, is well known. And this strong concern for the preservation and elongation of life constituted a core value for both philosophical Taoism and for the Taoist popular religion. In practical terms, especially among the educated and the upper class, it nurtured a lifestyle in favor of self-preservation of the physique, while for the larger masses it bred activities and ceremonies geared toward extending a healthy life.

The cult of longevity and immortality, when translated into demographical behaviors, helped to formulate an attitude toward carnal activities that was positive and yet modest. The positive value placed upon sex hygiene in connection with a Taoist search for health enhancement and eternal existence produced a pervasive belief in life-nurturing (*yang-sheng*) in historical and contemporary Chinese people and was always closely associated with people's practice in the bedchamber (*fang-chung*). The strong concern for longevity and the Taoist inclination toward material sparsity and spiritual thriftiness (or conservation) continued to be at the core of the cultural framework, and this seeped into Chinese medicine. Chinese culture once dwelled upon the value for a man of "taking in numerous virgins (*tuo-yü t'ung-nü*)," and it encouraged techniques for "absorbing the female essence to complement the male element (*ts'ai-yin pu-yang*)." The expansive cultural taste of the T'ang empire (618–907) provided a fertile ground whereby such an indulgent and male-centered sex culture reportedly prevailed, especially among the aristocracy, and this spread the reputation of a liberating and licentious Chinese attitude toward sex and sexuality (especially in comparison with the rigorous Christian mores) that European liberals like R. H. Van Gilik envied.[3]

A certain embedded suspicion against overindulgence and unconditional merrymaking (*chung-yü, k'uang-huan*), along with the emphasis on a healthy respect for physical satisfaction (*chung-yü*), came together in Chinese thought. The Sung (960–1279) Neo-Confucian philosophy that combined Buddhist contemplation and Taoist cultivation in a Confucian revivalism contributed much in bringing out this appreciation for prudence in a resurgent preference for modesty (*shen-yü*) and restraint (*chieh-yü*) in China's sex culture for the later imperial period. In the wake of this important intellectual turn and cultural movement in its eclecticism, a synthesis on classic Confucian value in biosocial reproduction was increasingly mixed with both the Buddhist wish to minimize human desires (*chüeh-yü*) so as to transcend the karma of endless suffering, and the Taoist emphasis on saving the essence in order to enhance physical well-being. This created a special blend of self-cultivation and careful handling of the human body.

In other words, at least from the tenth century onward, certainly after the twelfth century, this newly developed philosophical school of Neo-Confucianism had ushered in a heightened interest in meditation, self-control, and physical management among Chinese men, first as a vogue among the educated elite and later spreading out as a social trend and institutionalized ethics on the popular level. According to this Neo-Confucian brand of self-cultivation, an increasingly contemplative attitude toward life in general had materialized into a serious observation on one's daily conduct, and watchful inner eyes were kept to examine time and again the performative aspect of personal life. An almost combative distrust of "human (especially bodily) desires (*jen-yü*)" at the core of this cultural turn and social movement proved of grave consequence for the values and behaviors of the later era. Quietness and self-control gradually became the quintessential quality for commendable human character. Translated into tangible deeds, these could gradually trickle down to the minute handling of daily life and domestic management, as well as in the ritual activities and social mores.

Positive Sex and a Confirmation of Pleasure

Historically, therefore, how to reconcile the "positive" (or at least "no-fault") attitude Chinese culture held toward sex and sexuality with other puritanical trends becomes intriguing. The general character of this tradition must be appreciated from more than one angle. There was the Confucian affirmation of carnal desires and sexual consummation as constituting the most basic and "natural" of the human instincts and practical needs (functions). The Mencian observation that: "With (the activities of) drinking and eating, men and women, there exists the greater of human desires."[4] This expressed well the core value of such a "naturalist" and nonsuppressive stance toward sex, a philosophy the Taoists were only too happy to concur with. However, they would add their still stronger view in asserting the additional effect good sex may produce in maintaining and enhancing the physical and spiritual well-being of men and women to lengthen their earthly lives. When health-related concerns joined the picture, especially when medicine and the medical profession came increasingly into its own in the second millennium of the empire, it was often and emphatically said that "man cannot go without women, and women cannot go without men." The way sex was conducted could have a direct consequence on reproduction: i.e., on whether one was to beget any offspring, or whether a boy might be generated, and whether the child one received would live to maturity, or turn out to be smart and capable. Thus, philosophically, religiously, and healthwise, sex is important and should be considered in a positive manner. Whether one wants to act on the sexual expression of our nature, pursue longevity, and seek immortality, or simply to succeed in successful family procreation, sex is proper, and doing sex properly is key. Surely, then, there existed prejudice, pejoratives, and mystiques about sex, but the overall shadowing of a puritanical association of human sex with guilt, sin, or shame was never intrinsic to the Chinese picture.

Furthermore, since the contemplative, controllable, and positively manipulable and manipulative character (whether via behavioral, mechanical, or pharmaceutical means) of human sex was never a question, it opened up all sorts of possibilities for the development of coital methods and fecundity stratagems. In fact, only well-planned and carefully carried out sex could meet its many purposes and functions while satisfying the human desire in carnal pleasure. Sex also elevated people's spiritual virtue in the art of self-cultivation while at the same time enhanced their physical well-being in pursuit of immortality, and their earthly duty to breed.

To let sex have its full positive potential, the emotional and physical gratification of both the male and the female parties is essential, as the deficiency in either compromises the end effect in the four-in-one mission of spiritual elevation, health promotion, successful reproduction, and personal pleasure. The majority of this massive and long-existent literature on moral cultivation, physical exercise, and successful breeding was mostly authored by men and for the consumption of men, and, significantly, it contains many passages on the skills of pleasing a woman. However, passages preaching attitudes and techniques for self-gratification were even more prevalent. The irony that stood at the core of all this, nevertheless, was that for maximizing the pleasure, as well as for hitting the high mark of fertility, the less frequent sex was, the better.

Recipes for Planting the Seeds

In addition to proverbial wisdom, popular convictions, and ritual acts, social values and cultural forces favoring procreation in traditional China also brought about significant technical efforts to advance such goals. A key text, in the male branch (nan-k'o) of Chinese procreation medicine from early in the seventeenth century, illustrates for us in concrete terms the nature and composition of such a body of knowledge.

The Collection on Planting the Seeds: A Medical Aid from the Miao-I Studio, by Yüeh P'u-chia, from the Wu-ching district of Chiang-su province, stands out among its kind at the end of the Ming dynasty (1368–1644).[5] In addition to its openly pronatal proposition, naming the book after an explicit cause of fertility, "planting the seeds or sowing the offspring (chung-tzu)," it represents the best example of a separate medical concern for man parallel to gynecology. The text begins with a first section (shang-chüan) entitled nan-k'o (medicine or treatments for man) as a structured counterpart of the nü-ko (medicine or treatments for woman) that makes up the second half of the composition. As explained in his preface, the author's aim was to help those men and their wives with "difficulties in begetting an heir," or those who had lost hope of having any children (wu-tzu or chüeh-ss'u). His advice for men, roughly speaking, consisted of three aspects: the right attitude toward copulation, the techniques for fruitful intercourse, and specific recipes to facilitate a healthy and productive sex life.[6]

For the correct mindset toward copulation, he advocated such ideas as the importance of "maintaining the principle of humanity (ts'un-jen)," of nurturing kindness, of "achieving the magnificent pleasure for both women and men (liang-ch'ing ch'ang-mei)," and the restriction of both worldly desires and carnal activities, all of which were specific manifestations rooted in earlier traditions, as I explained. On technical details, he recommended such ideas as men looking for the right moment (women showing a desire to engage as if quite unsuppressible [yü chiao-chieh pu k'o jen chih chuang])," keeping to a simple lifestyle (avoid overexhaustion [chieh-lao], aggravation [nü], getting drunk [chieh-chueh], or overindulgence in taste [ch'en-wei]), and practicing special physical exercises to "cultivate the male essence (lien-hing)," and so forth.[7]

The pharmaceutics recipes Yüeh prescribed included those to enhance male potency and those aiming at "fruitful sex." In total he listed over five dozen concoctions (t'ang), recipes (fang), pills (wan), cakes (kau), prescriptions (tan), powder (ts'an), drink (chiu), and so on. All carried explicitly enticing names fitting for their purposes. They were described as wonderfully helpful methods (ch'i-fang, i-fang) with proven effects (ch'eng-hsiao chü-lüeh).[8] Many recipes were converted into rhymed verses for easy memory and transmission. Seemingly technical details were frequently referred to as principles (tao) to connect them with the spiritual implications behind techniques and to remind their users of the larger philosophical and cosmological systems and purposes involved.

Coming from a long tradition of Taoist notions concerning life nurturing (yang-sheng) and the Confucian concern for family reproduction, the special characteristics as well as the historical background of this late imperial literature on male medicine invites additional attention. A survey of emerging textual and material evidences indicated, first of all, that the suspected decline or subsiding of the yang-sheng culture, rooted in ancient Chinese religion and cosmology, was an unwarranted conclusion.[9] It is true that as a system of thought and practices this yang-sheng tradition was not without its own ebbs and flows. Yet many of the basic tenets in conviction and in technique remained intact from its earliest times until at least the seventeenth century. The two-sided effect of human sexuality, as a vehicle for both personal transcendence and contrarily for self-degradation, continued to stand at the core of the late imperial Chinese sex culture. Minute elements and technical details were stressed, including food and drug intake and self-management of the mind and body, as well as the vital importance of proper coital engagement. Furthermore, the mixture of the shamanistic Taoist origin of this sex culture with the medical-pharmaceutical practices, though amply manifested in the Sui-T'ang (581—907) "medical" texts, was a trait present at the very beginning.

These ancient origins remained even as these two branches evolved somewhat separately later in Chinese history. Thirdly, a proper evaluation of the Neo-Confucian stress on mental rectification and physical self-watchfulness and the art of "planting the seeds" is indeed crucial to a full appreciation of the historicity of this seemingly perennial Chinese preoccupation. Fourthly, on the other hand, the changing and dynamic character of China's medical and pharmaceutical practices guaranteed the addition of fresh ideas and new ingredients and prescriptions to facilitate old beliefs, revise conventional methods, or design entirely new possibilities.

Yüeh's text was not the only example of fertility medicine. Other medical authors provided similar manuals (e.g., Wan Chuan's *Important Principles for the Increase of Offspring* and Chang Chi-bin's (1563–1640) *Proposals for the Begetting of Fine Heirs*).[10] Indeed on the Ming (1368–1644) market of information, there was no lack of expert advice on the skills, art, or joy of spreading the seeds or increasing one's offspring. (Yü Mu-fu's *Important Words for Increasing the Offspring* provides another example.)[11] Nor were the contents of this particular compilation on "planting the seeds" entirely new. Many of Yüeh's suggestions may be traced to earlier precedents. But in revising or openly repudiating many familiar ideas and practices, the author also made a clear effort to reform China's heritage in this regard. The text attests to this attempt and accomplishment in absorbing, combining, assessing, and re-creating a medicine for men fitting to the thoughts and technological knowledge of his time. Yüeh's effort to focus on men in stressing the "enhanceability" of their fertility performance and in so doing to create the platform of *nan-k'o* makes *Chung-tzu Pien* stand out as a distinguished case in representing the late imperial Chinese culture of male reproduction.

A shared feature of the *kuang-ssu* literature appeared in the late imperial period (mostly during the Ming dynasty). It tended to combine the old *Yang-sheng* ("life-nurturing," now often termed *she-shang*, "life-managing") tradition with the new approach of heir begetting (*chiu-ssu*) then becoming increasingly in vogue. In mixing the two together, it stressed the pivotal value the former had toward the success of the latter. Whether in recaptioning the traditional concerns for the timing (called "heavenly moments," *tien-ssih*), the location (called the "earthy advantage," *ti-li*), or the preparation (called the "humanly affairs," *jen-ssih*) for the right kind of conjugal activities,[12] it tried to emphasize that no conflicts existed between an individual's search for personal cultivation and physical transcendence, on the one hand, and this same individual's family obligation to breed, on the other. Indeed, the paths to such distinct goals were identical, as effective copulation depended on saved-up, potent "male essence" that had been nurtured and intensified through carefully observed abstinence.

Contemporary elaboration on the various ways to "nurture the essence" (*ching* was the same word for semen) and "take the medicine, *fu-yao*," both vital methods toward successful self-cultivation and human breeding, celebrated their power in facilitating reticence and "desire control" as a positive means toward achieving a state whereby the quality (of sex and semen both) outweighs its quantity.[13] The clinical case records give full details of these procedures.[14] The pharmaceutical devices and the names of these recipes covered everything from "calming the spirit," to "securing the foundation," to "producing the essence."[15] The pills and medicaments that helped to lengthen one's life had in fact the exact same ingredients that were prescribed for "planting the seeds" so as to "carry on the line."[16]

Songs of Sleeping Alone

On a related though a different topic, traditional Chinese conviction on almost a "zero-sum" nature of the reserve of male essence (semen) and the progressive decline of human vitality through age combined to encourage men to exercise caution and constraint in their sexual life as they aged. The Taoist attitude toward self-control mixed perhaps with an element of the Buddhist negation on physical existence and material needs, when combined with Neo-Confucian beliefs, created a perfect environment for the increased cultivation of "sleeping alone (*tu-wo*)." Men, or the self-cultivating among them, as they approached 40, should try to retreat and sleep alone at night, so as not to confront the temptation of meeting with the desirable (*pu-chien k'o-yü*). Avoiding cohabitation may cut men entirely off from battling with carnal desires and save them the struggle with frustrated desire. From the Sung (960–1279) period onward, moreover, this also turned into a vogue in male aesthetics and a pursuit in personal morality. Therefore, as a rite of passage for middle-age men, this custom left behind an intriguing literary trail.

The famed poet from southern Sung Lu Yu (1125–1210) produced a verse describing his "Random Thoughts (*san-huai*)" after reaching his middle years.

> After mid-age I severed my desires and thought of them no longer.
> Now how much more difficult to contemplate (giving up) the meats
>   later on?
> What Heaven bestows upon me starts off thin,
> Only as I clear up all obstacles (against longevity) shall I gain my
>   small (slice of) peace.[17]

For those promoting the lifestyle, the supply of ancient wisdom or revealing anecdotes was never lacking. Mencius's reference to "being thrifty on human desires (*kua-yü*)" as the key to cultivating one's heart, or Lao Tzu's words on not seeing the enticing so as not to be disturbed had all been mobilized to add validity to this ideal. Stories continued to be circulated, or created, on the benefit of "sleeping alone." One famous story spoke of the Southern Sung (1127–1279) Prime Minister Chia Ss'u-tao's (1213–1275) encounter at court with his agile colleague Pao Hui (1182–1268). Seeing Pao getting up and down the stairs, and bowing and kneeling at this and that altar with little difficulty, Chia could not help but want to know the secret to Pao's long healthy life and agility. His special technique of maintenance and nourishment (*wei-yang chih shu*), Pao allegedly replied, had to do with a kind of special "pill" he took from an unspeakable source. Duly intrigued, Chia wanted the delightful recipe, at which point Pao smiled and disclosed his prescription: "What your humble servant myself has, in fact, been taking for fifty years is this pill of sleeping alone (*tu-shuei-wan*)"—a disclosure that brought roaring laughter from the audience.[18]

This secret medicine of *tu-shuei-wan* (sleep-alone-pill) had more than a humorous side to it. It embodied a culture that, as I mentioned, had always believed in medication in bringing about eternal living (physically not perishing) and life (physical existence). It reminds people of those legendary men who, as stories had it, tried hard to manage their bodily movements, thus slept alone to avoid cohabitation in order to achieve ethical and aesthetic self-redemption in body and in soul. Proverbial sayings from the Ming attested to such mentality in popular verses:

> Taking a thousand packages of drugs cannot compare with the
>   effect of sleeping alone for a single night;
> Receiving medicine for a thousand days cannot work as well as
>   lying down by thyself for one evening.[19]

Or:

> Taking drugs for one thousand days can never compare with
>   sleeping alone for a single night;
> Taking to a pitcher of wine can never compare with the satisfaction
>   of filling your stomach with one meal of congee.[20]

China's tradition of tying concerns for carnal activities (*fang-chung*) with the prevalent search for longevity (*ch'ang-sheng*) and nurturing of physical well-

being (*yang-sheng*), some would argue, went as far back as neolithic archaeo-
logical leitmotif.

Medieval authors give us fascinating evidence of all of this. The T'ang poet
Pai Chu-I (772–846), for instance, had a poem entitled "A Song of Reclining
Alone (*tu-mein yin*)" that goes as follows:

> Sleepless in this long night, I rose to the stairs.
> A few stars scattering the galaxy decorated the sky wanting to
>   dawn.
> For fifteen years under the moon light,
> whichever one night did I not sleep on my own?[21]

Verses of sleeping alone, at this point, had yet to become an emulated genre,
but with the charm and power that Pai had in T'ang society and Chinese
literature, they were on their way to becoming so.

Evidence suggests that as Neo-Confucian eclecticism absorbed medieval
Buddhist and Taoist accents on self-cultivation, interest in asceticism (*kua-yü*)
and in cutting off carnal desires (*chüeh-yü*) increased. The customary rites of
passage for men that stressed standing on one's own after the thirty-ninth or
fortieth birthday influenced the male process of aging in Ming-Ch'ing China.
Moreover, there was evidence from popular cults and folk medicine that this
was not an entirely elitist taste. The long-standing Taoist conviction in the
exhaustibility of male sexual vitality together with the belief in the relationship
of one's sexual acts and physical well-being helped to persuade the rural men
and village ordinaries that conservation and self-restraint in sex is probably a
useful and necessary habit. Anxieties over the premature depletion of the male
essence and an inadequate supply of "kidney water (*sheng-shui*, at the source
of male sexuality)" was a constant factor in Chinese giddy gossips and popular
medical advertisements. Men's apprehension about overindulgence or being
overly extracted could only be aggravated by the fear that their overused male
organ could fail them the task of successful coital performance in successful
reproduction.

By the sixteenth century and onward, many discussions on the goodness
of sleeping alone are found. Ancient quotes from Taoist mythology were elaborated upon. The legendary wisdom of P'eng Tzu, for instance, on "taking a
hundred packs of medicine may not compare with sleeping on one's own"
were exaggerated ten times over to add power and flavor for its late imperial
audience. Earlier poems eulogizing solitary dwelling were collected. Cautions
were even given to women warning against their "unwarranted" fantasy for
and danger of marrying a young groom. Free castes from Lu Yu (who called
himself "the old man who did as he pleases [*fang-wong*]") that "the bottom line

for his own strong health at ninety lies at the simple fact that half of those days were spent in a single nest (*tan-ch'i*)" encouraged this practice.[22]

Songs of sleeping alone were sung by men who accepted the practice. There was Hu I-tzu's "Lyrics of Dormant in Solo (*tu-shu yin*)" that tried to celebrate both the beauty and the noble discipline of this practice.

> Chilly and pure, a singular crane dormant in solo on this frosty
>   day.
> His shoulders tightly tugged in,
> A warmth stretching to cover the feet.
> The quilt encloses the burner,
> Incense release a fragrance full.
> The combat soldier at heart does not rise,
> Trying to seduce a date with the solitude.
> This evening I slept till the sun roasts over the window grid.
> A blissful kind of comforts, perhaps,
> The kind of life this brings.[23]

Not surprisingly, not all contemporaries agreed on the value or necessity of self-confinement. Some expressed doubts that this "sleep-alone-pill" really worked for longevity, citing medical classics that people past the age of 80 could hardly retain physical warmth other than from the human bodies they slept with. Others like the admired eighteenth-century poet Yuan Mei (1716–1797) confessed that "For the better half of my life I never slept by myself unless lying down in illnesses." Furthermore, there were cynical critics questioning the use of solitary sleep as incompatible with "run-away thoughts and uncontrollable desires (*hu-ssu luan-hsiang*)." What benefit was left after every ounce of energy and bit of spirit one had were spent suppressing unrequited sexual desire? Fascinating debates and discussions on male celibacy continued.[24]

Conclusion: Man's "Right" to Moderating Reproduction

Looking now at our modern world from the viewpoint of someone outside of Western linguistic, cultural, and social orbits, the adoption of such terms as "pro-life" and "pro-choice" to describe the two camps and different stands on family planning, contraception, and abortion seems at once mystifying and misleading. In most other times and places, life and choice appear intertwined and interrelated. Choices are usually made in favor of life, and life can hardly go on without a constant exercise of choice. It is a puzzle why both were not conceived as belonging to the same side, accomplishable through the same fashion.

The modern assumption that men are inevitably irresponsible and careless simply because they do not get pregnant can be questioned. It may be another slice of unhelpful modern mythology. Male reproductive culture in imperial China indicated that for reasons of health preservation and personal and social development, as well as concern for successful breeding of the next generation of wholesome, intelligent, and surviving heirs, sexuality can be seen as too serious to be left to insensitive personal indulgence. In a tradition that believed in the morality, aesthetics, and heavenly blessing as invariably involved in any meaningful reproduction, even ordinary men had to consider their own obligations regarding contraception. It was seen as it should be that sex not only gives pleasure and effects procreation; it is also an essential part of spiritual and physical cultivation, as well as a key pathway to longevity and even immortality. The acceptance of the legitimacy of sexual pleasure and ecstasy, and the acceptance of the lasting social obligations that sex implies, is not a "modern" invention. Adding health-enhancing and salvation-seeking potentials, Chinese Taoism actually identifies coital activities as a vehicle to arrive at a wide array of (at least four) different purposes. Any of these it is true may be achieved separately, but, more intriguingly, all can also be accomplished in the same fashion. Sex for fun, sex for birth, sex for health and immortality, or sex for self-cultivation and eternal salvation are not only mutually nonexclusive, they indeed call for the same principles and methods in theory and in execution.

This idea that we moderns entertain that the separation of sex and birthing, of copulation for fun and reproduction for duty, is an entirely modern phenomenon therefore appears, if I may say so, a kind of ignorance fed by self-congratulatory arrogance. The modern idea that contraceptive technology permitted a celebration of the joy of sex for the first time is erroneous. The so-called "sex-revolution" was not a human novelty brought on by the improvement of contraceptive and abortion procedures. The sex culture and reproductive medical literature in historical China provides us with direct counter evidences of the above theses. Coital intercourse as both a source of pleasure and potential opportunity for conception was appreciated. These were different aspects of the same act. The joy of sex was celebrated in the affirmative, not entirely in and of itself, but as part of a cosmological belief system that respected nature and valued human bodily experience as a vital channel to the wholesome self-cultivation. Chances of conception, on the other hand, were worth pursuing and avoiding at the same time. The quality of reproduction was seen as more important than the quantity. Born children should have a welcoming context to be born into, one in which they could prosper. Nature and nurture are not oppositional concepts. The philosophical school called "life nurturing (*yang-sheng*)" and the religious conviction of Taoism put respect for and the enhancement of Nature at the core of human existence. It was seen as natural to conjoin nature and nurture. The Chinese culture placed high value on the art of "planting the seeds" and the spiritual and physical value of "sleeping alone." These traditions called for men to wisely temper and carefully manage their sexuality and bodily activities. This expression of the yin and the yang is not something that applies only to the other sex. Mutuality of rights and obligations was the key to healthy sex and healthy living.

The fact that the main indigenous belief systems—Confucianism and Taoism—hold no inherent opposition to the notion of contraception or abortion, however, does not mean the Chinese way had no problems with family planning or population limitation. Ancestor worship and the strong tradition of son-preference related to it has been known to lead to discriminatory treatment of the female, even including infanticide. Even with progressive legal codification that permits the adoption of the mother's name and the strengthening of women's property rights, for instance, there is still in China a strongly felt need to give birth to a son so as to carry on the family line. This is a pronatalist force that leads to the support of sex-selective abortions. Waves of demographic explosion in the modern era, furthermore, demonstrated that in addition to the forces of modernization, the nationalist leader's plea to increase births so as to "preserve the nation/clan" could find abundant support from the profertility forces. However, there is also in Chinese culture a readiness to practice self-restraint in reproducing when that is asked for and needed, hence the considerable support for the "one child" policy. This only shows the fluid complexity and creative flexibility that most religious traditions contain historically and today. The serious problems with the overexploitation of the natural resources and the often callous destruction of the environment indicated that Taoist appreciation of nature, Confucian reverence for moderation, and the Buddhist advocacy of compassion are thin sources of inspiration in the face of the invasive allures of modernization. Paradoxically, nevertheless, people's long-held convictions and cultural practices should never be overlooked as potential energies to bring about needed change. Historical demography discovered a relatively moderate marital fertility rate for late imperial China. The study of ancient social customs and even medical intervention factors may hold secrets worth exploring in our world with its population and environmental problems.

NOTES

1. Hsiung Ping-chen, "More or Less: Culture and Medical Factors Behind Marital Fertility in Late Imperial China." Paper presented at the IUSSP/IRCJS Workshop on Abortion, Infanticide, and Neglect in Population History: Japan in Asian Comparative Perspective, Kyoto, Japan, October 20–21, 1994.

2. Hung Chi, *The Compendium on Life Management* (*Sho sheng tzung jao*, 1882).

3. R. H. Van Gulik, *Sexual Life in Ancient China: A Preliminary Survey of Chinese Sex and Society from ca. 1500 B.C. till 1644 A.D.* (Leiden: E. J. Brill, 1961).

4. "Li Yün p'ien" in *Li chi* (Taipei: Hsin wen fung, 1986), vol. 9, p. 10.

5. Yüeh P'u-chia, *The Collection on Planting the Seeds; A Medical Aid from the Miao-I Studio* (*Miao i chai i hsueh cheng yin chung tz pien*) (Beijing: Chung i ku chi ch'u pan sho, 1985).

6. Yüeh P'u-chia, *The Collection on Planting the Seeds*, p. 4.

7. Yüeh P'u-chia, *The Collection on Planting the Seeds*, pp. 5–7.

8. Yüeh P'u-chia, *The Collection on Planting the Seeds*, pp. 11–39.

9. Charlotte Furth, "Rethinking Van Gulik: Sexuality and Reproduction in Tradition Chinese Medicine," in Christina K. Gilmartin, ed., *Engendering China: Women, Culture, and the State* (Cambridge, Mass.: Harvard University Press, 1994), pp. 125–146.

10. Wan Chuan, *Important Principles for the Increase of Offspring* (*Kuang ssu chi yao*) (Beijing: Chung kuo chung i yao ch'u pan sho, 1999); Chang Chi-bin, *Proposals for the Begetting of Fine Heirs* (I lin tz'o), collected in Ch'iu Chin-ch'eng, *Chen pen i shu chi ch'eng* (Beijing: Chung kuo i yao ch'u pen sho, 1999), vol. 4.

11. *Important Words for Increasing the Offspring* (Kuang ssu yao yu) (Taipei: Shih-chieh, 1962).

12. Chang Chi-bin, *Proposals for the Begetting of Fine Heirs*, pp. 1023–1025.

13. Yüeh P'u-chia, *The Collection on Planting the Seeds*, pp. 7–11.

14. Yüeh P'u-chia, *The Collection on Planting the Seeds*, pp. 11–40.

15. Yüeh P'u-chia, *The Collection on Planting the Seeds*, pp. 14–15; 20; 27–28.

16. Yüeh P'u-chia, *The Collection on Planting the Seeds*, p. 33.

17. Lu Yu, "Ssan hwai chih erh," in *Chien nan shih kao* (Taipei: Shih-chieh, 1961), vol. 84, p. 1147.

18. Wu Lai, *Szan ch'ao yeh shih* (Beijing: Chung-hua, 1991), pp. 2–3.

19. Yang Hsen, *Ku chin yen* (Beijing: Chung-hua, 1985), p. 29.

20. Hu Wen-huan, *Lei hsiu yao ch'ueh*, collected in the *Chung kuo i shueh t'a ch'eng szan pien*, (Ch'angsha: Yeuh-lu shu she, 1994), vol. 2, p. 916.

21. Pai Chu-i, *Pai hsiang shen shih chi* (Taipei: Shih-chieh, 1961), vol. 12, p. 127.

22. Yü Pien, *Shan ch'iao hsia yü*, collected in the *Ssu ku ch'uan shu tzun ku tzung shu* (Tainan: Chuang-yen, 1995), vol. 152, p. 48.

23. Ch'u Jen-huo, "Tu wo yin," in *Huo hu chi: pu chi chiuan erh*, collected in *Li tai pi chi hsiao shuo ta kuan* (Taipei: Hsin-hsing, 1978), p. 5891.

24. Wang chih ch'un, "Tu shui wan," in *Chiao sheng szuei pi* (Taipei: Wen-hai, 1961), vol. 4, pp. 139–140.

10

Excess, Lack, and Harmony

Some Confucian and Taoist Approaches to Family Planning and Population Management—Tradition and the Modern Challenge

GELING SHANG

After the population explosion of the last few decades, the birth rate in China has, as is well known, decreased considerably, from 3.343 percent in 1970 to 1.603 percent in 1998.[1] As recently reported, the population will be held below 1.3 billion by the year 2006. The notorious effectiveness of China's campaign of family planning and its "one-child policy," initiated by the Communist government and propagated by the Marxist ideology, often puzzles us. Why does this campaign not meet much resistance from the majority of Chinese people, though it is seen as manifestly coercive and even violent when measured by the Western standards of human rights? How exactly do Chinese people understand the idea of family planning and population in relation to their general beliefs and the religious traditions they have lived with for thousands of years? There have been, of course, many works done by scholars in different fields, which have suggested explanations from the perspectives of politics, economics, sociology, population growth theories, and so on. This chapter undertakes to explore the significant role that Chinese religious traditions have played in the context of family planning and related issues. The argument I would like to make through the following analysis is that the idea of family planning or population management does not necessarily conflict with the long traditions of the Chinese religions. On the contrary, the compatibility between the modern idea of family planning and how it was conceived according to the Chinese traditions, I believe, is in fact an inherent cultural and spiritual resource that has enabled Chinese people to tolerate, accept, and even support the modern idea of family planning.

What I mean here by "Chinese religious traditions" designates the two major indigenous religions:[2] Confucianism (*juchia*, or *yuch'iao*) and Taoism (*taochia*, or *taoch'iao*), which have shaped the Chinese cultural tradition so pervasively since the Chou Dynasty (1066–256 B.C.E.), during which the classics or scriptures of both religions were composed by their initiators. The following ideas and beliefs on which this chapter focuses are for the most part shared by both religions, and have been absorbed into the larger contexts of Chinese culture. The differences between these two religions and their respective arguments about their differences are not the subjects of this short essay, although they are crucial and indispensable in the studies of both religions. I will leave Buddhism, usually conceived as the third major religion of China, for other chapters, which will deal specifically with the Buddhist traditions. I will also pass detailed discussion on women's rights to family planning and contraception in Chinese history to Dr. Hsiung's chapter.

The Ultimate Concern: Peace and Harmony of the Universe

Both traditions, Confucianism and Taoism, have long represented peace or harmony as the original and ultimate state of the whole universe, and the ultimate goal of human life. Every form and way of life, divine and secular, must strive to maintain this ideal state of peace and harmony. There is ample evidence in the earliest texts that it was a common recognition in early China that if the state of peace and harmony was disturbed or interrupted the world and human society would become corrupt and fall apart, while when the state of peace and harmony remains, the whole universe with its "ten-thousand-things" flourishes, prospers, and celebrates. It is for Chinese the divine commandment or heavenly mandate (*t'ienming*) from above that made the natural world and human society peaceful and harmonious, and so human beings are obliged to support the divine mandate in order to preserve their fortunes and live a good life.

What is meant by "peace and harmony" (*ho, p'ing, hoi, chün*, etc.) in the context of the Chinese religious traditions? "Peace and harmony" stands first of all for a conflict-free state of all kinds of relationships between nature and human beings, the individual and society, living persons and spirits, the secular and divine, and so on. Confucians, as well as Taoists, seem to be convinced that all natural disasters and social crises come always from conflicts that often break or destroy the balance and order of the harmonious universe. Therefore, human beings should eliminate conflicts of all types, so that the originally peaceful and harmonious state of existence will manifest itself in the living world.

Secondly, "peace and harmony" refer particularly in Confucianism and Taoism to the state of "the oneness of heaven and humankind" (*t'ien jen hoi*). The word *tien*, or "heaven" in English, has two basic meanings: one as simply the "sky," metaphorically implying "nature" or "spontaneity," and another as a divine being (equivalent to *ti*, or God) or a numinous force. Unlike Western counterparts, the Chinese story of creation presents the world as it is now as having originated from and been created by a primary state of nature called *hundun* and later *t'aiji*, which was conceived as an undifferentiated, undivided, and dynamic whole or One. It was from this One that the universe with its three major compartments (*sants'ai*), heaven, earth, and human beings, was born and the ten-thousand-things (*wanwu*) were produced. Since all things, including human beings, came from the same origin or mother, as Lao Tzu (b.c. 600 B.C.E.) likes to put it, they are expected to participate in the same patterns of existence. In other words, all things in the world ought to coexist peacefully, harmoniously, and intimately, like a family; they are not supposed to conflict or fight with one another. The theory draws axiological, moral, and social consequences from its cosmology. If this original oneness were eliminated and the harmony of the ten-thousand-things fell apart, there would result all kinds of disastrous and destructive consequences.

Thirdly, a peaceful and harmonious world is also understood by Confucians and Taoists as a world of order, hierarchy, and principle. It says in the *Book of Odes* (*Shih Ching*), one of the earliest classics in China, "Heaven produces the teeming multitude, with things and principles (*tse*)."[3] The universe was not created as a realm of contingent and unpredictable movements, but as a network of ordered and necessary interactions of natural elements and human individuals. Order and principle are believed to be what maintains and guarantees the harmony and peace of the world. The High Lord, the two primary forces of *yin* and *yang*, heaven, earth, and human beings, the four directions and the four seasons, the five natural elements, and mountains, rivers, plants, stars, as well as societies, families, and peoples, are all placed in proper orders. Acting or moving in correspondence to the proper order or principle is what Chinese have called Tao, or the Way, after which the world or society should follow or rediscover if its track were ever lost.

It is about this core or ultimate concern with the peace and harmony of the universe and human society that Chinese people have created their unique ways of life and established their entire sociopolitical system. For example, the *Book of Rites* (*Li Chi*), in the chapter "On Music" (*Yüe Chi*), thus articulates the origin of music and ritual:

> Music stands for the harmony of heaven and earth; rite stands for the order of heaven and earth. It is the harmony that unifies hundreds of things; it is the order that clarifies the differences of things. So heaven is conducting music and earth legislating rites. There would be turbulence if there were transgressions of the rites; there would be violence if there were disharmony in music. This is why one has to know [the nature of] heaven and earth to be able to advocate music and rite.[4]

In accordance with this, all the norms, values, rites, teachings, and principles that prevailed in the Chinese religious and philosophical traditions have so far been perceived, accepted, and practiced merely as means to achieve and obtain the universal peace, harmony, oneness, and order. *The Great Learning* (*Ta Hsüeh*), one of four Confucian classics, has it:

> Investigating things leads to knowledge. Knowledge leads to sincere intention. Sincere intention leads to right mind. Right mind leads to the cultivation of the person. A cultivated person can preside over a regulated family. A regulated family leads to a rightly governed state. A rightly governed state leads to the peace and harmony of the universe.[5]

Confucius (551–479 B.C.) makes this point more than explicit: the ideal or ultimate goal of life is to attain universal harmony, and everyone's concerted efforts in everyday life constitute the beginning of the way (Tao) to attain that. At this point, Taoism definitely shares the same religious orientation with Confucianism, though they are of course different in many other respects.[6]

Chinese people have become accustomed to thinking, under the influence of these traditions, that the way we act and the things we have done even in everyday life might affect the state of our family, community, nation, and the whole world (*Analects*, 1:12). If we fail to do things correctly to keep peace, order, and harmony in the world, consequences such as personal illness, family crisis, political disorder, and natural disasters necessarily follow. Everybody in Chinese society seems to bear responsibility with respect to those possible consequences. Hence, based upon the ideal of a harmonious universe, the Chinese religions and philosophies have not only built their own cosmological and metaphysical worldviews but also enacted very concrete and practical norms and values to rectify and cultivate everyone's behavior. Most Chinese would follow these norms and praise these values because they believe that good deeds could help to make their family, nation, and the entire world peaceful and harmonious, and that a harmonious world would assure them secure and happy lives.

When we come to the recognition of the ultimate concern of the Chinese religious traditions, it is not so hard for us to find a natural link to the concept of family planning and population management in China. The size of the population has been a pressing concern of Chinese people since the very early stages of Chinese history, because the population affects the immediate condition of society and of the world at large. It is reasonable for traditional Chinese to believe that in order to maintain the balance and order of the world we surely need to keep the population in balance with nature. They would also accept the idea that population management is not a matter of personal choice but of collective and even universal interest, and that it is everyone's duty to be concerned with the problem of population and to do something about it. The point I would like to make is that the idea of family planning is not something strange or daunting for most Chinese. As a matter of fact, the Chinese were perhaps the first people to speculate about and practice "family planning" and population restraint, simply because it has long been considered an organic part of the pursuit for universal peace and harmony. In the following sections I would like to examine specifically how the traditional Chinese thought about family, population, and reproduction, in relation to the community, government, and the entire universe.

Family, Marriage, and Family Planning

Even at the earliest stages of Chinese civilization, the family has occupied a central position among the highest values in the "human world" in Chinese thought. From its religious traditions of ancestral worship and ethics based on filial piety, we can detect easily how significant the role of family was in China, especially as these roots sprouted in the Confucian tradition.[7] In the *Book of Odes* we read,

> Of all the men in the world
> None are equal to brothers . . .
> Brothers quarrel inside the walls,
> But they stand united against insult from without

> While even the best of friends,
> However numerous, will not fight for you.
>
> . . . .
>
> Happy union with wife and children,
> Is like the music of lutes and harps.
> When there is concord among brethren
> Harmony strides delightful and enduring.[8]

From here we can get a picture of an ancient family and see how it was valued by the people of that time. Family represents the natural unity and provides the relationships into which we were born and upon which we can rely for our security and happiness. The intimacy and affinity of the family members are construed by Chinese to be the manifestation or representation of the cosmological and social harmony, order, and unity; the family is also what binds people together in an appropriate network of social, moral, political, and economic relationships. Before any individual and society, there is the family. As a person, one must first be a family member, a daughter or son, a mother or father, a sister or brother, before whatever she or he wants to be as an individual. In Chinese traditions there is very little room for individuals or private rights apart from the roles and duties one is to fulfill. In addition, the family functions for the Chinese as an archetypal or primary form of a society. That means, first, that a society consists of and grows out of not individuals but families; and second, that the structure or form of a society resembles that of a family. For instance, the nation has been called a nation-family (*kuochia*) ever since it was created, and the parallel relationships of the king to his subjects and father to his son represent the clarification and justification of the order, nature, and form of a society. This is perhaps why the Chinese traditions have put so much emphasis on family values and the establishment or regulation of the family.

To establish a good family and to keep it in good shape, *ch'ichia*, or regulating a family, is of paramount importance for Chinese people in terms of creating and securing a good society. What most Chinese seem to believe is that "If one family practices loving virtue (*jen*), the whole state becomes loving; if one family practices courtesies, the whole state becomes courteous."[9] And what they see in reality is the fact that "Few of those who are filial sons and respectful brothers will show disrespect to superiors, and there has never been anyone who is not disrespectful to superiors and yet creates disorder."[10] From these premises it follows that, as long as we make our family good and happy, the whole society or even the universe will soon celebrate its sought-after state of peace and harmony.

How is one to determine what has been commonly perceived of as a good and happy family? There are certainly many signs of a good and happy family, such as social and political status, education and moral reputation, wealth and economic security, and, of course, a congenial relationship among family members. But the most important project of all for a traditional Chinese family is to reproduce, to have children in order to pass on its kinship and all it has had so far. In Chinese tradition, the biggest tragedy of a family or a couple is its sterility or lack of descendants, and this is also considered the most serious violation against traditional morality. As is stated in *Mencius*, "There are three things which are unfilial, and to have no posterity is the worst of them."[11] Many Chinese, if not most, still believe in this today.

Some might jump to the conclusion that the Chinese would have strongly resisted the modern idea of family planning had they been so seriously concerned about having children. I think this would be false, because there is another side of the coin we should take into account. That is, Chinese do not merely want to have children, but to have good, healthy, and talented children; not only are they obliged to keep passing on their family but to pass it on with glory and prosperity. In this respect, the Chinese people have long been very conscious about how to manage or "plan" to have quality children, especially sons. Based on the religious and philosophical belief in universal harmony, the Chinese have from very early periods realized that the key to having good and healthy children is to follow the natural order. For "When *yin* and *yang* are in proper places, and wind and rain come right in time, good children are born and the descendants flourish."[12] In Chinese antiquity, time (*shih*) and place (*wei*) are emphasized strongly because nothing good would happen if its time and place are interfered with. This perhaps underlies the Chinese idea of "regulating the family," the art, as it were, of managing or "planning" through which a good and happy family can be established. In this sense, I do not see any incompatibility between Chinese tradition and the modern concept of family planning.

In establishing a happy family with good children, the most significant and decisive factor is the right marriage. Though we cannot actually date when the phenomenon of marriage originated in China, it is quite certain that the concept of marriage (*hunyin*) became significant and normalized at least during the Chou Dynasty (1066–256 B.C.E.) since the *Five Classics* (*wuching*) have preserved much of the material on this topic. According to the ancient Chinese, the marriage of a man and woman represents within the human world the natural correlation and intercourse between *yin* and *yang*, the two elementary forces, which are believed to be the parents of all beings. A good marriage often brings glory, prosperity, and good offspring to the family, for it manifests the balance and harmony of *yin* and *yang*. If a marriage were problematic, then domestic disasters surely would come along. On the other hand, marriage was during that period the way to connect different families, ethnic groups, political parties, and even states and nations. Marriage as the ultimate union of woman and man became the ideal for all kinds of human relationships, which led not only to the happiness of a family but also the harmony of the entire society.

In contrast to any merely sexual relationship, marriage appears to be a regulated, controlled, and conducted matter. *Li Chi*, or *The Book of Rites*, has it that "Marriage (*hun*) and wedlock are meant to join the good of two families, thus [the couple] can serve their ancestors in the shrine and continue to grow the family into the future. . . . Marriage was seen as the foundation of propriety."[13] In relation to the word *hun* there is another word *mei*, literally matchmaking or mediation. But in the *Shuo Wen Chieh Tzu*, the earliest dictionary of the Han Dynasty (100–121), *mei* stands for "deliberation" (*mou*), meaning "to join two families deliberately." This shows that for the ancient Chinese, marriage is the human effort to make the sexual relationship appropriate, *deliberately*.

There are many rules and regulations set up for marriage in early China. Some of them have much to do with reproduction, or "family planning." First, for instance, it has been taboo, as early as the Chou Dynasty, for the members of the same family or those who have same family name to marry each other (*t'ung-hsin-pu-*). In *The Book of Rites* and the *Spring and Autumn Annals with Tso's Commentary* (*Tso Chuan*), much has been recorded about this. Until the Tang Dynasty (618–907), the law prohibited marriage to one's nephew or niece. As Xie Wei-yang has observed, the main reason for this taboo is eugenic. According to Xie, there was a popular belief that "infertility results when a married couple has the same family name" (*Tso Chuan*), and "that to prohibit the marriage of the same family name is to avoid sterility" (*Kuo Yü/Chin Yü*). It seems that the Chinese knew long ago that the marriage between near relatives is problematic for the outcome of reproduction, though they may have been mistaken about the exact nature of the problem.[14]

Another example is the preference of the right age or right time to be married. Just as there is a right season for growing crops, there is a right time for marriage. Though the appropriate age may vary from time to time and place to place, the ancient Chinese seemed to understand that in order to produce quality children, men and women should marry in accord with certain time periods. The popular age for marriage during the Chou Dynasty was 15 for women and 20 for men. After the Chou, men between 15 and 20 and women of about 15 were considered fit to marry.[15] Some held, however, that men of the age of 30 and women of 20 would be better suited, according to the *Book of Rites* (*Li Chi* and *Chou Li*), for only at these ages would both man and woman have completed their physical and mental developments in preparation for marriage. Many rulers in Chinese history even made laws to encourage people to marry and have children at the right times; those who violated such laws would be fined or overtaxed by the government.[16] We are not quite sure what sorts of basis such concepts of marital age rested on, nor how well these suggested conventions were actually carried out, especially at the level of popular society, but it is obvious that the ancient Chinese did begin to take into account the appropriate age of marriage and its impacts on the results of reproduction.

There were other requirements for a *good* marriage regarding economic status, social classes, moral duties, health and education, and so on. In addition to the aforementioned regulations, there were also detailed norms and rituals set for husbands and wives to act properly. For example, men were to go out to work and women were to stay at home taking care of the household; a husband was expected to sexually satisfy his wife or wives, and the wife was to bear children for him; men were to love their wives and children, and women and children were to subjugate themselves to him unconditionally. All such requirements and norms sound very sexist to us moderns, yet in traditional China people did believe that the division of the sexes and their social roles were bestowed by the heavenly mandate (*t'ienming*) and mother nature, or decided by the spirits of the great ancestors. We have also already examined the idea that heaven, in giving birth to human beings, also implants in them the forms of order that ought to govern their behavior in their relations with each other. Following such divine orders would ensure the fortune and happiness of the family. All these norms and maxims, and the principles that inspired them, appear to have aimed at two main goals, a happy family and healthy descendants, both being thought essential in obtaining the ultimate state of universal peace and harmony.

Undoubtedly, these ideas and traditions created and practiced during the early period of feudalistic and patriarchal China have been changed in the last two centuries. Most of them were under attack by modern liberals and communists as oppressive and reactive fetters that had suffocated the spirit of freedom, human rights, and scientific thinking in China for thousands of years. Nevertheless, the traditional concerns with regulating the family and universal harmony do not seem to be incompatible with the modern concept of family planning. If the regulation of the family was traditionally meant to increase the population, then it is not wrong to limit the population now when it exceeds the limits and threatens to disrupt the harmony of the universe. The same idea could cut both ways.

Sexuality and Contraception

In Chinese antiquity sexuality was not an unknown or untouchable topic, but one of the primary themes that early Chinese thinkers probed in envisioning the whole picture of the universe, though often implicitly and metaphorically. Sexuality, or more commonly called "man and woman" (*nan nü*) by the Chinese, is conceived as a human action that corresponds immediately to the interaction between the cosmic forces of *yang* and *yin*. The ancient Chinese imagined, perhaps from their own experiences in sexuality and reproduction, that the whole cosmos was created and transformed by the intercourse of these two forces. As far as the human world was concerned, sexuality came to be the "root" (*ken*) or "origin" (*tuan*), as Confucius put it, of the entire network of human relations, for it manifests the origin of all things. The Chinese, similar to people elsewhere, have been very much aware of the importance of human sexuality and its impact upon both our sociopolitical and family lives.

The *I Ching*, or *The Book of Change*, perhaps the primal source for both Confucianism and Taoism,[17] constructed a worldview based on the principle of *yin* and *yang* by using the image of "woman and man" and their sexual relationship. According to the *Book of Change*, all changes are generated by the two basic elements called *chian* and *k'un*; the former signifies all *yang* or male elements such as heaven, the day, the man and male organ, and so forth; the latter signifies the *yin* or female elements such as the earth, the night, the woman and female organ, and so on. When the two mingle together, things start to change; when the man and woman have sex, everything comes to life. Representing the two forces of *yang* and *yin* or man and woman, the whole system of the *Book of Change* is composed of two kinds of linear signs: one simple unbroken lines (*yang*) and another broken lines (*yin*). The combination of three lines becomes a trigram and two trigrams form a hexagram. Thus, there should be eight basic trigrams and a total of 64 hexagrams with 384 lines, within which the changes of the entire universe are supposed to occur. The three lines constructing a trigram symbolize three primary parts of the universe, heaven, human beings, and the earth, representing three conditions—time, social circumstances and space—that are believed to be decisive for the outcome or fortune of the change in question. The idea of this is that if anything happens or one does something at the wrong time or the wrong place, an unfortunate consequence will certainly ensue. The whole system and function of oracle or divination of the *Book of Change* rests upon such a belief.

What we learn from reading the *Book of Change* about human sexuality is twofold. First, the early Chinese did not see sexuality as something obscene or evil; instead, they affirmed it as a positive and productive force that was responsible for the origin, growth, and flourishing of both the natural and human worlds. The second is that human sexuality should be well conducted in terms of the right time, persons, and place, so that everything good would accrue to a marriage or family and its reproductivity. At the beginning of the book we read, "The clouds pass and the rain does its work, and all individual beings flow into their beings."[18] At a later period, the Chinese expression "clouds and rain" (*yün yü*) became a very popular metaphor for sexual intercourse. The sixty-third hexagram, *Chichi*, or "cooperation and completion," is a combination of two trigrams, *li*, below, and *k'an*, above. *Li* represents water, clouds, the woman, and *k'an* represents fire, rain, the man; when the two appear to be in the right place, order, and time, their proper intimacy brings about harmony. The third hexagram, *chun*, or "difficulty at the beginning," tells us that "difficulty appears at the beginning of intercourse," stressing the timing of the act. Moreover, the eleventh, *t'ai*, or "peace," talks about marriage; the twelfth, *p'i*, or "stagnancy," shows when men and women are not in the right positions; the thirty-first, *hsien*, or "universality," indicates the joy of sexual interplay. And many other discussions and images are found in the book regarding human sexual relationship and sexuality.

These images and ideas of sexuality are also recorded in other major classics such as the *Book of Odes*, the *Book of History*, and the *Book of Rites*. For the early Chinese, there seem to be three purposes or consequences of human sexuality: reproduction (*sheng*), pleasure, and health (*ch'iangshen*). Confucianism and Taoism agree on this, and both are very cautious about the fact that improper sexual activity can harm its positive aims. However, the two traditions have very different approaches and attitudes toward the subject of human sexuality. Confucianism emphasizes the sociopolitical dimension of human life and thus holds that the sexual drive ought to be controlled or restrained by traditional morals and rites. The Confucians were convinced that the pleasure of sexuality could lead to promiscuous and licentious behaviors, which was what caused decadence and disorder, and had precipitated the fall of the preceding Hsia and Shang Dynasties. Except for the function of reproduction, Confucianism in general has been somewhat negative and evasive even in discussing the topic of sexuality, especially in its later development during the Sung and Ming Dynasties (960–1644).

Taoism, on the other hand, emphasizes Tao, or the Way of nature and human spontaneity, instead of politics, morality, and other human devices of regulation. It is not our natural desire or tendency but man-made rules and norms that have perverted and corrupted human nature, because social apparatus and political structures have drawn human beings away from nature.[19]

The central concern of the Taoist tradition is how to return to nature and spontaneity and become one with the natural flow of life as it is. By renouncing morality and knowledge and becoming one with nature, a Taoist is believed to be able to obtain its essential energy (*chingchi*) and to attain longevity and even immortality (*ch'angsheng*). Since the energy produced during the intercourse between *yin* and *yang* is considered the ultimate force of creativity, Taoism construes human sexuality as a natural way to exchange and balance the *yin-yang* energy and thus to enhance the life forces of one's body. Unlike Confucianism, Taoism, especially the religious Taoism first developed during the Han Dynasty (206 B.C.E.–220 C.E.), puts more emphasis on sexuality for the purpose of health and longevity rather than reproduction. For most Taoists, the religious goal is to transform themselves, their bodies and souls, to the state of universal harmony, which is beyond the dichotomies between good/evil, right/wrong, society/individual, and human/nature. If practiced correctly in the Taoist sense, human sexuality can become part of the Tao or Way and a religious practice to reach that end of transformation. Since sexuality is so crucial for personal health, human reproduction, and religious transformation, Taoism developed, along with its philosophy, a series of theories and techniques to rectify human sexual behavior. This was commonly referred to by the Chinese as "the art in the inner chamber" (*fang chung shu*).

The basic teaching of such Taoist art is coitus reservatus (*chih ching fa*), meaning to have sex or even orgasm without ejaculation, in order to preserve and strengthen the sperm or essential energy. A man was not to ejaculate in the course of sex unless it was necessary for pregnancy. This would prolong the time of intercourse and help the man and woman release and absorb *yang* and *yin* energy to and from each other, and thus enhance one other's health. For the purpose of pregnancy, men were also to ejaculate only within the five days after a woman's menstruation. This would enable men to provide the best sperm in helping the woman conceive a healthy child.

As Robert Hans van Gulik has noted, the technique of reservatus reveals to us at least two things in which the Chinese believed. First, sperm was for them the source of vigor and health; every time sperm are ejaculated, one's essential energy weakens. Only a woman's *yin* energy can nurture and strengthen a man's sperm and essential energy, and vice versa. Second, a man should help the woman reach orgasm as often as possible because the best *yin* energy often comes out at the moment of her orgasm. But a man may ejaculate only under some special circumstances.[20] In the course of Chinese civilization, as a whole, the Taoist texts and practice of sexuality remained esoteric and mysterious, perhaps due to the predomination of Confucianism, which tends to discourage sensuality in favor of social stability and moral propriety. But the majority of the Chinese people commonly accepted its general philosophy of sexuality, especially the idea of coitus reservatus. This indicates that the Chinese have in their tradition long realized at least two things regarding our discussion of family planning and contraception. First, the Chinese made distinctions between the functions of sexuality and reproduction. Human sexuality is not merely an activity for the purpose of reproduction but also for health, pleasure, and even self-cultivation. Second, the technique of reservatus was obviously a way to avoid an unexpected or unhealthy pregnancy. At this point, I would say that in traditional China the idea of controlling or preventing pregnancy has long been understood and practiced, even though the techniques involved differ from more modern forms of contraception. This is perhaps one of the reasons that the modern Chinese would not feel offended when they are told to use means of contraception.

Early Theories of Population

Population has been one of the central concerns for the Chinese. They seemed to be convinced at a very early stage of their civilization that the quality and quantity of population would affect the state of universal harmony and the order of society. On the other hand, for most of Chinese history, to increase population and to expand territories have been ambitions of tribal chiefs, local lords, and political leaders. Population has been an important and popular subject among philosophers and politicians since the early Chou Dynasty (about 600 B.C.E.); indeed they may have been the first to speak about it seriously in world history.

Most thinkers of the Chinese tradition encouraged the increase of population. In the *Book of Odes*, there are many songs praising women who could bear children like peach trees.[21] Confucius said, "A noble man would be ashamed of land wasted due to a lack of people."[22] To urge reproduction, Duke Ch'i ordered: "A man must marry when he reaches twenty and a woman when fifteen." He even released his maids to get married in order to ensure that his state would "not have discontented women inside and bachelors outside."[23] From the *Guan Tzu* we read: "Immense territory and riches, an enormous population and a mighty military, are the essence of a hegemonic state."[24] Mencius suggests that "land, people, and political ministration are the three treasures of a feudal lord."[25] Duke Yüeh ruled that if a 20-year-old man or a 17-year-old woman was unmarried, the parents would be charged as criminals. A family would be rewarded if children were produced, to the order of two gallons of wine and a dog for a son, two gallons of wine and a baby pig for a daughter; additional food would be supplied for two children, and the government would pay for a foster maid if a child were born. Furthermore, if the parents were ill or died, the government would look after their children.[26]

Some, however, were conservative on population growth; they were concerned about keeping a balance between territory and population. Shang Yang (390–338 B.C.E.), a famous reformist minister of Ch'in, maintained that the population should be controlled according to the acreage of available farmland. He said: "If the population exceeds the size of land, there will ensue a shortage of mountains and rivers to use; if the amount of land exceeds the number of people, there will occur a deficit of state power and military force."[27] Therefore, he suggests that if there is a shortage of population, the state should try to attract immigrants, while if there is a shortage of land, it should try to expand its territory.[28]

Han Fei (297–233 B.C.E.), a great student of the Confucian Hsun Tzu (314–217 B.C.E.), did not seem to appreciate the theory promoting the increase of population. He reasoned that it would be better to maintain a modest population and continue expanding the state's territory, so that the people could have more resources and natural supplies to make a better living. People never fought each other in old times because there were more resources but too few people.[29] But now, he says:

> For every family having at least five sons, each son will have another five, before the grandfather dies there will be twenty-five offspring. This is why there are too few resources to support the number of people. People now would like to fight because they work hard but can hardly make ends meet. The society as such will end up in turmoil no matter how much award or punishment the government offers or threatens to stop it.[30]

In order to prevent a state from falling into turmoil, Han called for controlling the growth of the population, in order to strike a balance between the people's needs and the natural resources.

Taoists, on the other hand, advocated the idea of a "little state with a small population" first promoted by the founder Lao Tzu. Since nature is supposed to be in harmonious order, we should not do anything to increase the population nor to expand the state's territory. Otherwise, a constant competition and struggle for resources, political power, social status, and so on, would result.

From all these references we find that it has been a common theme in Chinese thought to take the issue of population into serious account. The Chinese were aware that controlling the size of the population was significant for maintaining a society and its people. In addition to the aforementioned theories of population, the Chinese also created methods for both census and the recording of demographic information, which has been an indispensable and significant part of Chinese historical chronicling. To control the population for the Chinese is more a social matter than one's own individual or family issue. For the good of the whole society, it was deemed necessary to either increase or decrease the population, depending upon the perspective of the theorists.

Another thing to noticed here is that the government can be responsible for the overall control of the population. A ruler is supposed to take charge of the growth of population as an important element of his duties in keeping the nation strong and prosperous. For most of Chinese history, the population has been a measure of a nation's political, economic, and military strength. Since there were constant wars, natural disasters, and low birthrates during classical times, the Chinese government was always interested in ways to increase the population to address the shortage of manpower. The people felt obliged to marry and have children not only to preserve their families but also to make their country great. They seemed to be convinced that having children had more to do with the national interests than with personal ones, and the government was expected to have a role in such matters. Therefore, when the nation was overpopulated, it was thought to be the right thing to do for the government to control population and for the people to follow whatever relevant policies were issued by the government.

Abortions and Infanticide

No evidence has been found so far to indicate when the Chinese began to practice abortion. Yet at least one thing is certain: the Chinese have employed abortion for various purposes since ancient times. Generally speaking, abortion was not encouraged, although there was no explicit code to prohibit it, for it was considered only as a result of accidental events or an unexpected emergency that could not be dealt with in any other way. In most cases people resorted to abortion because of some sort of disastrous or disgraceful cause of pregnancy, for instance, the pregnancy caused by prostitution, having an affair, incest and rape, or diseases or physical problems that put the mother in peril. Most people perceived abortion as unfavorable because it would most likely bring about harmful, unhealthy, unnatural, and even shameful consequences to whoever did it. Abortion was therefore a secret or private matter and was carried out by midwives rather than official physicians.

Nevertheless, there has never occurred in the Chinese tradition a ban against abortion; rather, Chinese attitudes toward abortion were mostly tolerant and compassionate. People did not think it was wrong unless it was done unnecessarily. In the *Table of Merits and Errors (Kong Kuo Ke)* from the Yüan Dynasty (1279–1368), for example, abortion is counted as a three-hundred-point error, two hundred points less than that of marrying a widow or setting fire to someone's house, and carried the same penalty as enticing a person to gamble. Abortion was never counted even close to the crime of murdering a person, which was penalized one thousand points. From the Chinese perspective, it would seem that an unborn fetus was not considered a complete human being, and therefore aborting it could not be counted equivalent to taking a person's life. On the other hand, the Chinese religions have always prioritized family and social values over the concerns of the individual. Where conflict arose between a family and its members or society and individuals, the latter were expected to sacrifice their needs to serve the common interests. If abortion profits the family or society, then it is reasonable to do it. Even an adult is supposed to be ready to sacrifice his or her life for the family and society, and so why not a fetus? Another thing worth mentioning here is that the patriarchal Chinese family was used to treating children as part of their private property, and hence it had every right to determine the child's life and its destiny. For most Chinese, a necessary abortion is a matter of the parents' choice.

These ideas were rooted strongly in the Chinese tradition. It is therefore not surprising that little resistance occurred after the Communist government began to prompt a coercive campaign of family planning and use abortion as a supplemental means of birth control in late 1960s. The major issue for the people with this policy has always had to do with the number and gender of children they have wanted for themselves. Some may criticize the poor medical conditions in which abortions take place in China, or the forceful aggressiveness of some local officers in enforcing the policy. These objections are humanistic ones. But the issue has never been a religious one for Chinese.

Infanticide, or more accurately put, female infanticide, used to be a common phenomenon in ancient China. As Olga Lang has pointed out, "[G]irls were the main, if not exclusive, victims of infanticide, which was practiced in the poor families of China from time immemorial."[31] As early as the Chou Dynasty, Kuan Chung (d. 645 B.C.E.) had already undertaken an effort to stop people from abandoning infants.[32] Han Fei (279–233 B.C.E.) had also analyzed the phenomenon of infanticide, lamenting: "Parents often celebrate when a son was born and kill the baby when it is a daughter. But since all children come from the same parents, why do they bless their sons and kill their daughters? Because they are calculating the long-term profits, in order to ensure the survival of their families in the future."[33]

According to the historical references, infanticide was condemned by intellectuals and discouraged by the government. *The Table of Merits and Errors* counted infanticide as a one-thousand-point error, tantamount to murder. Yet among poor families, infanticide has been common, and more government regulations can be found dealing with them. The basic reason for people to resort to female infanticide was economic, and revolved around the pressing problems of poverty and starvation. But this also proves that in ancient China the concept of "family planning" and control of population had developed even among the lower classes of society and was not merely a matter of consideration for the political or social elite.

Conclusion

The evidence this essay has presented shows clearly that there are rich resources in the Chinese religious traditions that have in fact contributed to contemporary China's reactions to the crisis of overpopulation. The key to understanding the modern approach to family planning is the Chinese concept of universal harmony, which has for a long time developed as a religious belief, as well as a philosophical and sociopolitical ideal shared by Confucianism, Taoism, and later Chinese Buddhism. It is upon the foundation of the ultimate concern with universal harmony that the Chinese have created and maintained their cultural and religious traditions, within which family values are greatly celebrated. We have seen that the Chinese have taken the problem of population into account for thousands of years. They have believed that the human phenomena of reproduction, sexuality, and family life could gravely affect the balance, order, and harmony of human society and the natural world. In this light, it is hardly surprising that the Chinese have attempted in more recent years to control the rate of human reproduction and the consequent growth of the population, especially when the balance between the available natural resources and the population has been as upset, as in recent history. Furthermore, we can see now more clearly how the contemporary goals of family planning are nothing strange to contemporary Chinese; even the practices of modern contraception and abortion have been adopted readily. It is the traditional belief in universal harmony rather than Communist ideology or other Western influences that has made this possible on such a large scale. Traditions of such long standing cannot cease to become effective unless the problems of cultural life that they address were either solved or disappeared and the living conditions were drastically changed. The question is not whether the traditional approaches to these problems are still present in cultural, social, and political life, but rather how much the tradition can offer to support the contemporary confrontations of modern crises caused by our way of life.

NOTES

1. From Yang Kuifu's report at the United Nations Commission on Population and Development as the representative of China and vice-minister of the State Family Planning Commission, March 22, 1999 (www. Unescap.org/pop/database/ law_china). See also *The Little Data Book* (2000), *The World Bank* (2000), and *World Population Prospects* (1998 revision) (New York: United Nations Department of Economies and Social Affairs).

2. I use the word "religion" here to refer broadly to those belief systems which have something to do with the reality that is beyond ordinary experience and scientific proof, and with the moral or spiritual effort to transform and transcend the concerns of secular life.

3. *The Book of Odes and the Book of Rites*, ed. Wu Shu-ping and Lai Chang-yang, Four Classics and Five Scriptures in Modern Chinese, vol. 3 (Guo Ji Wen Hua Press, 1993). Five Scriptures are *The Book of Change, The Book of Odes, The Book of History, The Book of Rites, Spring and Autumn*. Quotation is taken from *The Book of Odes*, no. 261, *chengmin*.

4. *The Book of Rites*, "On Music."

5. *Great Learning*, 1.5. *A Collective Exegesis of Four Classics*, by Zhu Xi (Yue Lu Shu She, 1985). *Four Classics* refers to four Confucian classics: *Analects, Mencius, Golden Means*, and *Great Learning*.

6. See Lao Tzu, *Tao Te Ching*, ch. 54 and 55.

7. In *Analects*, 1.2, it says, "When the root or foundation is firmly established, the moral law (*Tao*) will grow. Filial piety and brotherly respect are the root of humanity." Also in *The Golden Means*, 18, "*Ren* means humanity. The greatest value in humanity is familial love."

8. No. 165, *hsiaoya or ch'angdi*.

9. *Great Learning*, 8.

10. *Analects*, 1.2.

11. *Mencius*, 4.1.26.

12. *Sayings of the States (Kuo Yü)*, pt. 2 (Shanghai: Guji Press, 1978).

13. *The Book of Rites*, Hun Yi, or the Meaning of Marriage.

14. Xie Wei-yang, *The Patterns of Family in Chou Dynasty* (Beijing: Chinese Social Sciences Press, 1990), pp. 58–77.

15. Yang Tian-yu, *The Book of Odes: The Songs of Spontaneity* (Hong Kong: Zhong Hua Shu Ju, 1996), pp. 20–22.

16. Dong Jia-zun, *A Study in the History of Marriage in Ancient China* (Guangzhou: Guangdong People's Press, 1995), pp. 230–233.

17. Richard Wilhelm observed correctly, "Lao Tzu knew this book, and some of his most profound aphorisms were inspired by it. Indeed, his whole thought is permeated with its teachings. Confucius too knew the Book of Changes and devoted himself to reflection upon it. He probably wrote down some of his interpretative comments and imparted others to his pupils in oral teaching. The Book of Changes as edited and annotated by Confucius is the version that has come down to our time." *The I Ching or Book of Change*, the Richard Wilhelm translation rendered into English by Cary F. Baynes (Princeton: Princeton University Press, 1997), p. liv.

18. Ibid., p. 4.

19. According to Lao Tzu, "When the great Tao is abandoned, morality and righteousness arise. When wisdom and intelligence come into being the great pretense develops. When the family falls apart, filial piety and care appear. When the state is corrupted and in chaos, loyal ministers are demanded" (*Tao Te Ching*, 18). Similar statements can be found in the *Book of Chuan Tzu*.

20. Robert Hans van Glulik, *A Investigation of Sex Life in Ancient China* (Shanghai: Shanghai People's Press, 1990), pp. 64–65.

21. *The Book of Odes*, no. 1, Kuo Feng, Chou Nan.

22. *The Book of Rites*, Tsa Chi, 2.

23. *A Collective Exegesis of Han Fei Tzu* (Shanghai: Shanghai People's Press, 1974), pp. 786–787.

24. *A Collective Collation of Kuan Tzu* (Beijing: Beijing Science Press, 1965), ch. Chung Ling.

25. *Mencius*, Liang Hui Wang, 2.

26. Wang Yu-ming, *The History of Chinese Population* (Nanjing: Jiang Su People's Press, 1995), pp. 57–67.

27. *An Exegesis and Interpretation of the Boon of Lord Shang* (Beijing: Zhonghua Book Company, 1974), ch. Suang Di.

28. Ibid., ch. Lai Min.

29. *A Collective Exegesis of Han Fei Tzu*, pp. 1040–1041.

30. Ibid.

31. Olga Lang, *Chinese Family and Society* (North Haven, Conn.: Archon Books, 1968), p. 46.

32. *A Collective Collation of Kuan Tzu*, ch. Ru Guo.

33. *A Collective Exegesis of Han Fei Tzu*, p. 949.

II

Religion, State, and Population Growth

ANRUDH JAIN

Religion, by its nature, pronounces its laws and edicts to govern various aspects of human behavior including sexual and reproductive behavior. Through this authority, religion has had a powerful role in many countries' population programs. Religion is also believed to have a profound effect on an individual's sexual and reproductive behavior, which, in turn, is one of the major determinants of population growth.[1] Religion and population growth, however, are rarely discussed together. The purpose of this chapter is to provide a framework for a discussion of religious teachings insofar as they impinge upon the issue of population growth.

My perspective on the relationship between religion and population growth is influenced by my upbringing and academic training. I was brought up as a Jain, i.e., following the teachings of *Jainism*, a religion founded in the sixth century B.C. in India.[2] I was trained originally as a statistician and then as a sociologist and demographer.

Analytical Framework

The analytical framework used in this chapter and shown schematically in figure 11.1 is influenced by my training as a sociologist, namely, that individuals do not live in isolation; they are members of a larger social system including "family," "community," and

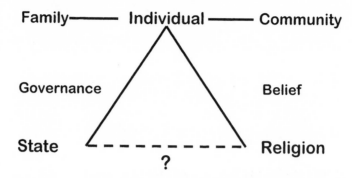

FIGURE II.I. Relationships between the individual and institutions.

other social institutions. In this sense, an individual's behavior including sexual and reproductive behavior is influenced not only by her/his own characteristics (e.g., education) but also by what is happening in the society at large.

Let us first consider the family system. Various forms of families have been identified in the literature. For example, an individual can be a member of a nuclear or a traditional extended family.[3] In terms of whether and when to have children, individuals living in a nuclear family are likely to have more independence and flexibility than those living in a traditional extended family. Similarly, an individual can be a member of a community as determined by residence, defined by geographic boundaries or ethnic, tribal, racial, or cultural affiliations, which cut across geographic boundaries. In practice, an individual typically is a member of many communities simultaneously. These community affiliations also exert influence on individuals' behavior, including their sexuality and reproduction. Naturally, the degree of the influence of familial and community affiliation on individual behavior depends upon many other factors and varies from individual to individual.

Two other important institutions that exert influence on an individual's behavior are religion and state. Since individuals live in a country, their behavior is governed by the rules and regulation of that country state. While an individual's relationship with the state is a matter of governance, her/his religion is a matter of her/his faith and belief system. It is important to note that in some countries, the state is synonymous with religion and in others the two are separate. The role of religion will be quite different under these circumstances.

In brief, the role of religion must be considered within the context of state, community, and the family (see figure II.I for the depiction of these relationships). While the familial and community affiliations are important determinants of individual behavior; in this chapter I focus only on the roles of the state and religion. The chapter is divided into three sections. The questions that need to be addressed in considering the roles of the state and religion are specified in the first section; the role of the state in the second; and the role of religion is discussed in the third section. In presenting this material, I make certain propositions and raise certain questions.

Two ethical issues are identified by discussion of religion, state, and population growth together. These are as follows:

1. Does the state have a right to coerce individuals to modify their reproductive behavior?
2. Does religion give a right to its followers to coerce its nonfollowers to modify their reproductive behavior?

The role of the state was deliberated by governments of developed and developing countries at the International Conference on Population and Development held in Cairo in 1994. In principle, all governments rejected the use of coercion in the matter of reproduction. Similar debate has not taken place about the coercive role of religion in the matter of reproduction. I hope that the propositions made and questions raised in this chapter will help the readers to address the ethical issue involved if followers of any religion try to coerce its nonfollowers to modify their reproductive behavior.

Questions That Need to Be Addressed

Two questions embedded in the title of this consultative group—right to family planning, contraception, and abortion in 10 world religions—are as follows:

1. Do individuals have a right to family planning?
2. Do individuals have a right to contraception and abortion *services?*

I have added the term services in the second question because, as is shown below, it is with respect to services that the obligations of the state may come into conflict with the desires of some religious organizations and leaders.

Right to Family Planning

In addressing the first question, we must distinguish between "family planning" and "family planning *program.*"

Family planning refers to individuals' intentions or actions taken by them to plan their families. *Family planning program*, in contrast, refers to an organized effort by the government and nongovernment organizations to provide services and information that would enable individuals to plan their own families. With this distinction, I make the following proposition:

Proposition 1: Every individual has a right to plan her/his own family according to her/his circumstances and needs.

I presume that all religious traditions will agree with this proposition. Whether and the extent to which individuals can exercise that right is another matter. As mentioned earlier, an individual's behavior is influenced by various institutions. Similarly, the degree to which an individual can exercise her right to plan her family would depend upon the influence exerted on that individual by the state, the religion, the community, and the family. Any of these institutions could facilitate, remain neutral, or create hindrances for an individual in exercising her right to plan her family. Any of these institutions could also influence an individual's desires about the number, sex composition, and timing of having children. For example, a strong son preference in India not only influences the number of children women end up having in order to produce a son but also influences the practice of abortion based on the sex of the fetus. At the extreme, any of these institutions can coerce an individual into having more (or fewer) children than she wants. For example, the one-child policy in China must have coerced many Chinese couples into having fewer children than they would have liked to have. Thus, while we are interested in considering the role of religion, we have to do so within the context of these other important institutions.

Right to Services for Contraception and Abortion

In addressing this question, we have to consider what individuals have done over the years and where the state or the religion may have played a part. Three circumstances can be distinguished.

First, individuals have and continue to exercise their right to plan their families by using methods like breastfeeding, postpartum abstinence, periodic abstinence, terminal abstinence, and withdrawal. These are culturally accepted means of behavior that also have some effect on fertility outcomes. Individuals have a right to these means and they learn about them from family members and friends. Neither the state nor any religion can take away individuals' right to use these means of fertility regulation. In fact, in some cases religion has prescribed days for abstinence and given its approval to use these means to regulate family size. Table 11.1 shows the percent of women who are practicing contraceptive methods according to national surveys conducted in the 1990s in selected developing countries. As can be seen, a substantial proportion of

TABLE 11.1. Percent of currently married women of reproductive ages (15–49 years) reported to be practicing contraception in selected developing countries

Regions/Countries	Current Use of Contraception (%)		
	Any method	Modern method	Traditional method
Asia			
Bangladesh (1997)	49.2	41.6	7.7
India (1992–93)	40.6	36.3	4.3
Indonesia (1997)	57.4	54.7	2.7
Nepal (1996)	28.5	26.0	2.5
Pakistan (1991)	11.8	9.0	2.8
Philippines (1998)	46.5	28.2	18.3
Latin America			
Bolivia (1998)	48.3	25.2	22.3
Brazil (1996)	76.7	70.3	6.1
Colombia (1995)	72.2	59.3	11.1
Guatemala (1995)	31.4	26.9	4.5
Haiti (1995)	12.3	8.9	3.2
Peru (1996)	64.2	41.3	22.9
Middle East			
Egypt (1995)	47.9	45.5	2.4
Jordan (1997)	52.6	37.7	14.8
Yemen (1997)	20.8	9.8	10.8
Africa			
Cameroon (1998)	24.0	10.0	14.0
Eritrea (1995)	8.0	4.0	4.0
Kenya (1998)	39.0	31.5	7.5
Madagascar (1997)	16.0	7.4	8.6
Sudan (1990)	8.7	5.5	3.2
Tanzania (1996)	16.1	11.7	4.3
Uganda (1995)	14.8	7.8	4.3
Zambia 1996	19.2	11.2	7.9
Zimbabwe (1994)	35.1	31.1	2.8

Source: Country-specific reports of Demographic and Health Surveys. Year of the report is shown in parentheses.

women have reported to be using these traditional methods in many countries. For example, about one in five women in Boliva, Peru, and the Philippines has reported using a traditional method.

Second, individuals have and can exercise their right to plan their families by using services offered through the private sector, provided they can afford them. Once again, religious organizations and leaders can do very little except to put "moral" pressure on individual followers not to use certain services or not to engage in certain types of behavior, such as not to lie or steal. Given enough demand, the private sector does find a way to offer services for contraception and abortion, even if the provision of these services is not legally approved by the state. Thus, even if there is no disagreement between the state and the religion about the need to provide these services, those who can afford it can always find a service. For example, where the consumption of alcohol is prohibited by the state, those who can afford it can always get it through the private sector. In this sense, individuals always have a right to services for family planning and abortion made available through the private sector.[4]

Third, individuals cannot exercise their right to plan their families if they do not want to use traditional methods and cannot afford services provided by the private sector. Thus, the question about individuals' right to family planning and abortion really boils down to their right to services and especially to the right of those who *cannot* afford these services provided by the private sector. Do they have a right to services for contraception and abortion? The two related questions are: Does the state have an obligation to provide these services? and What is the role of religion in influencing the relationship between individuals and the state? Let us first consider the role of the state.

Role of the State

Does the state have an obligation to provide services for contraception and abortion to those who want them but cannot afford these services provided by the private sector? I propose the following:

Proposition 2: The state has an obligation to provide services of adequate quality at an affordable price to those who want them and especially to those who cannot afford these services provided by the private sector.

This obligation of the state can be justified above all on the basis of social justice, because in the absence of such services those who need them but cannot afford to use the private sector will be unable to exercise their right to plan their own families according to their needs and circumstances. The provision of contraceptive services in the broader context of reproductive and general health services can also be justified on the basis of its effect on improving the health of women and children. A third reason the state should provide these services is the effect these services have on the reduction of unwanted fertility and thus on the reduction of population growth.

Role of the State and Population Growth

The governments of developing countries very recently became interested in reducing population growth because population growth is a recent phenomenon. These governments implemented direct policies to reduce fertility because rapid population growth was a result of a rapid decline in mortality. The state can potentially affect fertility in general by influencing an individual's desired or wanted family size and by providing services for contraception and abortion to those who want them.[5]

The growth in the world's population over the centuries is shown in figure 11.2. The global population at the time of Christ was about 300 million only. It was about 310 million at the time of the first millennium and 6,000 million or six billion at the second millennium. Consider the growth of the population in another way: it took hundreds of thousands of years to reach the first billion in around 1804. The second billion was reached in about 123 years, and the third billion in only about 33 years in 1960. The fourth and the fifth billion marks were reached in only 14 and 13 years, respectively, and the sixth billion in another 12 years. Thus, more than 50 percent of the population growth occurred in the second half of the twentieth century, or during the last 50 years.

Most of the population growth during the last 50 years occurred in the so-called developing countries. Consequently, the proportion of the global population that live in the "developed" countries declined substantially from 32 percent in 1950 to 20 percent in 1998. This proportion is anticipated to decline further to 13 percent by the year 2050 (see figure 11.3). This does not mean that the population of the developed countries did not increase rapidly at any time in the past. All countries either have gone or are going through a period of rapid population growth. The difference between the developed and developing countries in terms of their experience with rapid population growth can be understood better by considering a phenomenon called the "demographic transition."

Population growth of a country, in the absence of in- or outmigration, is equal to the difference between the number of births (or birth rate or fertility) and the number of deaths (or death rate or mortality) that occur to the people living in that country. Both the fertility and mortality levels in a country at the beginning of the demographic transition are high and of the same order of magnitude. Women have a large number of children to compensate for the high mortality conditions prevalent at that time. The decline in fertility follows the decline in mortality with some time lag. Both again become equal by the end of the demographic transition, but now at a low level. Consequently, the rate of population growth in a country is close to zero at the beginning and the end of its demographic transition. It is during this transition period that a country experiences population growth. The pace of this growth is determined by the difference between the fertility and mortality levels.

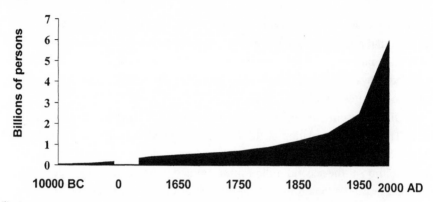

FIGURE II.2. Growth of world population. Source: R. Tomlinson, *Population Dynamics*, 1976; W. Peterson, *Population*, 1975.

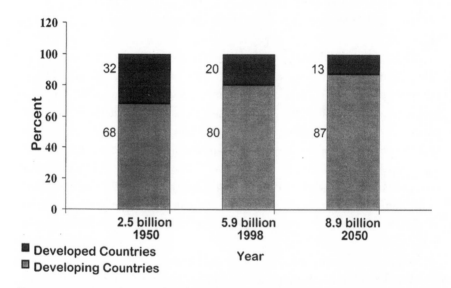

FIGURE II.3. Distribution of world population. Source: World Population Prospects, 1998.

Let us now compare the demographic transition in Western Europe with the ongoing transition in India (see figure 11.4). Both the fertility and mortality levels in Western Europe were high until about 1750. Mortality declined rapidly during the period of about 100 years from 1750 to 1850, and then gradually. Fertility declined with a time lag: first gradually and then rapidly during 1850–1900. The rapid decline in fertility occurred after mortality had declined to a reasonable level in 1850. This pattern of fertility decline reflected a gradual

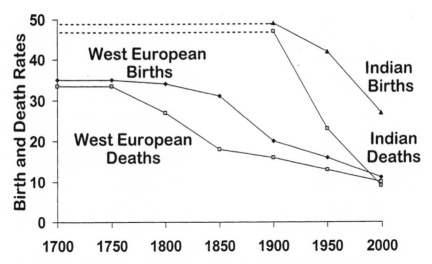

FIGURE 11.4. Demography transition: India and Western Europe. Source: A. Hawley, *Human Ecology*, 1950; World Population Prospects, 1998; Ministry of Health and Family Welfare, *Family Welfare Programme in India*, 1991.

adjustment in fertility behavior by individual couples to changing mortality conditions. The entire process of demographic transition in Western Europe took about 150 years. Countries in Western Europe also experienced rapid population growth during this period. For example, the population of northwestern Europe is estimated to have increased by 600 to 700 percent between 1750 and 1930. However, the population base of these countries was small. Moreover, colonization of developing countries and migration to the United States and Canada provided mechanisms to deal with the excessive population growth.

No such mechanisms were available to the developing countries. Moreover, morality in these countries declined at a much faster pace with the discovery of antibiotics and control of communicable diseases. Mortality in India, for example, declined from about 45 to 20 deaths per thousand in a short period of 50 years. Such a rapid decline in mortality did not offer sufficient time for a feedback mechanism to work on the fertility behavior of individual couples. Fertility remained high and, consequently, population started to grow rapidly. Moreover, there were no opportunities for outmigration of the magnitude required to act as a release valve for population pressure created by the rapid population growth that occurred during this period.

Faced with the challenges to deal with the increasing number of people, many governments of developing countries initiated population policies and programs to influence the fertility behavior of individual couples directly. While India was the first developing country to have a population policy in 1952, it was not until the early to middle sixties that these efforts took the form of organized family planning programs in many developing countries. The pace of fertility decline in India is considered much slower by the international standards. Nevertheless, the pace of fertility decline even in India has paralleled the pace of mortality decline.

The effectiveness of these efforts has varied from country to country. Fertility in some countries (especially in Southeast Asia) declined much more rapidly than others (especially in South Asia). In general, the population policies turned out to be effective in places where a large number of men and women wanted smaller families and where policies were implemented efficiently to provide the means of fertility regulation, including abortion.

There is less consensus on the appropriate role of the state in influencing an individual's desired family size. The justification becomes increasingly difficult as the means move through the following methods:

1. the implementation of those development policies (e.g., improvements in female education) that are more conducive to the reduction in desired family size
2. propaganda and motivation messages about having small families
3. incentives and quotas
4. coercion.

In many countries, the state has used means ranging from propaganda and motivational messages to incentives and quotas to coercion. The use of these means had been justified in terms of "common good," and had given rise to almost all the controversies in the field of population. The reasons for implementing some of these means include a general lack of appreciation about the process of demographic transition, international attention to "population explosion" in developing countries, lopsided development policies, and pressures felt by the state on its inability to provide basic services to its people.

The ethical issue raised by the use of these means is: Does the state have the right to coerce individuals to modify their reproductive behavior? This issue was discussed among the representatives from all countries at the International Conference on Population and Development (ICPD) held in Cairo in 1994. The consensus was that the means have to be just in and of themselves. The overall purpose of reducing population growth is to improve individual well-being. In this sense there is little justification for the state to use those means of fertility regulation that are not consistent with the overall objective of reducing population growth—improvement in individual well-being. Moreover, there is no need to implement means such as incentives and disincentives for providers or clients because there exists a large *unmet need* for fertility regulation methods in developing countries. Here, unmet need is defined as the percent of women who say they want to space or limit childbearing but are not using any means to do so. Table 11.2 shows the percent of women with unmet need for spacing and for limiting childbearing. The percent of women with unmet need ranges from about 10 percent in Indonesia, Cameroon, and Zimbabwe to about 29 percent in Uganda.

Role of Religion

What is the role of religion in exerting influence on individual behavior with respect to reproduction? I proposed earlier that individuals have the right to family planning, that is, to plan their families according to their circumstances. I presume that there will be very little disagreement with this proposition. But can religion prohibit individuals from exercising this right? I have argued that individuals have exercised this right by using traditional methods, which are sanctioned by almost all religions. Furthermore, they can exercise this right by using services offered by the private sector, provided they can afford them. Religion can have little effect on individual reproductive behavior in this sense. The issue is pertinent only for those who cannot afford the services provided by the private sector. Does the state have an obligation to provide these services? I have argued that the state has an obligation to offer services of adequate quality at least to those who cannot afford these services provided by the private sector. Does religion have a role in preventing the state from fulfilling this obligation?

In addressing these questions, we should also consider the context of population growth because the state's obligation in offering these services has also been justified on the basis of addressing the issue of population growth. As mentioned earlier, population growth is a recent phenomenon. Every country has experienced a period of population growth: countries in Western Europe experienced population growth for about 150 years and developing countries have been experiencing it for only the last 50 years. Contrary to popular belief, population growth is not caused by an increase in fertility. It has resulted from a decline in mortality. Individuals in developing countries are not having more children now, but more of the children born are surviving. This growth resulting from an imbalance between fertility and mortality has contributed to increasing diversity among countries and among people within a country.

The global population has just crossed the six billion mark. In comparison,

TABLE 11.2. Percent of currently married women of reproductive ages (15–49 years) estimated to be having unmet need* for contraceptive methods and percent of women reported not using contraception due to religious reasons

| Regions/Countries | Unmet need (%) | | | Women not using contraception due to religious reasons and % of those who were neither using any contraception at interview nor intending to use a method in the future. |
	For Spacing	For Limiting	Total	
Asia				
Bangladesh (1997)	7.9	7.9	15.8	9.4
India (1992–93)	11.0	8.5	19.5	3.5
Indonesia (1997)	4.2	5.0	9.2	0.5
Nepal (1996)	14.3	17.1	31.4	8.7
Pakistan (1991)	10.5	17.6	28.0	13.2
Philippines (1998)	8.6	11.2	19.8	4.8
Latin America				
Bolivia (1998)	6.8	19.3	26.1	5.1
Brazil (1996)	2.6	4.7	7.3	2.4
Colombia (1995)	3.2	4.6	7.7	0.7
Guatemala (1995)	12.4	12.0	24.3	15.7
Haiti (1995)	17.7	30.1	47.8	6.4
Peru (1996)	3.5	8.6	12.1	2.2
Middle East				
Egypt (1995)	5.3	10.7	16.0	2.2
Jordan (1997)	7.4	6.8	14.2	1.0
Yemen (1997)	17.2	21.4	38.6	17.2
Africa				
Cameroon (1998)	5.1	4.5	9.6	5.2
Eritrea (1995)	21.4	6.1	27.5	8.4
Kenya (1998)	10.4	8.5	19.0	5.8
Madagascar (1997)	14.1	11.4	25.5	0.6
Sudan (1990)	15.5	13.4	28.9	3.9
Tanzania (1996)	12.1	6.5	18.6	2.0
Uganda (1995)	18.3	10.7	29.0	3.1
Zambia (1996)	13.2	5.1	18.3	1.3
Zimbabwe (1994)	6.2	4.1	10.4	11.1

* See note 10.

Source: Country-specific reports of Demographic and Health Surveys. Year of the report is shown in parentheses.

the global population was much smaller when most of the major religions were first articulated. The approximate numbers of people inhabiting the globe around the time when major religions originated are shown in table 11.3.[6] For example, the origin of Hinduism is placed around the time of the Indus valley civilization, circa 3000 B.C.E. The global population around that time could not have been more than 50 million people. Today's global population is 120 times larger than what it was at the time of the origination of Hinduism in India. Even at the time of the evolvement of Protestant Christianity in the sixteenth century A.D., the global population would have been close to 450 million people—one-thirteenth of today's population.

Religion, by its nature, pronounces its laws and edicts to govern human behavior including their sexuality and reproduction. Through this authority, religion has had a powerful role in many countries' population programs and is believed to have profound effect on individual behavior. The influence of religious teachings included in sacred books on individual behavior is mitigated by religious institutions and religious leaders who are involved in interpreting these rules of human behavior for the lay people. But the question is: Are the rules articulated to govern human behavior when the global population was 50 or 450 million people applicable today when the global population has crossed the six billion mark?

At the individual level, women can reproduce between menarche and menopause (roughly between the ages of 15 and 49, a period called the reproductive period). The maximum *theoretical* fertility in a group of women who get married at the age 15, remain married throughout their reproductive period and use no contraception, abortion, breastfeeding, or abstinence is estimated to vary between 13 and 17 children with an average of about 15 children. Demographers call this number *Total Fecundity Rate*. While there are cases for indi-

TABLE 11.3. Estimated global population around the time major religions originated

Religion	Established Circa	World's Population (approx.)	Ratio to 6 billion (current population)
Hinduism	3000 B.C.E.	50 million	120
Judaism	2000 B.C.E.	100 million	60
Taoism	604 B.C.E.	150 million	40
Bhuddhism	600 B.C.E.	150 million	40
Jainism	600 B.C.E.	150 million	40
Christianity	0	200 million	30
Islam	610 A.D.	250 million	24
Protestant Christianity	16th century A.D.	450 million	13

vidual women giving births to that many children, the maximum recorded for a group of women is about nine children, among the Hutterites.[7] Demographers use the term *Total Fertility Rate* to measure actual fertility among a group of women. The average actual fertility among the Hutterites is higher than those reported for typical developing countries. For example, even in the absence of modern contraception, the average number of children born to women in India in the 1960s was about six children per woman.[8] The actual fertility in most developing countries was lower than the biological maximum because women breastfed their children for longer periods, couples practiced postpartum abstinence, and there was marital disruption due to widowhood and divorce.[9] The point here is to demonstrate that women have had fewer children than their biological maximum with or without the approval of their religion. That is, women have not followed the religious teaching that might have asked them "to multiply and grow." This type of dictum might have been relevant when most of the religious philosophies were articulated, at a time when conditions for survival were very harsh and life expectancy was extremely low. If individuals did not follow religious teachings all throughout history, then why would they follow now?

They would certainly want to adjust their reproductive behavior to changing conditions, especially to declining mortality among infants and children. This assertion is supported by the fact that a considerable percent of women around the world are practicing modern contraceptive methods (see table 11.1) and there exists a considerable degree of what demographers call the *unmet need* for fertility regulation methods (see table 11.2).[10] Various reasons for the existence of unmet need include inadequate availability and poor quality of services for contraceptive methods, lack of necessary knowledge about contraceptive methods, social opposition to their use, and health concerns about possible side effects.[11] While improvements in availability and quality of services will help individuals to meet their need for fertility regulation, unmet need is unlikely to be eliminated completely at the societal level. The assertion that individuals do not necessarily follow their religious teachings is also supported by the fact that only a small percent of those women who are neither using contraception nor intending to use a method in the future say that they are not using contraceptive methods for "religious" reasons (see table 11.2).

As mentioned earlier, the relation between individuals and their religion is a matter of their faith and their belief system. This relationship is guided by the religious philosophy about life and death: how and when life begins and what happens after a person's death. The degree to which religion and religious teachings can exert influence or control over individual behavior depends upon many factors, such as the extent to which a religion is "organized" and whether or not there is any direct link between the individual and the "supreme" being. In Jainism, for example, the belief system consists of a separation between the soul and the body. The soul is immortal and transmigrates from one life to another, and thus the death of a person is not considered as the end of the soul. The basic purpose of an individual person (soul) is to end the cycle of birth and death and achieve "nirvana." Religious teachings in Jainism provide general guidelines for behavior that could move the soul through this process. The Jain religion is not organized and there is little social pressure to conform to any particular way of living. There is no intermediary between an individual person and the supreme being. Some other religions, in contrast, are more organized; and there is another authority to mediate the link between an individual and the supreme being. In a religion like Jainism, there is much more room for an individual to deviate from any prescribed way of living than would be the case in an organized religion that involves regular group worship and may be able to exert more peer pressure.

In terms of the influence of religion on group behavior, followers of one religion can influence the reproductive behavior of nonfollowers by influencing the state's legal system through participation in its political system. This could only happen in democratic societies. In other circumstances, there is an ethical issue involved: Does religion give a right to its followers to coerce its nonfollowers to modify their reproductive behavior? While the ethical issue involved in the coercive role of the state was debated and discussed at the 1994 ICPD conference by governments of developing and developed countries, similar debate has not taken place about the coercion involved in the role of religion, religious institutions, and religious leaders. Perhaps that can be done by the present consultative group. The deliberations might be facilitated by the propositions I have made in this chapter and by addressing some specific questions such as the following:

1. Are the rules governing human behavior articulated when the global population was 50 to 450 million applicable today when the population has crossed the six billion mark?
2. How does religion explain the rapid population growth that has taken place?
3. How does religion explain other societal changes over time and differences among various societies?
4. How does religion explain the birth of an individual in more versus less advantageous conditions?

The explanations at the individual level may be simple. For example, the *karma theory* among the Jains and Hindus may explain the birth of an individual in a rich or poor family and the timing of the death of an individual by that individual's *karma*. However, could it also explain overall societal changes, such as massive declines in aggregate mortality and fertility that have taken place in the West and are taking place in the developing countries? It is true that the group experience, for example, mortality level in a country, is the sum of experiences of individuals living in that country. However, differences between mortality levels among countries and changes over time within a country, perhaps, would be difficult to explain by karmas of individuals living in different countries at different points in time. Such an explanation may imply massive improvements in karma of souls taking birth at different points in time.

Concluding Remarks

Most of the world's religions originated at a time when the global population was 50 to 450 million people in comparison to six billion at the beginning of the second millennium. Are the laws and edicts articulated at that time to guide (control) human behavior applicable now?

Throughout history, women have had fewer children than their biological maximum. They have achieved this lower fertility by using means such as breastfeeding, abstinence, and withdrawal. The average fertility thus achieved by these women has been consistent with the then-prevailing mortality conditions. Now that mortality has declined in many developing countries and has been declining in others, it is quite natural to expect that women in these countries would want to adjust their fertility behavior as well. Whether they do so by using traditional methods or by using modern methods such as the IUD or the birth control pill is another matter. Religious edicts to deny them the right to plan their families are unlikely to have significant effect on their behavior. If there were no pill or IUD at that time, how could religious teachings prohibit or sanction the use of these methods? The use of these methods has to be guided by the recent interpretations of old teachings and the extent to which an individual believes in those interpretations. The data presented here on contraceptive use and the existence of unmet need for contraception in developing countries suggest that in fact religious teachings, even if they prohibit the use of contraception, have had very little effect on individual behavior related to reproduction.

It is another matter at the group level. At times the role of religion comes in direct conflict with the obligation of the state in providing services of adequate quality to those who want them but cannot afford these services provided by the private sector. The followers of a religion can prohibit the state from providing these services by influencing the state's legal system through democratic means. Other circumstances raise an ethical issue: Does religion give a right to its followers to coerce its nonfollowers to modify their reproductive behavior? I hope that the propositions made and the questions raised in this chapter will help readers to address this issue.

NOTES

The author wishes to acknowledge with thanks valuable comments on earlier drafts made by his colleagues and by participants in the meeting of the Religious Consultation Group. Assistance of Heather Clark, Raji Mohanam, and Karen Schoepflin in preparing this manuscript is also acknowledged with thanks.

1. In the absence of migration, population growth of a geographic area equals the difference between the number of births and the number of deaths that occur to people living in that area.

2. According to historians, Jain religion was founded by Mahavira, but according to Jains, Mahavira was the 24th *Tirthankara* and the Jain religion has no beginning.

3. The nuclear family typically consists of husband, wife, and unmarried children. The extended family, on the other hand, can consist of married siblings, parents, and other relatives. There are other variations of family and kinship structures.

4. Safety of these services is another matter. If these services are legal, the state tries to regulate their safety.

5. Governments are involved in providing services for abortion in countries where it is legal to do so.

6. The global population around 5000 B.C.E. is estimated at between 5 and 20 million and at the time of Christ it is estimated to have been around 200 million. The annual growth rate of population at that time was too small. For religions that originated prior to Chrisianity, the number of people inhabiting the globe would have been between 20 and 200 million people. The numbers shown in table 11.3 are really approximate.

7. "The Hutterites are members of an Anabaptist sect descendent from Swiss settlers in the northern United States and in Canada. They live in small communities in which strict social and religious control exists over most aspects of daily life. Demographers have a strong interest in their society because the fertility rates of Hutterites is higher than that of any other populations with reliable records. In 1950, women who had reached the end of their childbearing years had borne an average of about nine children (Eaton and Mayer 1953). Their high fertility was made possible by spacing births about 2 years apart throughout their reproductive years, beginning with marriage in their early twenties" (Bongaarts and Potter 1983:8).

8. While the average number of children per woman in India has declined from six to about three, the population growth continues.

9. These practices may not have been used by individuals to deliberately control their individual fertility. These practices reflected societal and cultural norms of hu-

man behavior, which also had a dampening effect on fertility. It can be argued that these norms were evolved at the societal level over time to maintain a balance between the aggregate fertility and mortality levels. In this sense, societies can evolve normative behavior to practice modern contraceptive methods in order to reestablish a balance between fertility and mortality.

10. The extent of unmet need is estimated by comparing responses to questions relating to the current use of contraception and to the stated desire to have another child and its timing. Women who have reported being pregnant at interview or those who are amenorrheic, i.e., have not resumed menstruation since last birth, are treated differently by considering the status of their current pregnancy or last live birth. Thus, "unmet need for spacing includes pregnant women whose pregnancy was mistimed, amenorrhoeic women whose last birth was mistimed, and women who are neither pregnant nor amenorrhoeic and who are not using any method of family planning and say they that they want to wait two or more years until their next birth. Also included in unmet need for spacing are women who are unsure whether they want another child or who want another child but are unsure when to have the birth. Unmet need for limiting refers to pregnant women whose pregnancy was unwanted, amenorrhoeic women whose last child was unwanted, amenorrhoeic women who became pregnant while using a method (these women are in need of better contraception). Also excluded are menopausal or infecund women" (Demographic and Health Survey: Kenya, 1998).

11. See Casterline and Sinding for a recent review.

REFERENCES

Bongaarts, John, and Robert G. Potter. *Fertility, Biology, and Behavior: An Analysis of the Proximate Determinants.* New York: Academic Press, 1983.

Casterline, John B., and Steven W. Sinding. 2000. "Unmet Need for Family Planning in Developing Countries and Implications for Population Policy." *Population and Devleopment Review* 26(4): 691–723. New York: Population Council.

Hawley, Amos H. *Human Ecology: A Theory of Community Structure.* New York: Ronald Press, 1950.

Kenya Demographic and Health Survey 1998. Calverton, Maryland: Macro International, 1999.

Ministry of Health and Family Welfare, Department of Family Welfare, and Government of India. *Family Welfare Programme in India: Year Book 1989–90.* New Delhi, 1991.

Peterson, William. *Population.* New York: Macmillan Publishing, 1975.

Tomlinson, Ralph. *Population Dynamics: Causes and Consequences of World Demographic Change.* New York: Random House, 1976.

United Nations Secretariat Department of Economic and Social Affairs. *World Population Prospects.* New York: United Nations, 1998.

12

Reproduction and Sexuality in a Changing World

Reaching Consensus

JOSE BARZELATTO AND ELIZABETH DAWSON

For women and men to fully enjoy reproductive and sexual health and rights, legal systems must be modified and many social, economic, and political systems revised. Crucial to achieving these changes is promoting more equitable societies and, within them, just gender roles and the adoption of more positive attitudes toward sexuality. This is a difficult but not an impossible task, one that requires a focus on values and a search for new solutions. In doing so, religions have a major role to play by providing moral guidance and acting as a source of personal "power and motivation."[1]

An Emerging International Consensus

Reaching consensus has been difficult because sexuality and reproduction are among the most private and intimate aspects of the life of human beings, and until recently were considered inappropriate for public discussion. During the last 50 years, as modern methods of fertility regulation (pills, IUDs, and vacuum aspiration) began to be massively introduced, reproduction and sexuality have become extremely divisive issues. Opposing positions have been staked on issues from population control versus development, encouragement versus prohibition of contraceptive methods, and "pro-choice" versus "pro-life." While divisions—particularly regarding abortion—continue to grab headlines, the initial advances toward reaching a social consensus and the increased importance of values in the discussion have passed relatively unnoticed. Yet they are very significant and provide a base for developing more progressive social policies. There are two primary reasons that a consensus is emerging and that reaching it is not an impossible task. First, social and economic progress is changing all societies in a way that deeply affects reproductive and sexual behavior. There is a growing consensus that a small family is an advantage for all, enabling parents to provide a better future for their children and societies to progress at a faster pace. This is because people no longer die in great numbers at an early age and survivors live longer; hence, high fertility is no longer a prerequisite for the survival of families or of most nations. Moreover, modern fertility-regulating technology makes it possible to separate sexuality and reproduction with reasonable efficacy and safety. Consequently, fertility is dropping steadily almost everywhere. When fertility is lower, women need less time to bear and rear children. This permits them more time for activities outside the home, so they are able to play creative and productive roles in addition to motherhood.

A second factor is that agreement on smaller family size and the expanded role of women beyond motherhood is occurring in a shrinking world that is accelerating social change. Progressively more people of diverse origins and traditions are coming into contact with one another as a result of the proliferation of mass media and the increase of direct contact among persons via the Internet, travel and migration, and the globalization of the world economy. This contact is forcing people to contemplate and respect—or at least tolerate—each other's differences. Cultures, religions, ideologies, and moral systems are being compelled to explain their contrasting views to themselves and to "the others" in a rational and respectful way. As a result, we are witnessing an increasing dialogue among different people that includes the subjects of health and rights, reproduction and sexuality.

A New and Growing International Consensus

What is the evidence for believing that a consensus is emerging? First is the magnitude and extension of the decline in fertility as reflected in demographic statistics. Then there is the evolution of international agreements among governments and the trends of changes in national laws. Finally is the increasing involvement of civil society as advocates and agents of change.

Demographic Shifts

With few exceptions—most of them in Africa—fertility has plummeted around the world. In 1998, the global average fertility level was 2.7 births per woman, almost half the average of 5.0 births in 1950, when fertility started to drop in the less developed countries. During the last 25 years, the number of children per couple has fallen from 5.1 to 2.6 in Asia, from 5.0 to 2.7 in Latin America and the Caribbean, and from 6.6 to 5.1 in Africa. Also in 1998, the fertility in 61 countries representing 44 percent of the world population (2.6 billion) was already at or below the level necessary for the replacement of generations (or a total fertility rate of 2.1), including China and several other countries in the less-developed regions. Asia and Latin America are expected to reach replacement around 2025.[2]

The important point here is that the need for a social consensus is about the consequences of replacement fertility and not about the need for family planning. In fact, there is practically no serious religious or governmental opposition to family planning. The debate about fertility regulation focuses today on what methods are legitimate and under what circumstances, or on what is the appropriate role of governments. The debate is no longer about numbers; it is about values, and the consensus is needed whether the population is growing, stable, or decreasing. Such a consensus would also facilitate access to family planning in the half of the world where fertility is still above replacement and where improving family planning has a significant role to play in slowing population growth. Even more important, fertility regulation services will continue to be crucial for the well-being of society after population growth stops. Furthermore, for dealing with some of the negative effects of population growth, such as increased poverty and environmental deterioration, family planning now has a relatively small role to play. Given the magnitude of these issues and the inevitability of most future population growth, these problems require solutions today and must go well beyond family planning interventions.

Evidence from International Conferences

About 50 years ago, the attention of governments, as well as of public opinion, started to focus on the negative effects of population growth in the less developed countries. Understandably so, because the phenomenon was dramatic and connoted grave consequences for all countries, regardless of their degree of development. At the United Nations World Conference on Population in Bucharest in 1974, governments arrived at a consensus that population growth was jeopardizing the development of the South. However, there was serious disagreement on how to address the threat. The North offered family planning services as the solution, while the South countered that the best contraceptive was development. Ten years later, in Mexico City at the United Nations International Conference on Population, many participants appeared to have switched sides. The United States declared that population growth did not affect development while most developing country governments favored increasing family planning services to accelerate development. Nevertheless, as during the previous decade, the United States continued to be the main foreign aid supporter of family planning in the South.

The clearest expression of the emerging consensus is found in the Program of Action agreed upon at the United Nations International Conference on Population and Development (ICPD), held in Cairo in 1994. At the conference, governments reached a much broader agreement by recognizing that fertility and development were inextricably interconnected. They concluded that development generated a motivation to reduce fertility and modern fertility-regulating methods provided safe means to achieve this objective. Furthermore, these two factors act synergistically. In other words, when both factors coexist, fertility drops faster than the sum of the impacts of both factors acting separately. More importantly, the ICPD consensus was embedded within the context of health and human rights. Understanding health as "total wellbeing, physical, mental and social, and not the mere absence of disease," it recognized that reproductive and sexual health and rights were social goods of importance to all governments regardless of whether the population was growing, stable, or decreasing. Thus, international concern evolved from promoting population control—where people were the objects of policies—to promoting reproductive and sexual health and rights where people are the subjects of the policies. The concern had shifted from numbers of people to the well-being of individuals.

Before the ICPD, the objective was to stop population growth and consequently allow social and economic development to proceed. As the complex motivations for reproductive behavior were better understood, it became clear that the objective had to be the well-being of individuals, including their having the means to control their fertility. This was a social good in itself, of permanent importance, and not only for dealing with population growth, which is a transitory phenomenon. The well-being of individuals requires that governments make all efforts to enable their citizens to achieve the highest possible level of health, while fully respecting all their rights.

Changes in National Laws

Some governments have found it easier to participate in the international dialogue than to actually make these commitments at the national level, including revising their own laws. Nevertheless, at a country level, some bellwether changes in legislation reflect the start of a consensus on the importance of reproductive health and lower fertility. Contraceptives are now legal practically everywhere and increasingly laws are facilitating access to contraception. Even the trend in abortion law revisions is toward liberalization, particularly during early pregnancy, possibly indicative of an increased respect for pluralism. The fact is that 65 percent of the world's population lives in 75 countries whose laws permit unrestricted abortions (although most establish gestational age limits) or abortion for socioeconomic reasons or health reasons, including mental health. Ten percent of the population lives in 23 countries that authorize abortion for reasons of physical health, and practically all the remaining 25 percent live in countries that permit abortion only to save the life of the pregnant woman. There are five countries with less than 1 percent of the world population that penalize abortion under all circumstances.[3]

The Importance of Civil Society

Civil society, mainly through women-led nongovernmental organizations working on women's rights and health, has probably played the most important role in promoting change and in building a consensus with respect to reproductive and sexual health. The "international women's health movement,"[4] a loose but effective network, has created public awareness, demanded accountability, enriched understanding, and greatly influenced the adoption of international agreements. It has envisioned the possibility of a consensus built around a women-centered perspective[5]—the perspective agreed upon at the ICPD—and has emphasized the need for a broad consensus in order to make the international discourse a reality at a grassroots level.[6] It further stresses the need for an integrative approach to human rights and health, avoiding the fragmentation of policies, strategies, and activism, to realize this consensus.[7]

The influential role of women in the preparatory meetings leading up to the ICPD in Cairo in 1994, in the agreements of the conference, as well as in the follow-up, is well known. There is less awareness, though, of the financial support offered by a number of philanthropic organizations—yet another arm of civil society—for the institutional development of many of the national and international civil society organizations that constituted this network. On the eve of the Cairo conference, women's organizations were also successful in raising support from these foundations for organizing national and regional meetings to discuss the agenda prior to the conference. These meetings culminated in the worldwide gathering in Rio de Janeiro in January 1994, where close to 200 women from more than 80 countries, representing a wide diversity of women's health, development, and rights organizations, participated.[8] This forum allowed women leaders to get to know each other personally, to understand their differences, and to agree on what they all could fight for together. A successful common strategy was to seek inclusion into their respective governments' official country delegations to the Cairo Conference. Thus, they were able not only to speak with one voice but also to facilitate the consensus among governments, as well as the coordination with the NGO Forum that met in parallel to the conference itself. This network continues to function and grow today.

This influence of women on public policy is in large part due to the involvement of feminist movements, which hold a basic common banner in advocating women's control of their own bodies in their fight for more equitable gender roles. An excellent example of how these groups of women are contributing to the development of an international consensus on reproductive and sexual health is the influential role played first by English-speaking women, particularly in the United States, by the Boston Women's Health Book Collective series, starting with its first version of *Our Bodies, Ourselves*, published in 1972, when abortion was still illegal in the United States, to its last English revision in 1998. The importance of the series is that different versions have been published in dozens of other languages around the world, not as mere translations but as texts adapted to the local culture and reality by groups of local women leaders. The last of these adaptations, published in May 2000, in Spanish (*Nuestros Cuerpos, Nuestras Vidas*), was a collaborative effort of a group of Latin American women.[9]

The voices of ethicists and religious leaders, also supported by foundations, made their contribution to the consensus reached at the ICPD, as best illustrated by the two following examples.

(1) The Development Law and Policy Program of Columbia University's Center for Population and Family Health and the United Nations Population Fund (UNFPA) convened an international roundtable on Ethics, Population, and Reproductive Health. Thirty-two scholars, including ethicists, lawyers, theologians, and social scientists, from 21 countries agreed on a declaration that made an important contribution to the Cairo Conference by providing five ethical propositions to guide population and reproductive health policies and programs.[10] Their emphasis upon the need for governments to "devise strategies that are broadly integrated with social and economic development, im-

proved education, and political and legal reform"[11] was clearly echoed in the ICPD's Program of Action.

(2) The Park Ridge Center for the Study of Health, Faith, and Ethics convened two meetings in preparation for the ICPD. One allowed members of the U.S. delegation to discuss the agenda with scholars of the main religions in the United States and suggested specific language for the draft Program of Action. The second meeting was held in May 1994, in Belgium, with the cooperation of the International Forum for Biophilosophy. Thirty scholars of the world's major religious traditions produced a report that reflects the diversity of perspectives within and among the different faiths, while reaching a significant measure of consensus on several important items. The report was distributed and widely used by government and NGO delegates at the conference.[12]

The report began by emphasizing the importance of respect for "freedom of religion and even freedom from religion and religions . . . because no single faith may claim final moral authority in international discourse." Other discussion points included population and development; development, consumption, and the maldistribution of resources; humans and the environment; the role of women in issues of population and development; valuing families in their various forms; adolescents; contraception; abortion; sex education; and migration. In respect to contraception, the report recognized that "almost all of the world's religions endorse contraception . . . as a responsible option, even as a religiously motivated activity" and object to any form of coercion.

Another illustrative example of the involvement of civil society in seeking a consensus is the many workshops of the International Federation of Gynecology and Obstetrics (FIGO) in support of the ICPD agreements. The first workshop took place in November 1996, organized in collaboration with the World Health Organization (WHO), the UNFPA, and the International Planned Parenthood Federation (IPPF). Under the title "Better Reproductive Health for All: The Role of Obstetricians and Gynecologists," participants from 31 countries including obstetricians/gynecologists, women's health experts, family planning professionals, and representatives of government and industry met in Manila. Consideration was given to the primary components of reproductive and sexual health programs: safe motherhood, family planning, reproductive tract infections, and unsafe abortion. It was agreed that obstetricians and gynecologists should assume leadership as advocates for implementing the Cairo Program of Action; urge governments to allocate resources accordingly; work with other NGOs; recognize the obligation to educate fellow health professionals and the public at large; and exchange experiences and ideas among national societies. Their analysis and recommendations were transmitted to their colleagues around the world, encouraging action of individual professionals as well of their member national societies.[13] Numerous national and regional workshops have followed, contributing to the dialogue required to build a broad social consensus.

The Case of Abortion

To further illustrate our belief that a consensus is developing, we have chosen to discuss the case of abortion in more detail. Why abortion? Because it is the most controversial of all the issues related to reproductive health and rights, the one that elicits the most emotional reactions and possibly the most important stumbling block in attaining an international consensus.

It is estimated that one-third of all pregnancies, 80 million, are unwanted or mistimed. Fifty million end up in abortion, of which 20 million are performed under unsafe conditions, threatening women's health and lives. In fact, at least 78,000 women die every year and hundreds of thousands of other women experience short- or long-term disabilities.[14]

At the ICPD in 1994, the governments of the world reached what is the prevailing consensus on abortion. They recognized that unsafe abortion was a major worldwide public health problem, that unwanted pregnancies should be prevented and every attempt made to eliminate the need for abortion (Art. 8.25 of the Plan of Action).[15] At the United Nations Fourth World Conference on Women, held in Beijing in 1995, governments went one step further. They included among the recommended actions for governments the review of laws penalizing women who undergo an abortion (Article 106, k, of the Platform of Action).[16] Within individual nations, as mentioned earlier, the trend in abortion laws is toward liberalization. The decriminalization of abortion is, perhaps, the next area upon which international agreement will be reached.

In addition, the issue of decriminalizing abortions was addressed in the previously noted meeting of theologians from the main world religions that took place in Belgium in May 1994. When specifically discussing abortion, the report stated that "while (it) is universally treated as a serious moral and religious concern, it is treated differently among and within religious communities. Most religious traditions do not forbid abortion altogether, yet some limit the conditions under which it may be permitted. Others understand it as a matter that is to be left at the discretion of the individual." The report also noted that the consequences upon the life and health of women when abortion is illegal or heavily restricted could not be disregarded and, therefore, decriminalization "is a minimal response to this reality and a reasonable means to protect the life and health of women at risk."[17]

Obstetricians and gynecologists have also participated in a significant way in the abortion debate. In the aforementioned FIGO workshops held in Manila in 1996, it was recommended that obstetricians and gynecologists "promote safe abortion and fight the stigma attached to abortion by . . . documenting the reality of abortion in their countries . . . informing public opinion and promoting a respectful . . . public debate . . . to demystify abortion by emphasizing" and respecting the diversity of values; and by "promoting education and training on abortion care." The workshop also recommended "promoting regional exchanges of experiences among countries" and that the "FIGO Ethics Committee should address ethical guidelines in respect to abortion." The follow-up to these recommendations are described below:

(1) FIGO and the World Health Organization organized a Latin American meeting on "Abortion: A Professional Responsibility of Obstetricians and Gynecologists" that took place in Campinas, Sao Paulo, Brazil, in 1997.[18] The 32 participants from 16 countries included the present and a former president of FIGO, a former president and the secretary general of the Latin American Federation of Societies of Obstetricians and Gynecologists, three presidents of national societies, three parliamentarians, university professors, social scientists, and women's groups leaders.

The participants started by recognizing that obstetricians and gynecologists, both professionally and as private citizens, had a special responsibility in addressing the serious social and public health problem of voluntary abortion. They suggested that professional societies should inform their communities and promote a broad and respectful dialogue involving other sectors of society. Then the following recommendations were made, which addressed the three subjects of the meeting:

a. *Good professional practice for women seeking care for abortion complications* included local societies questioning and opposing laws that forced physicians to report self-induced abortions or requiring the presence of police where patients are treated.

b. *Good professional practice for women requesting legal interruption of pregnancy in countries with restrictive laws* entailed national societies endorsing the creation of specialized units for providing legal abortions at teaching hospitals as part of an effort to inform their members about abortion laws in their countries and empower them to act within the law.

c. *Role of physicians in liberalizing laws and regulations on abortion* involved leading an objective debate within the profession and within society at large to decriminalize abortion, emphasizing the magnitude, "the determinants and the social, cultural and economic consequences of unwanted pregnancies."[19] The recommendations noted that "criminalization of abortion does not decrease its incidence, but dramatically increases maternal mortality and morbidity" and results in "social inequality and social injustice." Hence, gynecologists and obstetricians have an "ethical imperative . . . to expand the conditions under which abortion is legal," following a tradition of influencing the adoption of laws that improve women's health.

Following the Campinas meeting, the Peruvian Society for Obstetrics and Gynecology convened two meetings: a national one, on the Medical Responsibility in Dealing with Abortion to Decrease Maternal Mortality (July 1997), and a regional one on the Responsibility of the Societies of Obstetrics and Gynecology in Dealing with Abortion to Decrease Maternal Mortality (January 1998). Both meetings discussed the Campinas report and expanded upon the analysis and conclusions.

(2) Since 1985, FIGO has had a Committee for the Ethical Aspects of Human Reproduction and Women's Health that offers FIGO and its member societies ethical guidelines for their consideration and discussion. The committee addressed the worldwide problem of unsafe abortion at three meetings (May 1997, March 1998, and September 1998), from which developed the "Ethical Guidelines Regarding Induced Abortion for Non-Medical Reasons."[20] The guidelines recognize the diversity of opinions for justifying an abortion, and the magnitude and characteristics of the problem, particularly of high levels of unsafe abortion as women try to circumvent restrictive legislation. This introduction is followed by recommendations including:

- "Governments and other concerned organizations should make every effort to improve women's rights, status, and health, and should try to prevent unintended pregnancies . . ."
- "Women have the right to make a choice on whether or not to reproduce and should therefore have access to legal, safe, effective, acceptable, and affordable methods of contraception."
- "Providing the process of properly informed consent has been carried out, a woman's right to autonomy, combined with the need to prevent unsafe abortion, justifies the provision of safe abortion."
- "Respect for . . . autonomy means that no . . . member of the medical team should be expected to advise or perform an abortion against his

or her personal conviction. . . . Such a doctor, however, has an obligation to refer the woman to a colleague who is not in principle opposed to termination."

Another example of civil society efforts edging toward consensus in the difficult area of abortion is the Meeting of Latin American and Caribbean Parliamentarians on Induced Abortion, convened by the Universidad Externado de Colombia in collaboration with the Center for Health and Social Policy. Held in Bogota, in October 1998, it was attended by 80 parliamentarians from 21 countries and from the Central American and Latin American Parliaments. The participants represented a variety of political perspectives.

The Bogota Declaration, unanimously agreed upon by all participants, acknowledges the "extreme gravity" of the problem and emphasizes its magnitude in Latin America—"one in three pregnancies end in abortion," at least four million per year, causing "close to ten thousand deaths"—and notes "that almost the totality of legislation fully or partially criminalize the practice of induced abortion" and "where legislation does consider exceptions to the penalization . . . it becomes impossible to apply." Then it states: "An analysis of the state of induced abortion in the region has demonstrated that current legislation not only has proved ineffective in reducing the prevalence of induced abortion but that it has led to a concentration of risks and inequities within the poorest sectors of the population."

The parliamentarians took upon themselves the responsibility to ensure that induced abortion is openly debated within their societies "from a pluralistic perspective," and concluded it was "indispensable" for them to act in their respective countries in different ways, including:

- "To acknowledge and deal with the question of induced abortion as a public health problem and as a human rights issue, with an emphasis on preventive measures."
- "To promote legal norms that protect and support pregnant women in general, and in particular . . . young single women, working women (eliminating the requirement of a pregnancy test and job dismissal due to a pregnancy); and women students (to guarantee scholastic nonsuspension)."
- "To create and strengthen legal and institutional mechanisms that foment nonviolence against women and children, responsible paternity and maternity, and the expansion or coverage of social security."
- "To make sexual and reproductive education compulsory from the earliest school-years, extending it to fathers and mothers, and to both male and female teachers."

- "Legislative norms relating to induced abortion must emphasize access to safe methods of family planning, easy access to legal abortions . . . emergency contraception, a humane treatment of women who are pregnant and during post-abortion care in health establishments, and a respect for the ethnic and cultural diversity that prevails in the region."
- "To allocate increasing resources in national budgets for the area of health and for sexual and reproductive education."
- "To revise and bring up-to-date existing legislation . . . so that it will conform with the recommendations herein agreed to."[21]

What Helps in Building a Consensus?

Building a social consensus of any sort is a process, one that merits discussion in light of our shared objective of achieving a consensus on reproductive and sexual health and rights. The first basic rule in promoting a consensus is not to frame the discussion as a confrontation or as a dilemma. Indeed, there are occasions when choosing between two options is inevitable. More often than not, though, there are alternative ways to proceed, even though many times it may not be readily apparent. Consequently, an effort should be made to avoid being paternalistic or defensive and, in particular, to avoid focusing narrowly on the means while ignoring the context or losing sight of the goal.

One must also be mindful that seeking a consensus is not about denying or ignoring differences, but rather is a process that starts with identifying common views and expanding upon them through a respectful dialogue. This process must be based on the best available objective evidence that is not manipulated by presenting it in a partial way or out of context. Hence, social consensus requires an equitable society and a strong democracy to allow for a very broad participation and a free flow of ideas and information.

It seems pertinent to mention a couple of examples of what is not helpful in building a consensus in our case.

(1) Frequently, discussions are framed as, or even meetings entitled, "Population Control versus Reproductive Health in the Developing World," stating a false dilemma and implying at least two questions. One is whether one must choose between reducing population growth and improving the well-being of individuals. The other is whether this is a problem limited to the South. Obviously, the answer is no to both questions, as discussed previously. A better title would be "From Population Control to Reproductive and Sexual Health and Rights," reflecting a real conceptual evolution of an international concern.

Furthermore, during the course of this evolution there was no serious confrontation suggesting that family planning and reproductive and sexual health and rights were two incompatible approaches. This was true despite the heated denunciations of the human rights violations by family planning programs that occurred when demographic goals predominated, on the one hand, and, on the other, concerns of policy makers for the economic viability of family planning programs if they became part of reproductive and sexual health programs. Conceptually, there is no conflict either. In fact, from the first time that reproductive health was defined,[22] it was recognized that family planning was one of the four pillars sustaining this concept.[23]

(2) Another example of what is unhelpful in building a consensus is posing the abortion debate as a dichotomy of either being solely in favor of or against it when in reality practically no one adheres to these extreme positions. Nearly everyone agrees that there are too many abortions in the world today, and nearly everyone agrees that, under certain circumstances, it is a necessary lesser evil. Let us not forget that treating an ectopic pregnancy is in fact performing an abortion to save the mother's life. The real debate is about how to reduce the number of abortions and about when an abortion is justified. The proposed solutions differ widely: from reducing abortion by "improving moral behavior," to legalizing all abortions; from justifying abortion whenever the woman decides to interrupt a pregnancy, to justifying it to save the life of the woman only when the pregnancy is ectopic or when it coexists with a cancer of the genital tract, as accepted by the Catholic Church. Starting the discussion on the basis of common views rather than as a confrontation provides an opportunity to expand this currently very limited consensus through a dialogue that respects intellectual integrity.

A final comment on prerequisites to build a consensus is the need to continue to document change and to expand our knowledge of the situation in all its complexity. Research, mainly social and demographic, has greatly facilitated our understanding of population growth and how family planning works, but only recently has it started to explore the consequences of fertility decline and its effects on individuals and families. Little attention has been paid, for example, to how to provide the needed education and socialization of children whose nuclear family consists of two working parents and who may lack siblings and an extended family. Another neglected issue is the trend toward delayed marriages. This trend brings into question the reasonableness of expecting sexual abstention until marriage, which may not take place until 20 years or more after the onset of puberty. The question begs the balance, one that does not promote promiscuity and inappropriate early sexual activity but still affirms the realities of human sexuality. Another pertinent question is how the separation of sexuality and procreation, the lowering of fertility, and the changes in gender roles affect the structure of marriage. These are the types of value-laden issues at the micro level that merit discussion and resources and yet are given short shrift by focusing only on population growth. Major macro-level issues are similarly neglected or falsely assumed to be solved by focusing on the population explosion, as in the case for the "poverty explosion."[24]

The Role of Religion in Forging the Consensus

As we have seen, people's reproductive and sexual behavior is creating a new international consensus. The debate with respect to sexual and reproductive health is now mainly about what methods of fertility regulation are morally permissible and under what circumstances. It centers, as well, on the social and cultural effects of fertility decline such as changes in gender roles and their impact upon family structures. The debate has moved from numbers to values, and thus religions have an even more important role to play in this significant process of social change.

Moreover, reproduction and sexuality are at the core of marriage and hence at the basic foundation of families and societies. The values underlying family structures have always been a major concern of religions. As such, it is significant to note that promoting high fertility is no longer a prominent strategy for increasing the number of the faithful. On the contrary, responsible parenthood is now frequently emphasized in different religious traditions. There is also greater recognition that procreation is not the main or only purpose of marriage, as illustrated within the Catholic Church when the Vatican Council II, which met from 1962 to 1965, agreed that marriage had two equally important primary purposes: procreation and the unity of the spouses. This changed the traditional Catholic teaching that procreation was the only primary objective.

Similarly, changes in gender roles are starting to challenge traditional patriarchal societies to accept new familial structures and new definitions of power among men and women that are more equitable. This, too, is a matter of values where religions have wisdom to offer. In fact, many religions are implicitly, and some explicitly, beginning to look at sexuality and gender roles more forthrightly than in the past. For example, they are highlighting the need for sexual education and getting involved in passionate debates on the appropriate content, not to mention the ongoing discussions within many organized religions about whether women should be ordained, whether gay couples should be permitted to marry, and whether priests should remain celibate.

Religion, too, has a role in the discussions about what constitutes "health." Despite the significant progress represented by the conceptual shift of the ICPD agreements, there are still numerous aspects of this new understanding that have not yet been properly discussed. Maybe the most fundamental is that health, understood as "total wellbeing" and "not the mere absence of disease" is inevitably part of a system of values, including political, social, cultural, and religious values that need a social consensus or at least a social agreement for new policies to be effective. This is particularly true when trying to balance the tensions between rights and responsibilities and between individual and common good.

NOTES

1. D. C. Maguire, "Introduction," in *Visions of a New Earth. Religious Perspectives on Population, Consumption and Ecology*, ed. H. Coward and D. C. Maguire (Albany: State University of New York Press, 2000).

2. United Nations, "1998 Revision World Population Estimates and Projections," Briefing Packet, Population Division, United Nations, New York, 1998. This does not mean in any way that the problem of population growth is stopping any time soon. The world population is estimated to reach 8.9 billion by 2050, increasing by almost 50% the present level and continuing to grow, although at a much lower pace, into the next century. What it means is only that the growth is slowing down. Furthermore, only 30 of those 61 countries with fertility below replacement will experience a decline in total population during the next 50 years and the rest will not, due to their young population structures and to immigration.

Further analysis of these figures shows that more than half of future population growth will be due to population momentum, that is, growth occurring after the decline in fertility has reached replacement, due to a young population structure. Unfortunately, there are only two limited policy options to influence this part of future population growth: promote greater delay of the first birth and greater spacing in between births. See J. Bongaarts, "Future Population Growth and Policy Options," lecture at the Advanced Leadership Program, Princeton, New Jersey, November 1998, unpublished. The effectiveness of these measures for populations that have reached replacement is limited, because they are normally quite advanced already in this respect. Unless coercive measures are adopted or if the culture of the present development process induces couples to reduce their fertility below replacement level, as is already the case in most of the more developed countries, populatioin pressures will continue to build. In such a case population growth will be smaller than projected, because projections assume that the decline of fertility will stabilize at replacement. Some countries have in fact already maintained fertility below replacement for more than two decades.

3. A. Rahman, L. Katzive, and S. K. Henshaw, "A Global Review of Laws on Induced Abortion," *International Family Planning Perspectives* 24:56 (1998), and R. J., Cook, B. M. Dickens, and L. E. Bliss, "International Developments in Abortion Law from 1988 to 1998," *American Journal of Public Health* 89:579–586 (1999).

4. M. Berer, "Editorial: The International Women's Health Movement," *Reproductive Health Matters* 10:6 (1997).

5. See M. Berer, "Introduction: Population and Family Planning Policies: Women Centred Perspectives." *Reproductive Health Matters* 1:4 (1993).

6. See J. Jacobson, "Transforming Family Planning Programmes: Towards a Framework for Advancing the Reproductive Rights Agenda," *Reproductive Health Matters* 8:21 (2000).

7. See R. Petchesky, "Human Rights, Reproductive Health, and Economic Justice: Why They Are Indivisible," *Reproductive Health Matters* 8:12 (2000).

8. Ford Foundation, "Sexuality and Reproductive Health," Reproductive Health and Population Program: A Progress Report to the Board of Trustees, December 1994.

9. The Boston Woman's Healthbook Collective, *Nuestros Cuerpos, Nuestras Vidas: La Guia Definitiva para La Salud de La Muier Latina* (Seven Stories Press: New York, 2000).

10. The five propositions that organized their ethical analysis were as follows:

(1) "Because reproductive health is an important social good, promoting reproductive health and improving conditions for its attainment are an ethical obligation."
(2) "Justice in reproductive health requires an equitable allocation of benefits and responsibilities related to reproductive decisions, including decisions about whether or not to have children."
(3) "For actions and practices to be ethical, persons must be treated with respect and the autonomy of individuals must be respected."
(4) "Ethically sound reproductive health programs and policies are ones that result in a balance of desirable consequences over undesirable ones."
(5) "Population policies are integral parts of social, economic, and cultural development, whose principal aim is to enhance the human dignity and quality of life of all individuals."

11. The Development Law and Policy Program, "Roundtable on Ethics, Population, and Reproductive Health: Declaration of Principles," Columbia University, March 8–10, 1994, New York.

12. The Park Ridge Center for the Study of Health, Faith, and Ethics, "World Religions and the 1994 United Nations International Conference on Population and Development: A Report on an International and Interfaith Consultation," Genval, Belgium, May 4–7, 1994, The Park Ridge Center, Chicago.

13. International Federation of Gynecology and Obstetrics (FIGO), "Better Reproductive Health for All: The Role of Obstetricians and Gynecologists," Report of a Workshop, November 14–15, 1996, Manila, Philippines. London, FIGO, 1997.

14. Family Care International, "Sexual and Reproductive Health: Briefing Cards" New York, 2000.

15. United Nations, "Report of the International Conference on Population and Development," Cairo, September 5–13, 1994, United Nations, New York, 1995.

16. United Nations: "Report of the Fourth World Conference on Women," Beijing, September 4–15, 1995, United Nations, New York, 1996.

17. The Park Ridge Center, "World Religions Conference."

18. FIGO/WHO Working Group, "Abortion: A Professional Responsibility of Obstetricians and Gynecologists," Final Report, CEMICAMP, March 2–5, 1997, Campinas, Sao Paulo, Brazil.

19. Ibid.

20. FIGO Committee for the Ethical Aspects of Human Reproduction and Women's Health, "Ethical Guidelines Regarding Induced Abortion for Non-Medical Reasons," *International Journal of Gynecology and Obstetrics* 64:318–320 (1999).

The guidelines start by defining induced abortion "as the termination of pregnancy using drugs or surgical intervention after implantation and before the conceptus has become independently viable." The Committee had defined pregnancy as that part of the reproductive process that commences with the implantation of the conceptus in a woman, and ends with either the birth of an infant or an abortion. Having previously accepted the WHO definition of 22 weeks of menstrual age as the limit to speak of an abortion or of a birth, it noted that this limit did not apply to the lethally malformed fetus and that from 22 to 28 weeks viability depended on the social and economic circumstances of the newborn infant.

21. Universidad Externado de Colombia, "Meeting of Parliamentarians from Latin America and the Caribbean on Induced Abortion," Centro de Investigaciones sobre Dinamica, Social, Bogota, 2000.

22. M. F. Fathalla, "Research Needs in Human Reproduction," in *Research in Human Reproduction: Biennial Report (1986–1987)*, ed. E. Diczfalusy, P. D. Griffin and J. Khanna (Geneva: WHO, 1988), p. 341

23. J. Barzelatto, "Continuity and Change," in *Research in Human Reproduction: Bienniel Report (1986–1987)*, ed. E. Diegfolusy, P. D. Griffin, and J. Khonne (Geneva: WHO, 1988), p. 11.

24. J. Barzelatto, "Socioeconomic and Ethical Aspects of Family Planning," Proceedings of the Twelfth World Congress on Fertility and Sterility, Singapore, October 1986, vol. 6, *Contraception*, p. 145–147 (Pearl River, N.Y.: Parthenon Publishing Group, 1986).

Conclusion

ARVIND SHARMA

It is customary, in Hindu philosophical discussions, to begin the exposition of one's point of view, not by stating the arguments for it, but instead by presenting first the position *against* it and the arguments on which this opposite stance is based. Thus, a discussion of the proofs of the existence of God usually commences, in the standard Hindu manner, with a catalogue of the arguments against God's existence. Such a statement is called the *p·arvapakùa*—or the preliminary view which is meant to be later refuted. Such a procedure may seem perverse to some of us, but it possesses one great merit—it leaves oneself, or others for that matter, in no doubt about the task one is engaged in.

It seems to me that the adoption of such a procedure might be particularly appropriate for this concluding chapter. After all, there is a widespread perception abroad that the religious traditions of humanity are uniformly opposed to family planning, contraception, and abortion. The word "uniformly" was used in the above sentence on purpose, as a double-edged sword, to imply that all the religious traditions of humanity are supposed to be opposed to family planning, contraception, and abortion, and further that each tradition in itself and of itself is totally so opposed. That is to say, it would be futile to suggest that perhaps Islam takes a more lenient line on abortion than, say, Christianity. Similarly, it would be futile to propose that within Christianity or Islam more than one view on the point may be encountered—and one more lenient, for want of a better word, than the other. Thus, not only are all traditions supposed to be opposed to family planning, contraception, and abortion, each is also supposed to be opposed to it in its entirety. This widespread negative view of religion in relation to family planning, contraception, and abortion can be painted in an even darker hue, if a subtle distinction is drawn between the *right* to family planning, contraception, and abortion and the *fact* of family planning, contraception, and abortion. It could be proposed, for example, in mitigation, that religions may be opposed to these practices in principle but take a more lenient view in practice. The prevailing view seems to be that this distinction also does not apply to the prevailing state of affairs.

Thus, whether it be the case that one religion is involved or many, or whether different strands within the same traditions are involved, or even when one tries to draw a distinction between theory and practice, the religions of the world are seen as opposed to contraception and abortion. Moreover, there is also the further assumption, to tighten the screw further, that there are no differences in opinion within these traditions on the two topics of contraception or abortion, so far as the religions are concerned. The religions, supposedly, are interested only in keeping women barefoot and pregnant.

The aim of this book is to challenge this perception. The various contributors have focused on challenging this stereotype, even as we grapple with the latest signals of the stereotypical perception as they stare at us from the newspapers or cause pauses in many a conversation. The reader who has gone through the various chapters is already familiar with the patterns of specific arguments and the details of particular data that can be presented from the religious traditions to call the stereotype into question, and come time, even to break it. I would therefore like to focus on questions of a more general nature, which are not any less relevant (and if anything more) on that account. I would specially like to single out two such questions: (1) How did the prevailing perception come to be what it is? and (2) What are the underlying principles that enable us to challenge these stereotypes from within the religious traditions themselves?

How did these stereotypes come to prevail? A little reflection leads to the conclusion that one is here dealing with a master stereotype about *religion* itself, as an entity that is opposed to contraception and abortion as much as the various individual religious traditions comprised by the term. In fact, it could well be that it is because religion as such is presumed to be opposed to contraception and abortion that the various *religions* came to be so considered, as particular examples of the generic religion that also shared its quality of opposition to contraception and abortion. In other words, the perception is perhaps more in the nature of a presupposition (prevailing in the intellectual circles as self-evident) than a conclusion (based on a careful consideration of the relevant evidence).

But why should religion be considered prima facie in a state of opposition to family planning, involving contraception and abortion as a backup when necessary?

I think one needs to take into account here the self-assessment (bordering on self-congratulation) of the modern age as an age of *science and progress*. It is common knowledge that the development of science, in the modern West, was seen as taking place at the expense of, and through the eclipse of, religion. To this mode of thinking religion became a metaphor for that backwardness out of which science was leading humanity forward. This resulted in a metaphorical metathesis—as whatever was religion was backward, whatever is backward became associated with religion. A good example of this is provided by a recent development. Because of socialist statist policies, according to many economists, the rate of economic growth in India remained low for decades. The rhetoric of socialist statist economics is also antireligious, so that anything Hindu is considered economically and socially backward. Some economists have now begun describing the old slow rate of economic growth in India as the Hindu rate of growth! In reality, Hinduism has nothing to do with the socialist statist policies that kept the rate down, but such is the logic of the rhetoric of metaphorical metathesis that the economists were apparently unable to resist the temptation!

The modern intelligentsia, which takes pride in science, seems to have found a similar temptation irresistible in relation to religion in general. Thus, just because contraception and (to a lesser extent) abortion had the aroma of modernity about them, they were automatically dissociated from religion because religion is passé. Of equal significance is the fact that religion came to be viewed in modern intellectual circles as a monolithic and static entity. All religions are so branded. Who wants to distinguish among the items of a garbage can when all of them seem to stink as badly? Similarly, why even distinguish, like rotten apples, among the religions!

This modern habit of holding one's nose when treating of religion has produced unhealthy consequences. It has had the unfortunate consequence of demonizing religion in the context of progress. The view, then, that religions are opposed to contraception and abortion seems to possess this dubious pedigree.

This is not to say that the religions themselves may not have contributed to it, although modern trends are implicated in the process as well. The major religions assumed normative shape in the past in a socioeconomic environment that put a premium on population growth for various reasons, secular as well as sacred. Those aspects of the traditions that favored such an ideolog-ical salience then became identified with the basic positions of the religions; other elements were ignored or marginalized. The spokespersons of the traditions then presented them as the only options within a tradition, and their voice carried the day in earlier ages characterized by massive nonliteracy.

The two main groups who could speak on behalf of the religious traditions as the modern world emerged were either traditional leaders or modern schol-ars (who had by the middle of the nineteenth century initiated the scientific study of religion). Such scholarly study, almost until the middle of the twentieth century, was heavily historical and philological in nature in the case of most of the religions being considered here (with the possible exception of primal religions). Modern voices within these religions, which were partly echoing the West, also shared the negative Western assumption about religion, which they transferred to their own religions, sometimes with the accompanying assump-tions that their own religious traditions were also monolithic and static entities. The misunderstanding that the word *sanatana dharma* acquired in India in relation to Hinduism—as implying its unchanging character—provides just one example of this process.[1]

The fact that the scholarly study of these religions was mainly carried out by those outside the religion (with the exception of Christianity and the partial exception of Judaism) further complicated the situation. The interpretations now offered by modern scholars in some cases challenged the traditional ones. This led to a debate pertaining to the *contents* of the tradition, undermin-ing the credibility of the traditional and the modern elements in each other's eyes to some extent, although the balance kept tilting in favor of the modern. Most of the progressives in these cultures had already accepted the interpre-tation of progress as progress *from* religion, rather than *with* religion (or even *through* it).

This explanation helps one to appreciate what an advance this book rep-resents in the field, for it rescues the study of religion on the point of family planning, contraception, and abortion from the hands of both traditionalists and modernists of this ilk. All its contributors have had a modern education and yet feel at home in their respective traditions. Thus, each chapter has been written by an insider who is familiar with the scientific-historical interpreta-tions of these traditions. Each of them bridges the two solitudes.

But why, one might ask, are such informed insiders particularly qualified to bridge them?

The answer to this question lies in a simple consideration: that a religion possesses a quality that exceeds its contents, and while an outsider might easily gain an access to its contents, this quality is more likely to be accessible to the insider than the outsider.

The statement is not as mysterious as it might appear at first sight and the following consideration might serve to immediately divert us from its mysteriousness: that *science* possesses a quality that exceeds its contents. How else are we to understand the phenomenon that the conclusions reached by science sometimes, some would even say often, change, but science continues to remain the same without fear of self-contradiction?

It is in the subtle margin wherein the quality of a religion exceeds its contents that the creativity of a tradition is to be located. It is the margin by which the whole of the tradition is greater than the sum of the parts. It is this margin that gives definition to the vaguely constructive character of traditions. It is this quality of a tradition that keeps a tradition from being frozen in time or in a position. Therefore, it is in this margin that the cutting edge of a tradition is found. It is also this margin that transforms a religion from a concept into a symbol, and it is the semantic difference between these two that is alluded to when it is said that to insist on "reason" is to sadly undervalue "metaphor." Sadly, because religion rather than science is more likely to be available as a means of knowledge to the consciousness of the ordinary human beings, for it is religion which, by and large, enables most human beings to sustain a coherent vision of the world over time. This remark is not meant to take anything away from the value of science but to point to the danger that the assumption of a state of axiological self-sufficiency on the part of science might unnecessarily inflame its border with religion.

But back to religion. Religions, if they do not succumb to the pressures of change, react to this pressure by degrees. They begin by trying to be innovative. If this does not work the ante is upped—they become inventive. If even this does not work the ante is upped further—they become creative. And all these responses flow from that margin between the quality of a tradition and its contents alluded to earlier. The traditions, however, are not identical. Therefore, they will not respond to the same pressures in the same *manner*, even if the outcomes in relation to the various religions were comparable in *nature*. This leads us into the next section.

Let us now try to see where precisely we may locate such creativity in terms of the various individual traditions. I should clarify, as I do so, that this exercise is being carried out in the context of the chapters included in this book and therefore possesses a specific context. One needs to say this since generalization without context can be potentially misleading.

Surprise could be expressed that the same religious tradition should be capable of providing a different response to the same issue at another point in time, thereby undermining our faith in faith. One discovers, however, that the sciences do this often enough, yet it does not make us lose faith in science. Why should this be so? Because in the case of science we distinguish clearly between the *scientific method*, which remains consistent, and the *results* of this method, which vary over time, as the method is pressed into service for the discovery of truth—the final truth about matter, which remains elusive—without engendering pessimism. We may similarly distinguish clearly between the *method* of a religion and the *results* it produces. We need not lose faith in religion any more than in science on account of the variability of the answers, as religions pursue their own cherished values, which remain elusive but which, no less than in science, need not lead us into cynicism on that account.

But just as the precise method of each science such as physics, chemistry, or astronomy differs while still falling within the shade of the umbrella called the scientific method, so may the precise method that each religion uses to calibrate its eternal verities to temporal reality differ from religion to religion, as was hinted earlier. And it does. What follows is an attempt to identify a major element of the method of each tradition, through which it copes with the kind of changes it is called upon to make when new circumstances seem to call for such changes. Because of the importance attached to scriptures in the world religions, I focus on their role in the present context,[2] especially as, in some form or another, they are considered sources of authority in terms of normative conduct, which bears directly on questions of family planning, contraception, and abortion.

Judaism

The following question, when answered in a Judaic context, may help us unlock some of the secrets in the case of Judaism: how may one change the meaning of a text without so much as touching it? The answer, of course, is "through commentary"!

In Judaism commentary takes the more juristic form of decisions by the rabbis on the basis of the compelling insight that although the Torah *came* from heaven, it is no longer *in* heaven. What it means precisely is determined by the rabbis down here; it is not determined up there. Hence in Judaism the space for fresh interpretation is created by the tradition of rabbinic interpretation.[3]

Christianity

In Christianity, with the emphasis coming to rest on faith rather than law, two interesting developments follow, especially after the rise of Protestantism. One is the demarcation between the secular and the sacred realms—with the secular arm being left free to deal with a host of issues that in other traditions would involve religious decision making. Second, the emphasis on faith here means individual faith, so that individuals become the numerous interstices through which the meaning of the gospel reaches out into the world.

But now turn to Catholicism, in relation to which the subject is more agitated. The chapter on Catholicism notes the divergence between papal teaching and historical fact—and explores how the further fact that both display variance provides scope for finding a place for the right to family planning, contraception, and abortion within the Catholic tradition. The word *tradition* was used earlier advisedly, for it is on the basis of its own perception of itself as being based on tradition that the Catholic Church has often sought to distinguish itself from the various other manifestations of Christianity.

Thus, irrespective of whether Christians choose to interpret their heritage more individualistically or more corporately, resources seem to be available to articulate the right to family planning, contraception, and abortion within Christianity in general.[4]

Islam

More than both Judaism and Christianity, Islam takes its definitive stand literally on the word of God as revealed in the Qur'an. But as the chapter on Islam abundantly illustrates, even a position so impervious on the face of it to any accommodation to change contains within itself the very source of it, if we distinguish clearly between divine and human activity. The Qur'an is the result of divine initiative and is the final word of God, but the *interpretation* of the Qur'an must forever be a human activity so that while the Qur'an as a revelation is the final revelation, no interpretation of the Qur'an can be final, for such interpretation is a human activity. It is, moreover, a continuous human activity, which must take changed human circumstances into account.

The Abrahamic Religions

The Abrahamic religions rely on divine revelation, but we have now seen how this common fact involves different understandings of its exact modality and significance, and how each understanding provides its own resources to prevent the revelation from becoming a prisoner of history—to enable the revelation to go on revealing, as it were, continually.

Hinduism

Hinduism tackles the issue in its own way, which becomes obvious once the techniques of the traditions already dealt with are summarized on this point. In Judaism it is the vastness of the commentarial literature that provides room for accommodation for new situations; in Christianity it is the secular vastness within it; and in Islam it is the space provided through time. In Hinduism, it is the vastness of the body of revelatory literature itself, which is allowed to grow with time through accretion, extension, or analogical expansion, as the canon was never formally closed.[5] The chapter on Hinduism provides a good example. The main body of revealed literature in Hinduism frowns upon abortion, but a body of literature called Ayur Veda allows it, and this Ayur Veda enjoys the status of a revelation as part of the larger corpus.[6]

Buddhism

Buddhism does not focus on revelation as such, although Buddha's words, or those attributed to him, enjoy a similar status. However, the point to consider here is not the text but the value that it inscribes—namely, its ethical and soteriological *intentionality*. Since Buddha's words embody this intentionality, the true understanding of his words requires that such intentionality be indefinitely extended to all issues.[7]

The Indic Religious Tradition

Both the Hindu and the Buddhist religious traditions, though the Buddhist more than the Hindu, place much greater emphasis on the values that are inscribed through the words than on the words themselves. Thus, even when revelatory in theory, they are hardly so in practice, which can always bypass the text in the name of its intention, should the need arise. Often, even the need does not arise because Hinduism supplies enough scriptural words to choose from to fulfill a pressing need, while the need itself often provides enough justification in Buddhism for it to be compassionately accepted.

Confucianism

The Indic religions are less revelation-oriented than the Abrahamic (which are more fully imbued with the weight of their scriptures), and the Chinese traditions are even less revelation-oriented than the Indic because their scriptures, although no less sacred, are more pedagogical[8] than apodictic in nature. Thus, what the carriers of the vessels believe becomes more significant than the vessels themselves, when it comes to determining what is being carried in the vessels.

In the case of Confucianism it is the self-conscious reflection within the tradition on the population problem, as a topic of political economy, that provides a more direct parallel to its secular consideration in the West, than is the case with other traditions. But while the West tends to separate the secular from the sacred, Confucianism has less difficulty locating the sacred in the secular. This renders the kind of exercise we are engaged in less problematical in the case of Confucianism.

Taoism

Although Taoism formally possesses a body of literature more clearly defined as revelatory than that of Confucianism, it is generally nonrevelatory in character perhaps as an indication of a culture shared with Confucianism. However, there is an interesting aspect of the teachings of Taoism that is of great contemporary relevance: the clear recognition within it of double function of sexuality as consisting of both recreation and procreation and of the whole-hearted acceptance of the distinction between the two. In this respect, Taoism was ahead of its time and sometimes even seems ahead of ours.

The Chinese Religious Tradition

The main locus of adaptation, as this discussion proceeds, seems to shift from text (Abrahamic) to general meaning (Indic) to specific content (Chinese), as we progress in our consideration of the various religions, while exploring their scriptures as the basis of their responses to fresh changes.

Primal Religions

When we come to the primal religions, we move a step further in this process: from textual syntax, through semantic breath, through thematic participation, directly to the context itself, for primal traditions are by definition nonliterate. In African religions, for instance, there are no sacred scriptures.[9] Heretofore by texts we had meant written texts, even in the case of those traditions such as Hinduism and Buddhism, where the original transmission may have been oral, but no longer.

Rootedness to the earth constitutes a fundamental anchor of the primal religious tradition, a sentiment famously articulated as follows in the speech of Young Chief, a Cayuse, who refused to sign the treaty of Walla Walla because, he felt, the rest of the creation was not represented in the transaction.

> I wonder if the ground has anything to say? I wonder if the ground
> is listening to what is said? I wonder if the ground would come alive
> and what is on it? Though I hear what the ground says. The ground
> says, It is the Great Spirit that placed me here. The Great Spirit ap-
> pointed the roots to feed the Indians on. The water says the same
> thing. The Great Spirit directs me, Feed the Indians well. The grass
> says the same thing, Feed the Indians well. The ground, water and
> grass say, the Great Spirit has given us our names. We have these
> names and hold these names. The ground says, The Great Spirit
> placed me here to produce all that grows on me, trees and fruit. The
> same way the ground says, it was from me man was made. The
> Great Spirit, in placing me on earth, desired them to take good care
> of the ground and to do each other no harm.[10]

If the issues of family planning, contraception, and abortion represent the population element in an equation, in which this population is then set along-side resources to assess the prospects of sustainable development, then the primal religions saw the future a long time ago, for it is not far-fetched to assume that such an intuition pervades them. After all, the primal religions did not create either the population problem or the consumption problem. On the contrary, they were the ones who kept population and consumption in exquisite balance partly by exercising what we are now calling the right to family planning, contraception, and abortion.

However, there was trouble in paradise, from their point of view at least, when these religions came in contact with the modern West, a contact that had negative implications for them, ranging all the way from benign neglect to attempted genocide. This history has complicated the current attitude of primal religions toward the right of family planning. The term *family planning* almost automatically carries with it the connotation of limitation of the family, but the followers of many of the primal religions may need to plan for the expansion of the family to respond to the genocidal pressures they managed to overcome in the past few centuries—but only just.

The case of primal religions, then, may reveal an ironical but perhaps not unsurprising situation: The religious tradition that enshrines this right most naturally may be the one that needs to exercise it the least. If anything, the opposite.

This book, then, is an invitation to consider not just the topic of the moral right to contraception and to abortion as a backup when needed. The scholars who write here invite us also into a needed dialogue on the relationship of religion to science and to culture. There is sunlight in these pages that can begin to dissipate the fog of naïveté that surrounds much modern discussion of religion in society.

NOTES

1. Benjamin Walker, *The Hindu World* (New York: Frederick A. Praeger, 1968), vol. 2, p. 347.

2. Miriam Levering, *Rethinking Scripture: Essays from a Comparative Perspective* (Albany: State University of New York Press, 1989).

3. Erich Fromm, *Psychoanalysis and Religion* (New York: Bantam Books, 1967).

4. See W. C. Smith, "The Study of Religion and the Study of the Bible," *Journal of the American Academy of Religion* 39 (1971): 131–140.

5. See K. Satchidananda Murty, *Vedic Hermeneutics* (Delhi: Motilal Banarsidass, 1993). Also see Thomas B. Coburn, " 'Scripture' in India: Towards a Topology of the Word in Hindu Life," *Journal of the American Academy of Religion* 52 (1984): 435–459.

6. Percival Spear, ed., *The Oxford History of India*. 4th ed. (Delhi: Oxford University Press, 1994), p. 54.

7. K. N. Jayatilleke, *Early Buddhist Theory of Knowledge* (London: Allen and Unwin, 1963).

8. See Tu Wei-Ming, *Way, Learning, and Politics: Essays on the Confucian Intellectual* (Singapore: The Institute of East Asian Philosophies, 1989).

9. John S. Mbiti, *African Religions and Philosophy*. 2nd ed. (Portsmouth, New Hampshire: Heinemann International, 1969), p. 4.

10. See Vine Deloria, Jr., *God Is Red* (New York: Grosset and Dunlap, 1973), p. 95.

Appendix

Editor's Note on Japanese Buddhism

DANIEL C. MAGUIRE

William LaFleur, Professor of Japanese and the Joseph B. Glossberg Term Professor of Humanities at the University of Pennsylvania is the author of *Liquid Life: Abortion and Buddhism in Japan* (Princeton University Press, 1992). He shows in this remarkable study how a contemporary Japanese woman could accept Buddhism with its "first Precept" against killing, have an abortion, and still consider herself a Buddhist in good standing.

Japanese Buddhists have a long experience with family planning including abortion. In fact, during the period from 1721 to 1846, population growth stopped. It had been climbing rapidly. Suddenly it stopped and population leveled. There was no government effort to stem growth. In fact, on the contrary, government policy wanted increased growth because they thought it would strengthen Japan. Thomas Malthus had famously said that what stops population growth are the terrible three: war, famine, and epidemic. However, there is no evidence that these factors were sufficiently present to explain the stabilization of population. LaFleur's conclusion is that the "decisions about having fewer children than had once been the custom were being made within the 'bedrooms' of the Japanese citizenry." Their main method of limiting births? LaFleur and other scholars say "infanticide and abortion" were widely used.

Does this mean that Japanese Buddhists were coldhearted and cruel, and should we invoke the old saw that Asians hold life as "cheap"? If we would do that, we should first recollect what we saw in chapter 2 about the widespread use of infanticide and abandonment in medieval Christian Europe when people had little access to reliable contraception or safe surgical abortion. Also, there is no evidence that Japan had a deficient sense of family values. When Saint Francis Xavier (1506–1552) visited Japan he remarked: "Judging by the people we have so far met, I would say that the Japanese are the best race yet discovered and I do not think you will find their match among the pagan nations." As LaFleur says: "This is, to say the least, rather high praise for the moral tenor of a society that, exactly at that time, countenanced both abortion and infanticide."

There has, in fact, always been a strong sense of the value of children in Japan. Francois Caron, who lived in Japan in the early seventeenth century, made this observation: "Children are carefully and tenderly brought up; their parents strike them seldom or never, and though they cry whole nights together, they endeavor to still them with patience; judging that infants have no understanding, but that it grows with them as they grow in years, and therefore they are to be encouraged with indulgences and examples."

What LaFleur sees in all of this is "evidence that there is no necessary correlation between the allowance of abortion and the quality—or even the overall tenor—of family life in a given society. . . . Apparently it is possible for a society to practice abortion and still have what is generally called a 'strong' conception of the family." Additional proof may be found inversely in those modern right-wing resisters to abortion rights who, with all their talk of "family values," display no great concern for born children, their schools, their families, or their welfare. There are lessons here. Do not equate the use of abortion with cruelty or resistance to it with gentleness. It's just not that simple.

Learning from Rituals

How did the Japanese Buddhists come to decide that abortion was compatible with their very gentle religion? The answer is found not so much in texts, as we Westerners would want, as in rituals and symbols. Because the symbols and the rituals surrounding them are unfamiliar to us, we could easily scorn them. That would be a mistake. We should never belittle the ways in which people deal with pain. Even today we can see that Japanese Buddhists do not take their abortions lightly. They do not forget the aborted fetus, which they see, in LaFleur's words, "not so much as being 'terminated' as being put on 'hold,' asked to bide its time in some other world." Remember the doctrine of reincarnation that is common in Buddhism. A being was going to be born.

For reasons judged good by the would-be parents, that birthing was stopped, but the being who would be born is put back in waiting. The "life" that was rejected or the being who died through miscarriage or early infant death is called a *mizuko* and parents pray for their well-being in the sacred realms to which they have been "returned." Elaborate rituals are employed to remember these rejected "lives." Little child-size statues of Jizo, a sweet savior-figure associated closely with children, are found in abundance and are visited by parents who lost children or had abortions. In some images, Jizo wraps the *mizukos* under his protective cape and gives them comfort. In a time when infant mortality was high, as LaFleur says, "the idea that such children were being pulled back into a basically 'good' world of the gods and Buddhas to some extent palliated parental pain." There is nothing coldhearted about the care of the *mizuko*, and it is not all that dissimilar to the belief found a century ago in Catholic Ireland, that the many children who died were being taken to heaven by God as angels to pray for their surviving families.

Also, in much of Buddhism, birth is looked on as a gradual process, not a specific moment. Progress was celebrated, but it was not until age 15—or today age 20—that the child was considered to be a full human. Prior to that the child was slowly moving out of the sacred realm of the Buddhas. Returning children back into that realm through abortion was not the same as killing an adult, especially since they had a chance to return in better circumstances or to even enter Nirvana. Some Christian leaders rejected any such gradualism and decided gratuitously that the "image of God" was stamped on the earliest embryonic manifestations of life. Even male masturbation was called homicide. Potential life was simply stipulated to have full personal status. The yellow flower on the tomato plant was to be treated as a tomato. Common sense is offended by such thinking and sensible debate on abortion is short-circuited.

Index